A Divine
Discontent

Nathan S. S. Beman
(Engraved by J. Cochran from a painting by H. Room; courtesy of the Rensselaer
Polytechnic Institute Archives)

Owen Peterson

A Divine Discontent

The Life of Nathan S. S. Beman

MERCER

ISBN 0-86554-170-1

The paper used in this publication meets the minimum requirements
of American National Standard for Information Sciences—
Permanence of Paper for Printed Library Materials, ANSI Z39.48-1984.

Library of Congress Cataloging in Publication Data
Peterson, Owen, 1924–
  A divine discontent.
  Bibliography: p. 215
  Includes index.
  1. Beman, Nathan S. S., 1785–1871. 2. Presbyterian
Church—United States—Clergy—Biography. I. Title.
BX9225.B5335P48   1985   285'.13 [B]   85-18765
          ISBN 0-86554-170-1 (alk. paper)

Contents

To
Helen Beman Byrne
and the late
Catherine Marston Anderson

Acknowledgments

I first became interested in the Reverend Nathan S. S. Beman upon learning of his unusual relationship to William Lowndes Yancey. In his biography of the Alabama secessionist, John Witherspoon DuBose mentions only that Yancey studied under Beman, his stepfather, and spent ten years in the Beman home in New York. Additional investigation revealed that Yancey had actually spent his formative years in the household of one of slavery's most determined foes.

Subsequent research into Beman's life began to unfold an important and almost wholly untold story, for in his day Nathan S. S. Beman played a prominent role in a variety of religious, educational, and reform movements that greatly influenced the social and political development of the country. He was one of the best known and most controversial clergymen of his time.

This biography develops a comprehensive and impartial account of his life and character. Because Beman's private life was inextricably bound to his public career, I have sought to reveal the personal considerations that influenced his actions. The task was complicated by the controversial nature of the subject, the variety of movements and places with which he was associated, and his almost total neglect by students of the period in which he lived.

I am indebted to the many people who aided me in locating materials for this study. Among those are: James W. Patton, Southern Historical Collection, University of North Carolina Library, Chapel Hill; John W. Bonner, Jr., J. Larry Gulley, and Vesta Lee Gordon, University Libraries, University of Georgia, Athens; Fanny Howe, Public Library, Troy, New York; Kay Lauster and Louise Robinson, Middlebury College Library, Middlebury, Vermont; Edna L. Jacobsen, Juliet Wolohan, and Ida M. Cohen, the New York

State Library, Albany; Theodore Lesley, Tampa, Florida; Don A. Yancey, Atlanta, Georgia; Howard H. Peckham, William L. Clements Library, University of Michigan, Ann Arbor; Ruby Kerley, University Libraries, Southern Illinois University, Carbondale; Thomas H. Spence, Jr., Historical Foundation of Presbyterian and Reformed Churches, Montreat, North Carolina; Charles A. Anderson, Presbyterian Historical Society, Philadelphia; Peter A. Brannon, Edwin C. Bridges, Albert K. Craig, Jr., and Mimi C. Jones, Alabama State Department of Archives and History, Montgomery; Edward A. Chapman and Mrs. Rebecca R. Gould, Rensselaer Polytechnic Institute Library, Troy, New York; Mary C. Venn, Oberlin College Library, Oberlin, Ohio; and Mrs. Hugh M. Foster, Union Theological Seminary Library, New York, New York.

Others include: Mrs. Mary G. Bryan, State Department of Archives and History, Atlanta, Georgia; Dwight Marvin, editor, The Record Newspapers, Troy, New York; Samuel Rezneck and Elizabeth C. Stewart, Rensselaer Polytechnic Institute, Troy, New York; Marguerite H. Packer, secretary, First Presbyterian Church, Troy, New York; Robert F. Scott, Philadelphia, Pennsylvania; Lois M. Fawcett and Mildred Ostvold, Minnesota Historical Society, St. Paul; Ruth C. Brill, Historical and Philosophical Society of Ohio, Cincinnati; Harold Merklen, New York Public Library, New York, New York; Arthur Monke, Colgate University Library, Hamilton, New York; Wyllis E. Wright, Williams College Library, Williamstown, Massachusetts; and Irene M. Poirier, Lenox Library Association, Lenox, Massachusetts.

I am also deeply indebted to the staffs of the Middleton Library, Louisiana State University, Baton Rouge, and of the British Library, London, England, for help in locating and obtaining materials.

I am especially grateful to Catharine Marston Anderson, Beman's great-granddaughter, and Helen Beman Byrne, his great-great-granddaughter, in Seattle, Washington, for their assistance, encouragement, and patience throughout the several years required to complete this study. Appreciation is also expressed to Waldo W. Braden and Francine Merritt of the Department of Speech Communication, Louisiana State University, for careful reading of the entire manuscript and valuable suggestions.

Baton Rouge, Louisiana   Owen Peterson
15 January 1985

A Beman Archive

Mount Zion Academy in Hancock County, Georgia, where Nathan S. S. Beman served as rector from 1812 to 1823. (Courtesy of the Broadsides Collection, University of Georgia Libraries)

Carlisle Beman, who succeeded his older brother as rector of Mt. Zion Academy and later became the first president of Oglethorpe University. (Courtesy of University of Georgia Libraries)

Caroline Bird Yancey Beman, who as a young widow with two small sons became the second wife of Nathan S. S. Beman in 1821. (Courtesy of the Alabama Department of Archives and History)

William Lowndes Yancey, elder son of Caroline Bird Yancey Beman. While much like his abolitionist stepfather in temperament, Yancey became the leading "fire-eater" in Alabama, an outspoken exponent of slavery and secession. (Courtesy of the Georgia Department of Archives and History)

First Presbyterian Church of Troy, New York, which Nathan S. S. Beman served as minister from 1823 to 1863. (Courtesy of Rensselaer Polytechnic Institute)

Scene on the campus of Rensselaer Polytechnic Institute, founded in 1824. Nathan S. S. Beman served as president from 1845 to 1865 and led a complete reorganization of the school and its curriculum. (Courtesy of Rensselaer Polytechnic Institute Archives)

Nathan S. S. Beman in his later years. (Courtesy of Rensselaer Polytechnic Institute Archives)

Chapter I

Growing Up
in New England

On Thursday, 28 November 1861, the Reverend Nathan S. S. Beman stepped into the pulpit of the First Presbyterian Church in Troy, New York, as had been his habit for more than three decades, and prepared to launch still another attack on sin. In the seventy-six years of his life, Beman had earned a reputation as one of the most fearless, influential, and controversial clergymen both in his state and in the country. He had spoken out against intemperance, corruption, gambling, prostitution, foreign influences, violation of the Sabbath, and a host of other activities that he regarded as unchristian or undemocratic. But, of all iniquities, he regarded slavery with the greatest abhorrence. And with the country in the throes of civil war, the venerable clergyman prepared once more to lash the monster of human bondage.

Because of his prominence in the Presbyterian Church and the "outspoken yet terse" character of his theological and political opinion, Beman usually had capacity crowds for his special sermons, and local newspapers frequently published summaries of his remarks. Yet, on this Thanksgiving Day, the press displayed an unusual interest in what the clergyman would say—even New York City papers assigned reporters to cover the event. The factors giving rise to this special attention were Beman's long opposition to slavery and the well-publicized trip of his stepson William Lowndes Yancey to England to negotiate for the rebel government. The press was not disappointed. The New York Herald correspondent pronounced the sermon "an immense politico-religious columbiad upon the rebellion."[1] He also provided an account of the marital difficulties that had led to Beman's separation from his wife, Caroline Bird Yancey Beman, William Yancey's mother. Of this report, Beman characteristically observed: "The article in the Herald was written by a regular scoundrel and has some truth, some falsehood, and much gas."[2]

If for no other reason than to understand his peculiar relationship with the Yancey family, Beman's life is of interest. However, his importance extended beyond his association with the Yanceys. In his prime he occupied a position of the first rank among reformers, theologians, and educators. Of his stature among the clergy, one man who shared with Beman the tumultuous events of the era later observed, "I think that from 1830 to 1850 there was scarcely any other man in the northern states who carried with him the confidence and secured the approval of our people to the same degree as Nathan S. S. Beman."[3]

Born a few years after the founding of the republic, he lived in an important and dramatic period of American history. Highly conscious of the significance of the institutions being created and of their effect upon the future, Beman labored untiringly to extend Christianity, democracy, and education. Although he never sought public office and failed to gain the recognition or notoriety accorded statesmen, military heroes, and the eccentric, Beman nonetheless exerted an important influence on the events of his era. He occupied the pulpit of one of the largest religious congregations in the country for forty years, served as president of Rensselaer Polytechnic Institute for nearly a quarter of a century, was moderator of the General Assembly of the Presbyterian Church, where he was the leading supporter of Charles Finney's "New Measures" revivalism, and founded

---

[1]New York Herald, 29 November 1861.

[2]Nathan S. S. Beman to L. S. Cist, 18 January 1862, Pennsylvania Historical Society, Philadelphia.

[3]Martin I. Townsend, Proceedings of the Centennial Anniversary of the First Presbyterian Church, Troy, N.Y., December 30, 31, 1891 (Troy: Troy Times, 1892) 24.

the distinguished Mount Zion Academy in Georgia and a theological seminary in New York.

Teacher, clergyman, college president, planter, editor, author, abolitionist, temperance lecturer, and hymnodist, Beman championed causes that left a deep imprint. For most of his eighty-five years, he sought to influence the lives of his parishioners, associates, students, and family. Many Troy young people grew to maturity knowing no theology other than his. Thousands of students felt the impact of his personality and ideas on everything from proper conduct to the classics. Within his own family, he imparted a sense of duty and belief in principle. Nationally, his attacks on the Presbyterian Church led to a division that lasted for thirty years. He traveled to all regions of the country, to England, and to the Continent. He was acquainted with most of the leading religious, political, and philanthropic figures of the time.

That a man of Beman's temperament achieved such eminence and influence is remarkable. Although he claimed to prefer "the steadier, though less brilliant, light of the sun" to a "vivid flash of lightning," Beman often acted with haste and recklessness. Sometimes arbitrary, sometimes rude, he was not always just. And he was not always tolerant of those who opposed him. Although he encountered opposition, often vehement and occasionally violent, Beman was his own greatest enemy with his love of authority, his temper, and his physical infirmities. With demoniacal regularity, he could be overbearingly intolerant or vain, or stricken with illness, almost as if he were possessed.

But Beman had learned to cope with adversity. During his New England childhood, he had faced both difficulty and uncertainty. The son of rugged Vermonters, Beman had been brought up to be self-reliant, industrious, and persevering. His parents, Samuel and Silence Douglas Beman, were hard-working, God-fearing individualists.

Born in New Lebanon, New York, on Sunday, 26 November 1785, Nathan Beman was five years old when his family moved to a farm straddling the Vermont-New York state line in the valley of the Poultney River not far from the villages of Hampton (then Greenfield), New York, and Poultney, Fair Haven, and West Haven in Vermont. In that day sons began to make themselves useful soon after they could walk—feeding the chickens, bringing in wood and water, and performing simple chores. When they were eight or nine years old, boys were assigned "stints," which they had to complete before they were free to play.[4] As they grew older, they took their places at the sides of their fathers in the fields. Beman's father, in partnership with Peter French, also kept the village store in Hampton, and Nathan often had to sweep the rough floors, chop firewood, and sort stocks.[5]

All, however, was not work; nature had provided a superb setting for a growing boy. Low ranges of hills that rose into precipitous summits stretched in every direction. In these hills, Nathan frequently came upon small lakes locked in on every side without apparent outlet or inlet, as smooth as a mirror and as silent as a grave. Much of the original timber in the valley had been cut, but ample forest remained for the boy to explore. Fish were plentiful in the lakes and streams; game, wild grapes, berries, and honey abounded in the woods.[6]

Trips to neighboring villages constituted another diversion. In the valley, business that was normally done in cities or large towns was divided among the several hamlets. Hampton was very small, but nonetheless exciting compared to the isolation of the farm. Nathan would often accompany his father to Poultney and occasionally be sent to the tiny village of East Poultney. There were also trips to Fair Haven, a community of nearly five hundred people and the most prosperous in the valley. The village lay on the route of north-south travel, and the coaches and travelers added to its "cosmopolitan" atmosphere. Fair Haven even had a newspaper. But in spite of these signs of progress, Fair Haven, like its neighbors, remained a sleepy hamlet. When a customer arrived in the village, his first difficulty very likely might be to find the storekeeper, who had locked his shop and gone to hoe in his garden or to talk to the blacksmith. Each village had its tavern, but Samuel Beman early taught his sons to avoid these haunts.[7]

---

[4]J. Parton, *The Life of Horace Greeley* (New York: Mason Brothers, 1855) 51.

[5]Horace Greeley, *Recollections of a Busy Life* (New York: E. B. Treat, 1872) 58; J. H. French, *Gazetteer of New York* (Syracuse: R. Pearsall Smith, 1860) 683.

[6]Parton, *Life of Horace Greeley*, 57; Greeley, *Recollections*, 54, 57.

[7]Parton, *Life of Horace Greeley*, 57, 82-83; Greeley, *Recollections*, 54; Fairfax McLaughlin, *Matthew Lyon, The Hampden of Congress* (New York: Wynkoop, Hallenbeck, Crawford, 1900) 195-97; Timothy Dwight, *Travels in New England and New York* (London: Baynes and Son, 1823) 2:455; Andrew N. Adams, *History of Fair Haven, Vermont* (Fair Haven: Leonard and Phelps, 1870) 86-87.

Holidays were few, but the Fourth of July was a gala celebration for the hard-working farmers who gathered with their families in Poultney for the event. For a day, toil was forgotten and personal animosities laid aside as the independent Vermonters joined to celebrate the great revolt from British domination. Close-mouthed, work-worn farmers and villagers donned uniforms and cockaded hats and, armed with swords and muskets, suddenly blossomed forth as adventurous heroes of the Revolution. Throughout his life Samuel Beman held to the customs and dress of colonial days, arranging his hair in a queue and wearing short breeches and knee buckles.

Although important to all New Englanders, the Fourth of July was especially exciting for the Bemans, for Nathan's uncle and namesake had been Ethan Allen's guide in the famous capture of Fort Ticonderoga. Nieces, nephews, and grandchildren never tired of its retelling. One grandson recalled the hero's version of the story.

In the town of Shoram Vt. on the lake shore at about dusk as my grandfather has often told me two men came to his father's house, and turned out to be Eathen [sic] Allen & annother [sic] man. And Allen spoke to my father and called him to one side. And asked him to go & pilot him into the Fort. And my father replied he could not. Allen pressed him and swore it must be captured before morning. My Father then remarked that Nathan might go. He said Nathan knows much more about the Fort than I do. And has been there all day. Wal I had just got home from the Fort where I had been playing with the boys. And the fact was I knew much more about the Fort than any man could. As we most every day spied every hole. Allen turned and said where is Nathan and I said here. He says wal will you go and I says yess [sic] Sir.

I soon saw a lot of soldiers coming up the road. And Allen & my Father made preperations [sic]. Allen & the other man, myself & about 20 soldiers went on the first trip. After the boat or scow returned again he asked me to take him to the Armes. On passing a sentry a soldier snapped his flint to fire. Whereupon Allen struck him with his sword and says, Dam you if you open your head or say one word you are a dead man.

I took him [to the] Arshnal or where the Armes were. And he secured them. He said now take me to Capt. Dillaplass [Delaplace's] Quarters. We then went and rapped. And he got up & let us in. And Allen then said I demand the surrender of this Fort & that Damd Quick. To that he said in what name do you demand the surrender. Allen says in the name of the Great Gehovier and the Continental Congress. And Dam you no more questions or it all goes up in smoke. Dillaplass then rang a bell & told his orderly to give the order for the men to parade without armes. Allen says

Dam your armes I have taken care of them. This boy has shown me the Armes and I have them all safe. Then Capt. Dillaplass turned to me and said Nathan are you here, and I said Yess sir. This was the only time Capt. spoke to me. Wal Allen got every thing just as he wanted it. And told me my name would go along with his in the history of the world.

When Capt. Dillaplass was dressing his shirt was verrey short & did not cover him verrey well. And Allen replied your Government or King is damd stingy of his linen. Not enough to cover your. . . .

I have given you the above in the same language as near as possible. . . . There were many people would come to our house to have him tell the good old story.[8]

Nathan listened to the story of the capture of old Ti numerous times, as well as the exploits of his father, who also had served in the war. He was proud of his father and uncle for the parts they had played, but never more so than on the Fourth of July when they paraded and sat on the platform with the veterans while an orator recounted the brave deeds of the Green Mountaineers.[9]

Sundays were solemn days for the boy. The day began with the family assembled for morning prayers before the sermons, prayers, and sombre reflection at the Congregational Church—a remodeled barn—in nearby Fair Haven. Whistling, singing, games, pranks, and other forms of diversion were forbidden on "the Lord's day." Occasionally, as occurred when Nathan was sixteen years old, an intense religious fervor rolled across the state and, eventually, into the remote Poultney valley. Prayer meetings were held from house to house, and preachers from Rutland, Brandon, and other nearby communities fanned the fires of frenzy in the "Lord's barn." They prayed for salvation and attacked the intemperate use of liquor. What effect these revivals had on the youth is conjectural—in all probability they simply strengthened an already strong religious conviction.[10]

---

[8]Nathan Beman (grandson of the original Nathan Beman) to Rev. L. L. Beman, 18 January 1801, in *New York History* 28:2 (April 1947): 197-98.

[9]Greeley, *Recollections*, 65; Jedidiah Morse, *The American Universal Geography* (Boston: Isaiah Thomas and Ebenezer T. Andrews, 1796) 355; Henry Hall to Arthur S. Gibbs, 30 September 1895, scrapbook, Catharine Marston Anderson, Seattle, Washington.

[10]David M. Ludlum, *Social Ferment in Vermont, 1791-1850* (New York: Columbia University Press, 1939) 42, 65, 135.

The emotionalism of the revivals was not, however, without its influence on some young men of the valley. William Miller, a mild-mannered and reticent youth three years Nathan Beman's senior, unlike others, moved farther and farther from the established faith of the community. He began to spend hours in meticulous study of the Bible and became obsessed with the vision of the second coming of Christ. In later years, applying a meager knowledge of mathematics to clues he found in the Bible, he concluded that 1843 would be the year of the Advent. He and his followers elaborately prepared for the occasion. Undaunted when the event failed to materialize, Miller spent years rechecking his calculations and revising his predictions. Beman must have known Miller well, for both were close friends of Matthew Lyon's children. Years later Beman was dismayed when the prophet established a colony of Millerites not far from Troy.[11]

Among the leading families of the region, the Bemans were on intimate terms with the Lyons, Witherells, Gilberts, Frenchs, and other prominent residents. Especially interesting to Nathan was the family of Colonel Matthew Lyon, who had come to the valley in 1783, founded Fair Haven, built an imposing home, and established lumber and paper mills on the Poultney River. Ingenious and ambitious, the Colonel opened an iron works, literally beating the broken mortars, cannon, and small arms found around Fort Ticonderoga into plough shares, spades, shovels, nails, hoes, and tradesmen's tools. The commercial success of the fiery Irishman led to his election to the United States Senate. In 1798, in order to give wider circulation to his views, the Colonel established the imposingly titled newspaper *The Scourge of Aristocracy and Repository of Important Political Truths*. In this journal Lyon published the libel for which he was tried, convicted, and imprisoned under the famous Adams Sedition Law, which led to his removal to Kentucky.

Nathan Beman became closely acquainted with the Lyon family through his friendship with Chittenden Lyon, who was less than a year older than Beman. Chit was a constant companion, but since both boys were highly impulsive and quick-tempered, they frequently quarreled. Beman's contact with the Lyon family was an important part of his education as it brought him into association with an eccentric family of individualists whose home was filled with luxuries and fine appointments not to be

---

[11]Ibid., 251-52.

found in his own and whose conversation ranged from politics to literature and music. He was keenly disappointed when the Lyon family left Fair Haven, but the sight of the procession of covered wagons remained vivid in his mind for many years.[12]

Another favorite of young Beman was James Witherell, the family physician. A native of Massachusetts and veteran of the Revolution, Witherell had made the acquaintance of Samuel Beman following the surrender of Burgoyne at Saratoga. After the war, Witherell went to Connecticut to study medicine. He later returned to Vermont and resided at the Beman homestead, where he began his practice. Once established, he moved to Fair Haven and became the leading physician in the vicinity. Inclined to facetiousness and levity, Witherell quickly won the friendship and devotion of Nathan, who later recalled that the doctor's good humor and jokes made illness almost agreeable. Beman discovered that the physician was also well versed in philosophy and possessed a large library, which he made available to the youth.

During these early years, Nathan received a sporadic and, at best, rudimentary education. When the boy could be spared from the farm, he attended the Poultney district school, a small, one-room log cabin at the intersection of two roads. The wall opposite the door was filled by a vast fireplace four or five feet wide where a carman's load of wood burned in one prodigious fire. Along another side was a low, slanted shelf, which served as a desk for those students who wrote. The pupils sat on planks supported by sticks and without backs. The older pupils sat along the sides of the room, the girls on one side and the boys on the other. The younger children sat nearest the fire, where they were as much too warm as those who sat near the door were too cold. Among the pupils were a few full-grown marriageable young men and women who had been too occupied helping at home to attend school at an earlier age. In the winter, freed from planting, cultivating, and harvesting, married men and, occasionally, their wives also attended the school.

The teacher was usually a farmer's son who knew a little more than his older pupils—too often only a little—or a student working his way through college, frequently no more than sixteen years old. He received about the

---

[12]Letter from Nathan S. S. Beman quoted in McLaughlin, *Matthew Lyon*, 407-409, see also 195.

same wages as a farm laborer and "boarded round," staying a few days at each home and stopping longest at the most agreeable place. The teacher's most important qualification was his ability to "do" any sum, for to know arithmetic was to be a learned man. In spite of his extreme youth, if the teacher possessed the required expertise at figures, could read the Bible without stumbling over the long words or mispronouncing the proper names, could write well enough to set a decent copy, could mend a pen, and had vigor enough to assert his authority and strength enough to maintain it, he would do.

The teacher convened school at nine in the morning by rapping upon the window frame with a ruler, and the pupils came tumbling in from their snow-balling and sledding. The beginning lesson was in reading. The "first class," consisting of those who could read best, stood up and read around once, each student reciting half a page from the English reader. Then the second class read, then the third. Last of all, the youngest children, who had yet to learn fully the alphabet, said their letters. This generally consumed about a third of the morning. The reading was then begun again, for the parents demanded that the teacher hear every pupil read four times a day, twice in the morning and twice in the afternoon. Those pupils who were not reading worked—or were supposed to work—on ciphering and writing. If they wanted to write, they went to the teacher with writing-book and pen and he set them a copy—"Procrastination is the thief of time," "Contentment is a virtue," or some other wise adage—and mended the pen. When they were puzzled with a "sum," they interrupted the teacher and his readers to have it explained. The pupils seem to have written and ciphered as much or as little as they wished, at whatever time they chose, and in what manner they pleased. The morning exercises concluded with a general "spell," the teacher giving out the words from Webster's Spelling Book and the pupils spelling them at the tops of their voices. At noon school was dismissed. At one o'clock it was resumed, to repeat the morning's routine exactly.

In this rude way, Nathan Beman learned to read, write, and cipher. But he learned something more in that log-cabin schoolhouse; he learned obedience—not that discipline had been lax in the Beman household, but at school it was continued with no less diligence. It basically consisted of a ruler and five feet of year-old sapling, designated as the "heavy gad." These two implements were plied vigorously and often. Girls received their full share, and young ladies old enough to be wives were no more exempt than the young men old enough to marry them. In accordance with stern Calvinism, parents thought that if a youth was not too old to do wrong neither was he too old to suffer the consequences. To a certain extent, the severity of a teacher's discipline was perceived to be a direct correlation to his ability, and if he was backward in applying the ferule and the gad, parents became uneasy. Nathan and his younger brother Carlisle seem to have profited from this severity, for when they became teachers both were notorious for the rigidity of their discipline. Carlisle was so strongly impressed that nearly forty years later he felt compelled to resign from the presidency of Oglethorpe University because the trustees forbade the flogging of students above the sophomore level. [13]

In spite of the primitive methods and the severity of the discipline, Nathan enjoyed learning and early decided that he wanted a college education. Realizing that the district school was ill equipped to provide him the necessary training, he urged his father to let him begin a preparatory course for study. He finally succeeded in wresting a partial consent from Samuel Beman: he could go as soon as he could be spared from the farm. Months and then years passed, but the convenient time never arrived. While waiting, Beman was able to study with a teacher considerably more knowledgeable than the district schoolteachers. Mr. Bolles, a graduate of the University of Dublin, taught one year at Hampton Hill near the Beman farm, two years in Poultney, and a year in Fair Haven. Whenever he could get away, Nathan attended the Irishman's school.

In spite of Bolles's ability, Nathan knew his training was inadequate and that unless he was allowed to devote his full attention to studying for an extended period he would never be able to prepare himself for the college entrance examinations. Disheartened and afraid that he might never escape the farm, he made up his mind to confront his father with his doubt that the older man ever meant to let him go. Irritated by the boy's impudence and the prospect of losing a strong farm hand, Samuel Beman impatiently replied: "If you are so determined to go, you may go tomorrow!" At dawn the following morning, his most valuable possessions tied in a

---

[13]Parton, *Life of Horace Greeley*, 39-41; Allen P. Tankersley, *College Life at Old Oglethorpe* (Athens: University of Georgia Press, 1951) 10-11.

bundle, Nathan set off for Williamstown, Massachusetts. He made the seventy-mile journey in two days, on foot and alone.[14]

Although Beman returned to the Poultney valley to visit, to teach in the district school, and to live on the Beman homestead for several years following the death of his father, he was on his own thenceforward. In spite of—if not because of—the severe winters, hard work, and inadequate educational system, Beman had profited from the years spent at Hampton. He had developed a strong feeling of self-reliance, a deep fear of God, and an independence in thought and action. He was not afraid of hard work and not unfamiliar with suffering. The peculiar characteristics of the region and the era were also conducive to leadership training, for this small corner of New York-Vermont, in addition to Beman, produced Stephen Douglas, Horace Greeley, Ethan Allen, Matthew Lyon, and Theodore Weld.

A year of study in Williamstown was sufficient to complete his preparation, and in 1803 at the age of eighteen he was admitted to Williams College. However, less than a year later, financial difficulties cut short his education. Beman returned to the family farm, uncertain of where he would obtain the necessary funds and, indeed, of whether he would actually ever complete his studies.

The year at Williams College aided Beman. With his certificate of freshman standing and his father's friendship with Dr. Witherell and Major Tilly Gilbert, two of the valley's most influential citizens, Beman secured the position of Fair Haven's schoolmaster. Now on the other side of the desk, the young man found himself teaching the subjects which a few years before he had sought to master, wielding the ruler and the gad, and doing his best to maintain strict discipline.

The Fair Haven schoolhouse, according to Beman, "was just respectable and hardly that." During the bitterly cold days, the wind whistled through the loose boards. Beman later recalled that his only difficulty as schoolmaster concerned the heating. To keep the room warm, he established a schedule by which the boys took turns tending the fires. One day,

---

[14]Jonathon H. Noble, *Memorial Sermon on Rev. N. S. S. Beman, D. D., LL. D., Delivered Sunday Evening December 17, 1871, in the First Presbyterian Church, Troy, N. Y., by Rev. Marvin R. Vincent, D. D., Pastor* (Troy: A. W. Scribner Co., 1872) 30; Adams, *History of Fair Haven*, 245-47.

after repeated negligence on the part of the students, Beman issued an ultimatum that the school was to be warm the next morning if the pupil in charge had to sit up all night and burn the entire woodpile. Taking him at his word, the youngster with a prankish sense of humor kept the fire blazing all night. The following morning, when Beman entered the classroom, he was met by near-suffocating heat and the prankster sitting demurely in a corner studying his lessons.

As was the custom, Beman "boarded round" with the families of his scholars. He enjoyed his visits to the homes of Witherell and Gilbert, but the schoolmaster's favorite was that of Dan Smith, one of the wealthiest men in the community. Smith had come to the village in 1788 and, upon Matthew Lyon's departure, had purchased the iron works. However, the principal attraction lay not in the polished conversation or elegant furnishings, but in Smith's sixteen-year-old daughter, Lorane. The third of five children, Lorane was accomplished, intelligent, and well educated. She had also experienced a spiritual conversion, and Beman was pleased by her piety and interest in theological matters. Although Beman was then only a poor schoolteacher, the friendship between the two continued until, after his ordination as a minister, he was able to ask Lorane to be his bride.[15]

While at Fair Haven, Beman learned of a college, opened at Middlebury, Vermont, a few years before, where the terms were arranged so that needy students might drop out for the winter, teach to secure funds, and resume their studies in the spring. Deciding that this arrangement suited his particular situation, he bade farewell to his family and Lorane and made the trip north to Middlebury to seek admission. There he translated and parsed the classics of Tully, Virgil, and the Greek testament, displayed knowledge of the rules of vulgar arithmetic, and exhibited sufficient moral character to satisfy his examiners. He was accordingly admitted as a student and began study that summer.[16]

To a traveler from New York City or Boston in 1804, the village of Middlebury presented a bleak appearance, but to Nathan Beman, it must

---

[15]Noble, *Memorial Sermon*, 30; Letter from Nathan S. S. Beman, 5 October 1869, quoted in Adams, *History of Fair Haven*, 273-77, see also 245-47, 468-69.

[16]Adams, *History of Fair Haven*, 273-77, 245-47, 468-69; *Middlebury College—A Souvenir* (Rutland VT: Tuttle, 1897).

have appeared quite fashionable. No place north of Williamstown offered such educational advantages, and the town could even boast half a dozen "palatial" houses. In a letter to her parents, Miss Emma Hart, a teacher at the local female seminary, observed, "I find society in a high state of cultivation, much more than any other place I was ever in. The beaux here are, the greater part of them, men of collegiate education. . . . Among the older ladies there are some whose manners and conversation would dignify duchesses."[17]

The college itself consisted of a single three-storied white frame building erected in 1798 for the Addison County Grammar School. Being granted a charter by the state legislature in 1800, the building had been designated as a college. About eighty feet long and forty feet wide, it contained classrooms, housing for the students, a small library, and a chapel. Tuition was four dollars a quarter for the two lower classes and five dollars for the upper classes, with a dollar added for the privilege of attending the philosophical lectures. The principal items of expense were room and board, but even so the college estimated that $350 was quite enough to cover all costs during the student's four years.[18]

Beman quickly learned that the young scholars were held highly accountable. Apparently the president and faculty had thought of everything that a student might do to waste time and had passed a law expressly forbidding it. If absent from his rooms during study hours, the student was subject to a six-cents fine; absence from a recitation, lecture, declamation, or disputation meant payment of three cents. Students had to take care with books borrowed from the college library, for fines were levied for a spot of ink or grease, for turning down a leaf, or for tearing off a cover. In fact, the books were so carefully guarded that no student was permitted to enter the library or to glance through any book without the express permission of the librarian.

The founders of Middlebury had established the college primarily to prepare men for religious work. Accordingly, the first duties of the president and tutors were to watch over manners and morals and to set an ex-

---

[17]W. Storrs Lee, *Father Went to College* (New York: Wilson-Erickson, 1936) 59-60; George G. Bush, *History of Education in Vermont* (Washington: United States Bureau of Education, 1900) 132.

[18]Bush, *Education in Vermont*, 170, 174; Lee, *Father Went to College*, 39.

ample of the blameless life they hoped their charges would emulate. The faculty sought to fulfill this obligation by requiring attendance at frequent religious services and by imposing fines for unseemly conduct. Compulsory chapel services were held both morning and evening every day; absence resulted in a fine of two cents and tardiness cost one cent. On Sunday almost the entire day was spent in public worship. The price for absence from church was only six cents, but the regulations further provided that "If any scholar shall profane the said day by unnecessary business, by diversion, or by walking abroad; or shall thereon admit any other student, or a stranger, into his chamber, or on the preceding or following evening shall make any indecent noise or disturbance; or shall behave indecently or profanely at the time of public worship, or at prayers, he may be punished by fine, admonition or otherwise, as the nature and demerit of the crime shall require."[19]

In order to guarantee order and good conduct, rules had been enacted to cover almost every other contingency: fighting, striking, quarreling, challenging, turbulent words, lying, fraud, defamation, blasphemy, robbery, fornication, theft, forgery, duelling, profanity, and even wearing women's clothing. To enforce these rules, the president and tutors had authority to open and enter any room at any time. Although most of the scholars acquiesced to the severity of the college laws, there is evidence that the faculty was not without fear of reprisals, for the statute book also contained the provision that "If any scholar shall assault, wound, or strike the President or a Tutor, or shall maliciously and designedly break their windows and doors, he shall be expelled."[20]

In spite of the imposing list of restrictions, students did not entirely limit their activity to study and religion. Because of the size of the college, teachers and students lived on intimate terms, and under these conditions, the nineteenth-century equivalent of the "bull session" came into being. Surrounded by disciples stretched on floors and beds, on window ledges and desks, the more popular professors frequently discoursed for hours in the flickering light from a fireplace. The students also enthusiastically discussed news of current events, although it arrived late from

---

[19]Edwin J. Hendrie, *History of Middlebury*, manuscript, Middlebury College Library, Middlebury, Vermont, 1931; Lee, *Father Went to College*, 38-41.

[20]Hendrie, *Middlebury*; Lee, *Father Went to College*, 34.

southern New England. Nevertheless, the austere atmosphere of a monastery pervaded the campus: contacts with female society were permitted only at prayer meetings and in the households where students took their meals; dancing, drinking, and gambling were forbidden. Thus, students devoted most of their time to learning and salvation, safe from the temptations of frivolity and sin.[21]

In 1805 Beman began his second year at Middlebury, studying English grammar, geography, history, algebra and geometry, mensuration of superficies and solids, and conic sections. The year was one of excitement and the stimulant to the already over-sermonized student body was, of all things, a religious revival. At the time, New England was convulsed in religious ferment, and Middlebury did not escape the wave of evangelism. Although they were normally kept in a constant religious uproar, the students displayed a keen interest in the revival. Professions of faith, prayers, fasts, and conversions among the theological students aroused others to a feverous pitch.

The Philadelphian Society played an important part in the revival. Composed of the most devout members of the college, the organization met every Friday evening for worship, mutual religious instruction, and debates on theological topics such as, "Are the Scriptures the word of God?" "Is conscience a natural faculty?" and "Does the Sabbath begin at the setting of the sun on Saturday?" Even the more exclusive Philmathesian Society, which normally was concerned only with national and international affairs, experienced a spiritual awakening and devoted several meetings to religious discussions. While the effect of this revival and religious instruction upon the students cannot be measured, it is interesting to note that nearly half the graduates in the college's first ten years entered the ministry, including Nathan Beman.[22]

During his junior year at Middlebury, Beman studied trigonometry, navigation, surveying, natural philosophy, and astronomy, and during his final term rhetoric, ethics, logic, metaphysics, civil polity, and the law of nature and nations. The rigidity of the curriculum is suggested by the student who complained that he was "fed upon Latin, Greek and mathematics in endless repetition with a little chemistry, rhetoric, and

---

[21]Lee, *Father Went to College*, 38, 51, 77.

[22]Ibid., 70-76, 40.

philosophy for three years," while in his fourth and last he "might regale himself with Locke 'On the Human Understanding,' Butler's 'Analogy,' and such trifles."[23] If he felt this way, Beman was careful not to let his feelings interfere with the diligent pursuit of the prescribed course of studies.

In his last year, Beman came under the tutelage of Jeremiah Atwater, the young president of the college. As the youngest member of the class of 1793 at Yale, Atwater had so distinguished himself that he was granted a fellowship and hired by Yale's President Dwight as a tutor. In 1799 he became principal of the Addison County Grammar School and in 1800, at age twenty-eight, he was made president of the newly created Middlebury College. A disciplinarian first and a scholar second, Atwater reflected in his overhanging brows, solid jaw, and penetrating eyes the sternness of a Calvinistic temperament. If Beman's future conduct is any measure, Atwater exerted a profound influence on the young scholar.[24]

When the day of graduation finally arrived in August of 1807, Beman was awarded the choice position on the commencement program: the valedictory. His final examination—open to the public—consisted of questions over the entire course of study. In addition, he was required to produce "satisfactory evidence of a blameless life and conversion." This challenge necessitated answering questions concerning the origin of sin, free will, eternal damnation, the observance of the Sabbath, and the punishment of sins. There was only one answer the examiners wanted for each question, and Beman knew it.

What were the feelings of the young man on that warm August day? Surely he felt joy in finally obtaining the long-sought diploma, pride in the honor of heading his class even though the graduates numbered only seven, and at least a twinge of relief at being free of the close supervision and restrictions. In his years at Middlebury, he had become strongly attached to the struggling little college, and for the rest of his life he was to regard the school with affection. Years later, Beman regularly attended alumni reunions, frequently addressed the student body, and served as a member of the board of trustees. The college twice invited him to serve as its president, but he refused both offers. In 1852 he was awarded an

---

[23]Ibid., 33-34; *Middlebury College—A Souvenir*.

[24]Lee, *Father Went to College*, 41.

honorary doctor of laws degree, and upon his death, to the surprise—and chagrin—of his children, he left the bulk of his estate to the school.[25]

Following graduation, Beman obtained the position of preceptor of Lincoln Academy in Newcastle, Maine (then Massachusetts), through the intervention of Rev. Kiah Bayley, a native of Newbury, Vermont, who had founded the academy and served as its treasurer. Beman's arrangement not only provided him with an income, but also permitted him to board and study theology with Bayley.

Newcastle was a village of approximately a thousand citizens situated on Damariscotta Bay. After the Revolution, the attractions of cheap land, forests, limestone and clay for making brick, materials for shipbuilding, and a lucrative fishing trade had lured large numbers of southern New Englanders to this region. The early emigrants prospered and, envisioning continued good times, they encouraged their relatives and former neighbors to migrate to the bay area.

This growth created a demand for schools. Instead of the classical school, however, the residents insisted that their children be trained in shipbuilding and industrial work. Thus, the academy that offered courses in science, navigation, and surveying without sacrificing classical studies was popular in the region. Lincoln Academy had come into existence when citizens along the Damariscotta River united under Bayley's leadership to build the academy. The school opened its doors in October 1805, and Beman was its second preceptor.[26]

Newcastle contrasted with the villages of western Vermont in several ways. The most noticeable difference was the activity surrounding the river where vessels of all kinds and sizes—schooners, brigs, sloops—in various

---

[25]Henry B. Nason, *Biographical Record of the Officers and Graduates of Rensselaer Polytechnic Institute, 1824-1866* (Troy: William H. Young, 1887) 30-34; E. C. Scott, comp., "Carlisle Pollock Beman," *Ministerial Directory of the Presbyterian Church, U.S.* (Austin TX: Von Boeckmann-Jones Co., 1941); Samuel S. Beman to Benjamin C. Yancey, 12 May 1872, Southern Historical Collection, University of North Carolina Library, Chapel Hill; Final will and testament of Nathan S. S. Beman, Jackson County Courthouse, Murphysboro, Illinois.

[26]Frank L. S. Morse, "The History of Secondary Education in Knox and Lincoln Counties in Maine," *University of Maine Studies* 41:12 (April 1939): 11-12; David Quimby Cushman, *The History of Ancient Sheepscot and Newcastle* (Bath ME: E. Upton and Son, 1882) 300-301.

stages of construction lined both banks. The extensive forests of the region provided all of the materials necessary for shipbuilding—oak for frames, juniper or hackmatack for knees, and pine and spruce for the masts and boards. The brick-making establishments were also unfamiliar to Beman. Fishing boats sailing down the river to the sea presented still another unusual sight. In spite of these differences, however, Newcastle was much like the Poultneys, Hamptons, and Fair Havens which Beman knew—a village of pioneers striving to earn a livelihood in what a few years before had been rugged wilderness.

The townspeople were not much different from the hardy Vermonters among whom Beman had been reared. Hard-working, independent, and courageous, they sought to create a life that embraced and nourished both the newly acquired freedoms—political, religious, and economic—and the institutions for which many had fought the British. An integral part of this democratic process was the right to an education, an opportunity that many residents had been denied. Not surprisingly then, Beman found a great interest in education. The most enthusiastic, however, were the Reverend Kiah Bayley and his wife.

Upon his arrival in Newcastle, Beman moved into the Bayley home. However, he was not the only guest at the table, for the household included several student boarders and teachers from the academy. As a young Dartmouth graduate, Bayley had come to Newcastle in 1797 to supply the Congregationalists for the summer, but he had proved so satisfactory that they invited him to become permanent pastor. Unmoved by such worldly considerations as a new meetinghouse and the congregation's approbation, the minister consented to remain only because of the "truly lamentable . . . low state of religion" in Newcastle. A Calvinist of the sternest kind, Bayley nevertheless possessed a missionary-like zeal that led him to organize the academy, to welcome theological students into his home, and to promote almost every charitable and educational program endorsed by the Congregational Church in Maine.

Equally zealous in the promotion of religion was the clergyman's wife. Born Abigail Goodhue, the daughter of "a useful mechanic and respectable citizen" of Newburyport, Massachusetts, Mrs. Bayley grew up in a highly devout home. By the time she was four years old, her piety and biblical knowledge were matters of wonder to the family and neighbors; this preoccupation with religion continued throughout her life. In 1793, deeply moved by a religious experience in which "for an hour or two [she] had a great sense of divine things," she resolved to become a minister of the gospel. But since such a calling was closed to even so remarkable a woman as Abigail, she settled for study with Dr. Nathaniel Emmons, a prominent theologian. In the Emmons home, she met her future husband, then a ministerial student. Although Abigail Goodhue was fourteen years Kiah Bayley's senior, within the year the two were married.

Determined to "do something for my dear Master's cause," the clergyman's wife prayed daily that the boarders in their home might hear the call of the Lord, spent her evenings assisting the theological students and evangelizing the other scholars, and organized societies for the study of the Bible and for promotion of the Lincoln and Kennebeck Tract Society. Beman often returned to the Bayley home from the academy to find thirty or forty young ladies, each with Bible in hand, reading, singing, or praying, but more often listening to Abigail expostulate on the Scriptures. These meetings were the nearest she came to filling a pulpit.[27]

On 6 October 1807, Nathan Beman opened Lincoln Academy with ninety-nine students registered, more than double the enrollment when the school started two years earlier. In the two-story frame building, Beman taught substantially the same lessons he had learned in Vermont and exercised the same rigid discipline. He was quickly recognized for his ability, although some villagers resented his temper and firmness. On one occasion, after punishing the daughter of a leading Newcastle citizen, also a man of spirit, the young schoolmaster barely escaped a caning.[28]

Beman spent his evenings in theological study in the Bayley library, which contained the works of the leading theologians, an extensive collection of Congregational tracts, and many classics. Sometimes he was assisted by Bayley, but equally as often by his wife. At the end of the second school term, Beman had prepared himself well enough that on 14 May 1808, he was formally received into membership in the Congregational

---

[27]Oscar W. Peterson, *Manual and History of the Second Congregational Church in Newcastle* (Newcastle ME: n.p., 1917) 21-22; Oscar W. Peterson, *Abigail Goodhue Bayley* (privately published, 1917) 11-17; Morse, "History of Secondary Education," 13.

[28]Cushman, *Ancient Sheepscot and Newcastle,* 300; *Collections of the Maine Historical Society,* 8:166.

Church of Newcastle—a small, exclusive band whose members had proved their piety by public examination.[29]

Although occupied with duties at the academy and the study of theology, Beman was not insensitive to the economic distress of the villagers because of federal acts restricting foreign shipping. These laws had been enacted in retaliation against the British closure of West Indian ports to American vessels and impressment of American seamen. As the restrictions tightened, contracts were cancelled and unfinished hulls were left standing.

Only a few Newcastle residents were directly engaged in shipping, but the consequences of the federal acts were felt by shipbuilders, by young men who hired out to man the ships, and by numerous support industries. As the suspension of ship construction and enforced inactivity of builders and sailors continued, the townspeople became increasingly hostile to Jefferson and the national legislature. They sent protests to Congress, seamen openly disobeyed the law, and townspeople talked of separation from the Union. Beman sympathized with the villagers and bitterly opposed the actions of the government.[30]

During his second year as preceptor, Beman continued to study theology, and on 14 June 1809, he was licensed to preach by the Lincoln-Kennebeck Congregational Association. Although he returned to Lincoln Academy in the autumn of 1809, Beman did not complete the school term,[31] departing in the spring of 1810 to serve the Third Congregational Church in Portland, a congregation organized in 1807 and incorporated the following spring. After the departure of Johnathon Sewall, who served as a temporary pastor, Beman had been invited to preach several times.

---

[29]Cushman, *Ancient Sheepscot and Newcastle*, 283; Nason, *Biographical Record*, 30-34.

[30]Allen Johnson, *Jefferson and His Colleagues* (New Haven: Yale University Press, 1921) 146-47; Edward Channing, *The Jeffersonian System* (New York: Harper and Brothers, 1906) 215-25.

[31]Cushman, *Ancient Sheepscot and Newcastle*, 283; Nason, *Biographical Record*, 30-34.

When the congregation issued him a call, he accepted and was ordained pastor in March with Rev. Bayley preaching the sermon.[32]

Portland's Third Congregational Church was no small backwoods ministry, but a church with a new meetinghouse in one of the leading ports of New England. The growing church offered opportunities for an ambitious young minister, especially one of Beman's zeal. In 1810 Portland had more than seven thousand inhabitants, nearly double its population of 1800. Gathered upon the Neck between Casco Bay and Back Cove were seven hundred dwellings and three hundred shops, distilleries, warehouses, rope walks, iron works, tanneries, and other business enterprises. In spite of the economic recession of 1807-1808 caused by the federal restrictions on commerce, the economy of the town had almost returned to its predepression peak by the time of Beman's arrival.[33]

Beman had been in Portland only little more than a year when consumption, with which he was to be afflicted throughout his life, forced him to request a leave of absence. Upon his doctor's advice, he departed for a warmer climate and traveled to Georgia, where he spent the winter of 1811-1812. In the spring, much improved, he returned to Portland to resume his duties as pastor.[34]

Shortly after his return, Beman was invited to preach at the June dedication of the new Congregational meetinghouse in Fair Haven, which replaced their renovated barn, a proud occasion for the villagers. While in Fair Haven, he visited his family and at the dedication ceremony preached a sermon on "The reasons why the house of God is dear to his people."[35]

---

[32]William Willis, *History of Portland from 1632 to 1864* (Portland: Bailey and Noyes, 1865) 664; William Willis, *Journals of Rev. Thomas Smith and the Rev. Samuel Deane, Pastor of the First Church in Portland* (Portland: Joseph B. Bailey, 1849) 391; Nason, *Biographical Record*; *The Adviser, or Vermont Evangelical Magazine* 2:8 (August 1810): 255.

[33]Willis, *History of Portland*, 554, 561, 574; Willis, *Journals of Smith and Deane*, 393-95.

[34]Willis, *History of Portland*, 664; Nason, *Biographical Record*; Nathan S. S. Beman to L. S. Cist, 18 January 1862, Pennsylvania Historical Society, Philadelphia.

[35]Nathan S. S. Beman, *A Sermon Preached at Fairhaven, Vermont, June 18, 1812, at the Dedication of the New Meeting House* (Middlebury: n.p., 1812); Adams, *History of Fair Haven*, 263, 276.

More significant than this dedicatory address was a sermon on the war with England that he delivered on 20 August 1812. Following Beman's departure from Newcastle, relations between the United States and Britain continued to deteriorate; shipping had been curtailed and grass literally began to grow on the wharves in Portland. Several of the most reliable commercial houses had failed; the shock of these disasters had occasioned panic and additional closures. Expansion had come to a standstill; laborers were roaming the streets in search of work. On 2 February 1811, President Madison had suspended all commercial intercourse with the British. Finally, on 18 June 1812—the same day Beman dedicated the church in Fair Haven—war was declared. From the outset, the war was unpopular in Portland. Two months after its commencement, most New England congregations set aside 20 August as a day of fasting and prayer to protest the actions of the government. Beman delivered the principal address in observance of the day at the Second Parish Church in Portland.[36]

Deeply affected by the suffering of his parishioners, Beman vehemently denounced war as a means of national policy and attacked the leaders who had plunged the country into conflict. The clergyman regarded war as "one of the sorest judgments with which a nation can be visited, . . . [the] disgrace of Christendom and scourge of the world." "Ever since the apostasy of man . . . , " he proclaimed, "the lawless and ungovernable passions of the human heart have burst forth in the expression of contention and war, so that a history of our race has been little better than a register of the blackest crimes." He designated pride, ambition, and a desire for gain as the principal causes of war. Imploring the benediction of heaven upon the country, Beman asked the congregation to contemplate the evils of war: loss of property, depraved morality, the sacrifice of human life, and violation of the bond of brotherhood that should unite all nations.

In particular, Beman was disturbed by rumors that President Madison and others at the nation's capital seldom attended church. To the published sermon he appended this note:

It has for some years past been a popular doctrine in our country that a man's private character has nothing to do with his qualifications for pub-

---

[36]Willis, *History of Portland,* 574, 603; Willis, *Journals of Smith and Deane,* 393-95; Johnson, *Jefferson and His Colleagues,* 179, 212.

lic office. . . . But this doctrine is fraught with absurdity and impiety. . . .
After a tour through the United States I am thoroughly convinced that
most of our national calamities may be traced to our inattention to the
character of rulers! In some states, I am sorry to say, that infidelity is a
passport to honor. In the city of Washington, the Sabbath day is hardly
known; and the Chief Magistrate of this Christian land rarely, if ever,
graces a church with his presence. Surely the people of New England—
the descendants of the pious pilgrims—ought to set a better example.[37]

Although many persons at that time felt that sermons touching on political subjects had no place in the pulpit, throughout his life Beman never
hesitated to speak out on such matters. While he usually reserved discourses on political questions for special occasions, he was not adverse to
including such discussions in his regular Sunday sermons when he felt that
the question's seriousness warranted public attention. In defense of this
practice, Beman argued that in times of crisis the clergy, no less than other
members of the community, had a duty to defend right and virtue. He argued that the minister could not "in any circumstances or under any pre-
text . . . ignore, or repudiate, or shoulder aside those obligations which
bind him to the social structure of which he is an individual element or a
constituent." To opponents of this point of view, he replied, "The great
mass of those who shudder at political sermons as profane are those who
care not a fig for religion." Beman's vigorous attack on war and the nation's leaders in 1812 prophesied the interest in national affairs that was
to characterize his entire career.[38]

One of the happiest events during Beman's years in Maine was his
marriage to Lorane Eliza Smith. Although the exact date is not known,
the wedding took place while Beman was serving as pastor of the Third
Church in Portland. The young bride's solicitous care was to prove par-

---

[37]Nathan S. S. Beman, A *Sermon Delivered at the Meeting House of the Second
Parish in Portland, August 20, 1812, on the Occasion of the National Fast* (Portland:
Hyde, Lord and Co., 1812).

[38]Marvin R. Vincent, *Memorial Sermon on the Rev. N.S.S. Beman Delivered
December 17, 1871, Troy, New York* (Troy: A. W. Scribner and Co., 1872) 5;
Letter from Robert Aikman, *Proceedings of the Centennial Anniversary of the First
Presbyterian Church, Troy, N.Y., December 30, 31, 1891* (Troy: Troy Times, 1892)
72; Nathan S. S. Beman, *Thanksgiving in Times of Civil War* (Troy: A. W. Scrib-
ner and Co., 1861) 1.

ticularly comforting to Beman, for shortly after his return to Portland he was again stricken with consumption. The illness recurred with such seriousness that the twenty-seven-year-old minister reluctantly conceded that he would have to relinquish his pulpit and return to the South for an extended stay. Accordingly, he requested and received a dismissal from the Third Church.

Although he would not return to New England for quite some time, he would not repudiate its culture and traditions. The rugged individualism, stern Calvinism, and indefatigable enterprise of the New England character were to influence Beman's actions throughout his life. The strenuous work on his father's farm, the God-fearing piety of Samuel and Silence Beman, the rigid discipline in the village school, the regimentation and religious fervor of Middlebury and, finally, the exemplary conduct of the Bayleys made a lasting imprint upon Beman's character during these formative years. A New Englander he was and a New Englander he would remain.

Chapter II

Sojourn
in the South

Go ye into all the world
and preach the gospel to every creature.
—masthead of the Mount Zion
Missionary

Deeply attached to New England by ties of family, background, and sentiment, Beman did not expect to remain in Georgia for ten years when he went south in 1812. But he did stay and these years were to be significant. In addition to giving him insight into a different way of living, Beman gained valuable experience in the two fields in which he would labor profitably in later years: preaching and teaching. His experience with the institution of slavery vitally affected his private and public conduct in the future. And, not the least important, his remarriage following the death of Lorane marked the beginning of his tempestuous relationship with the Yancey family.

Even though he had spent the previous winter in the South, Beman found the countryside strange as he traveled from Washington through Virginia and the Carolinas to Georgia. Beyond Savannah the settlements became progressively smaller and farther apart. He passed through the villages of Washington, Greensboro, and Eatonton. The latter community lay less than thirty miles from the Ocmulgee River, beyond which was Indian territory and home to the Creeks, Choctaws, and Chickasaws. Not many years before, these villages had been under constant threat of attack by foraging tribesmen. Beman showed a keen interest in the Indians and was especially fascinated by the remains of abandoned forts and villages in the area.[1]

Oak, hickory, pine, and dogwood trees lined the crude, rough road as the stage bumped along toward the small state capital, Milledgeville. Interspersed among the trees were patches of corn, wheat, rye, and barley, as well as fields of cotton and tobacco, fig, peach, and mulberry trees, and even a few vineyards. For one who had grown up among the rocky foothills of the Green Mountains, there was nothing resembling a mountain, not even a little hillock. Perhaps the most striking difference between New England and Georgia was the balmy climate, with the autumn afternoons as warm as the hottest summer days in Maine and Vermont.[2]

In addition to his wife, Beman was accompanied by his fifteen-year-old brother Carlisle. The journey undoubtedly occasioned considerable introspection by the young minister: he was forced by illness at the age of twenty-seven to relinquish a promising pastorate, was faced with a sojourn of undetermined length in a region where customs, traditions, and habits differed sharply from those he had known all his life, and he realized that both his wife and brother were dependent upon him. But he was not a man to submit easily to fatigue or discouragement. Although the land appeared strange, the warm breezes told him that this was the place he sought. If sparsely populated Hancock County appeared alien, it did not frighten him; and if the prospect of leaving a church in one of the leading cities of New England for a rural congregation in the South seemed a step backward in his career, he was undaunted. Beman knew that a milder climate was essential to his recovery and that the rough and unfinished state of Georgia was badly in need of preachers. Exactly how and where the trio lived that first winter is not known, but by April Beman had resumed active preach-

[1]Adiel Sherwood, *A Gazetteer to the State of Georgia*, 3d ed. (Washington: P. Force, 1837) 56-61; Letter from Benjamin Gildersleeve, 16 October 1815, in *Literary and Philosophical Repository* 2:3 (March 1815): 375-78.

[2]Sherwood, *A Gazetteer*, 335; Adiel Sherwood, *A Gazetteer of the State of Georgia, 1827* (Athens: University of Georgia, 1939) 10-11; George White, *Statistics of Georgia* (Savannah: W. Thorne Williams, 1849) 38, 311.

ing, and the Cumberland Association of the Presbyterian Church had assigned him to fill a vacancy in the village of Madison.[3]

The scarcity of men trained to preach and to teach soon afforded Beman an unusual opportunity. Two years before his arrival, the Presbyterian Church had only five ministers and eleven congregations in all of Georgia, far from enough to satisfy the religious needs of the state. The wide distances separating the churches worked additional hardship upon the handful of men trying to minister to the faithful. A similar story was true of education, which suffered from inadequate facilities and too few trained teachers. Although funds had been made available as early as 1792, few counties maintained public schools, and the shortage of teachers retarded their establishment. Those created were only partially successful, for among the wealthier classes the term "free school" quickly became synonymous with "schools for poor people"; thus, although a blessing to some, many planters felt that it was better to remain uneducated than to attend a free school. Often, even teachers shrank from the stigma of association with these institutions. As a consequence, in the country where the largest plantations were widely separated, education was largely confined to those whose wealth enabled them to retain a private tutor.[4]

In order to provide education and religious instruction for their children, planters banded together to establish academy towns. The leading families within a twenty- to fifty-mile radius selected some spot among the sand hills or mineral springs noted for its healthy climate and erected summer homes, a church, and an academy. This nucleus soon attracted tradesmen, laborers, and professional men who were able to sustain the schools, churches, and activities of the communities throughout the year. Between 1800 and 1825 many Georgia towns were created in this manner.[5]

Beman's new home, Mt. Zion, was founded as an academy town. In 1811 the planters along Shoulder Bone Creek—a rich agricultural re-

---

[3]Hopewell Presbytery Minutes, p. 116, Presbyterian Historical Foundation Library, Montreat, North Carolina.

[4]James Stacy, A *History of the Presbyterian Church in Georgia* (Elberton GA: Press of the Star, 1912) 285; White, *Statistics of Georgia*, 69-70; Emily P. Burke, *Reminiscences of Georgia* (Oberlin OH: James M. Fitch, 1850) 197.

[5]Burke, *Reminiscences of Georgia*, 198-201.

gion—selected a spot in the central part of Hancock County, built a church and a schoolhouse, and erected summer residences. Set in the heart of one of the most populous and prosperous areas of the state, the village drew additional support from nearby Milledgeville, Sparta, Powelton, Devereaux, and other villages in the vicinity. In the autumn of 1812, Beman was called to this community to serve as a teacher and pastor. The quiet, rustic village, consisting of a scattering of new frame buildings nestled in a grove of trees, presented a singularly uninspiring picture to the new pedagogue. However, Beman and the planters who had hired him little realized that from their mutual effort would emerge one of the most celebrated educational institutions in the early history of Georgia.[6]

For someone accustomed to the neat-spired little churches of New England and the Calvinistic piety practiced unremittingly throughout the Sabbath, Beman found Sunday in Georgia a disquieting experience. In the morning, planters drove their wives and children to the church in the family coach. Accompanying them at a distance, on foot, were those slaves who could be spared for the day. All attended church; the planters and their families sat in the front near the pulpit, while the slaves were seated in the rear. The services were similar to those in Northern churches, except for the singing. Since the slaves could not read, the minister was required to accommodate them by reading two lines of the hymn at a time. When these had been sung, two more lines were read, and so on to the end of the anthem.

At the close of the morning service, the white members of the congregation repaired to a picnic ground adjoining the church. There, seated on benches, they exchanged news and gossip, discussed crop prospects, told stories, and laughed at jokes—Sabbath pastimes almost unknown to New England church-goers and intensely irritating to Beman. Letters and papers that had arrived at the post office during the week were distributed, strangers were introduced, and the state of the cotton market was discussed. While the planters and their families greeted neighbors, slaves circulated among them passing trays of fried chicken, baked hams, fresh strawberries, oranges and melons, fluffy biscuits and honey, tasty pastries, nuts, and other delectable items. When they had completed the repast and

---

[6]Sherwood, *Gazetteer of Georgia*, 1827, 79.

exhausted the conversation, the parishioners returned to the gaunt sanctuary for another haranguing before departing for their homes.[7]

Believing that Sunday had been set aside exclusively for worship, Beman rebelled against treating the Sabbath as a day for social intercourse. He commanded his flock to refrain not only from labor, but also from pleasure. His ire bristling, he reminded them that "visiting on the sabbath, particularly after publick worship, is calculated to destroy the good effects of preaching. All the solemnity inspired in the house of God is often in a single hour overwhelmed and lost amidst the convivial gaiety and mirth which pervade the social circle."[8]

Among the other customs of the rough, backwoods country that Beman could not tolerate were drinking, profanity, dancing, chicken-fighting, amateur theatricals, horse racing, and betting. Within a few years of his arrival, he had organized a committee of Protestant ministers to stamp out Sabbath violations and other iniquities.[9]

Upon his settlement at Mt. Zion, Beman embarked at once upon the dual duties of preacher and pedagogue with typical zeal. The Sunday services were just the beginning of Beman's clerical tasks, for he was called upon to fill a variety of appointments throughout the area. Whenever sermons were to be preached, blessings to be asked, prayers to be said, funerals to be conducted, or ordinations to be administered, the clergyman was required to pack a bag, saddle his horse, and set off to perform these duties. Twice a year he attended the sessions of the Hopewell Presbytery which met at one of the churches to lay plans for ordinations, to provide supply preachers for ailing or departed members, and to make whatever cooperative arrangements were necessary to serve the spiritual needs of the people of Georgia.[10]

From the very outset, Beman's association with the academy at Mt. Zion was auspicious. The school was ideally located and had the support

---

[7]Burke, *Reminiscences of Georgia*, 144-48.

[8]*The Missionary* (Mt. Zion, Georgia), 4 February, 1 April 1822.

[9]Hopewell Presbytery Minutes, 128; *The Missionary* (Mt. Zion, Georgia), 4 July, 27 August, 1 October, 5 November 1821, 21 January 1822.

[10]Hopewell Presbytery Minutes, 116, 187; Allen P. Tankersley, *College Life at Old Oglethorpe* (Athens: University of Georgia Press, 1951) 3.

and patronage of some of the leading families of the state. But more important, Beman was determined to make the school succeed. A man of intellect and almost boundless energy, he communicated much of his enthusiasm for learning to his young charges. His goal was "to make *thorough* scholars rather than to acquire an ephemeral reputation by teaching 'a mass of things, but nothing distinctly,' and thus leaving the pupil to become a mere smatterer."

Although the academy originally was open only to boys, in May 1813 Beman inaugurated a department for girls in the newly completed church. The curriculum for boys included Latin and Greek, literature, mathematics, composition, elocution, and logic and moral philosophy. The girls' course stressed music, etiquette, and practical skills such as sewing, in addition to spelling, geography, and English grammar. Although the school accepted students of any age, most of the pupils were old enough and sufficiently advanced to pursue a high school or college preparatory curriculum.

Beman served as rector and taught the boys, following a Draconian teaching system such as he had used in his New England schools. He knew but one penalty for the broken law—the rod—and, according to William Northen, who was both a pupil and a teacher at the academy and later governor of Georgia, he applied it to all violators with equal vigor, irrespective of sex, age, or social status. During Beman's association with the academy, the girls were taught by several different teachers, including his brother Carlisle. Mrs. Norton, the wife of one of the members of his congregation, taught music.

As might be expected, the enrollment of boys far exceeded that of girls. Students, except for those residing in Mt. Zion, were accommodated in nearby boardinghouses. Known initially as Hancock Private Academy, Beman changed the name to Mt. Zion Academy in August 1814. In 1815 he divided the boys' department into two sections, one offering a classical college preparatory curriculum and the other stressing basic skills and subjects for boys not planning to attend college. Fostered by satisfactory financial support and Beman's leadership, the school quickly became the most famous in the state. By May 1815, Beman was compelled to announce that enrollment for the next term would be limited to ninety students, thirty in each department. A year later six teachers were required to operate the academy.[11]

Beman did not achieve his success without toil, disappointment, and discouragement. He was not ignorant of the contempt with which many treated the ministry. He once told a group of his parishioners, "Men who devote themselves to this profession are deemed by a certain class as a dead weight upon the community—and all the time and talents and education consecrated to this object are considered as lost to their possessors and to the world."[12] Teachers stood in no higher repute with many Georgians. "Why is it that school-keeping is so disreputable an employment in our State?" asked one teacher. "If learning is honorable," he reasoned, "you cannot separate the teacher from a share in it. But how inconsistent is it in parents to desire their children to rise to stations of honor and yet provide no means for their permanent education!"[13]

Although they did not hold the ministry and teaching professions in high esteem, the pioneers of Georgia were proud of the educational and spiritual training of their sons and daughters. Paradoxically, parents whose educations had never progressed beyond reading and writing traveled as far as a hundred miles and incurred great expense in order to observe the academy's annual examinations. Several weeks preceding the examinations announcements were inserted in the newspapers inviting the public and "literary characters in particular" to attend. The examinations extended over a period of two days, with the boys being examined on the first day and the girls on the second day. On the evening of the second day, the students presented a candlelight exhibition.

The examinations and student orations and disputations were similar to those that terminated the school year in New England institutions. However, Beman must have been amazed by the festive air and gala cel-

---

[11]*The Missionary* (Mt. Zion, Georgia), 5 November, 19 May, 17 December 1821, 28 January, 24 June, 9 December 1822; *The Georgia Journal* (Milledgeville), 31 March, 17 May, 5 July, 19 August 1815, 11 December 1816; Lucian Lamar Knight, *Georgia's Landmarks, Memorials and Legends* (Atlanta: Byrd Printing Co., 1913) 659-60.

[12]Nathan S. S. Beman, *Sermon Delivered February 27, 1820 Before the Mt. Zion Auxiliary Education Society at the First Annual Meeting* (Mt. Zion, 1820) 4.

[13]Sherwood, *Gazetteer of Georgia*, 1827, 267-68.

ebration of the exercises in the South. The night before the examinations, parents sent their slaves to the schoolyard where preparations for the following day were begun. Pits were dug and filled with live coals. A short distance away a huge bonfire was built to furnish hot coals for replenishing the pits. Then several whole swine were placed on spits to roast throughout the night and the following morning. At the conclusion of the morning's exercises, parents, students, teachers, and guests repaired to picnic tables. The barbecued pork was carved and served with dishes containing almost every delicacy common to the region. When everyone had eaten his fill, the crowd returned to the examinations. The effect of the repast on masters, scholars, and parents can only be guessed. A final banquet concluded the event, followed by singing, speech-making, and toasting of the health of the schoolmasters, their scholars, and the leading military and political heroes of the day.[14]

In the autumn of 1815 Beman's brother Carlisle completed his college preparation and left for Middlebury College. The void created by his departure was filled by Benjamin Gildersleeve, a recent graduate of Middlebury who came both to teach and to study theology with Beman. Gildersleeve was taken into the Beman household where he resided for several years and, during that time, proved to be an able assistant to the clergyman. Gildersleeve was the first of several Middlebury graduates—including Alonzo Church and Remembrance Chamberlain—to follow Beman to Georgia and to labor with distinction in both religion and education.

It is likely that Beman exerted some influence in attracting them to Georgia. If so, Georgians are greatly indebted to Beman, for these men made notable contributions to the state: Church became president of the University of Georgia; Carlisle Beman served as president of and Remembrance Chamberlain as an agent for Oglethorpe University; and Gildersleeve, after organizing a church at Macon, moved to Charleston where he issued *The Observer*, a religious newspaper that promoted the Presbyterian cause throughout the South.[15] In 1816 another addition to the Be-

---

[14]Burke, *Reminiscences of Georgia*, 188-200; *The Missionary* (Mt. Zion, Georgia), 13 April, 5 November 1821, 18 November, 9 December 1822.

[15]E. C. Scott, comp., "Carlisle Pollock Beman," *Ministerial Directory of the Presbyterian Church, U.S.* (Austin TX: Von Boeckmann-Jones Co., 1941); Hopewell Presbytery Minutes, 125; Tankersley, *College Life at Old Oglethorpe*, viii; A. B. Hull, *A Historical Sketch of the University of Georgia* (Atlanta: Foote and Davies, 1894) 47.

man household was made when one of the clergyman's sisters arrived from Hampton to assist with teaching the girls.[16]

In the spring of 1818 Beman was recruited for the presidency of the University of Georgia, or Franklin College as it was also known, in Athens. The offer followed the death of Dr. Robert Finley, who had held the office for less than a year. An invitation to head the struggling state university was not an occasion of unrestrained rejoicing, for the college seemed on the verge of collapse. Beman had preached the funeral sermon for President Finley and had seen firsthand the state of the institution. In 1817 only twenty-eight students had enrolled and, as Finley had noted upon his arrival a year earlier, the university "was at its last gasp; the scorn of its enemies and the pity of its friends; forgotten in the public mind, or thought of only to despair of it; neglected and deserted, the buildings nearly in ruins and the trustees doubtful if it can be recovered." In spite of these drawbacks, the position interested Beman. Remembering Middlebury in its early years, he was convinced that the obstacles were not insurmountable. The office would also afford him greater influence than this current position as well as an annual salary of $2,200.[17]

The Board of Trustees offered Beman the presidency on 21 May, but acceding to his request, they waited until commencement in late June for his answer. Originally Beman's judgment told him to refuse. He was well established at the academy—an institution which, in fact, was more highly regarded than the state university. Beman communicated this initial reaction to his friends at Mt. Zion, and hoping to retain his services, the planters promised to build additional dormitory facilities and immediately began construction.[18]

During the next several weeks while the clergyman sought to reach a final decision, his wife became seriously ill. Although she insisted that he not let her illness influence him, Beman found it impossible to ignore this consideration. Yet he could not bring himself to notify the university that he would not accept the appointment, for he saw an opportunity to be

---

[16]*Georgia Journal* (Milledgeville), 5 July 1815, 11 December 1816.

[17]Hull, *Sketch of the University of Georgia*, 34, 50; Hopewell Presbytery Minutes, 154; Sherwood, *Gazetteer of Georgia, 1837*, 118-19.

[18]Minutes of the Board of Trustees of the University of Georgia, 2, 21 March 1818, University of Georgia Library, Athens; Letter, Isaac M. Wales to Leonard Wales, 17 July 1818, University of Georgia Library, Athens.

useful. Rectors of academies throughout the state urged him to accept. Perhaps most important, Beman feared that if he should refuse, the presidency and the management of the university might fall to someone unfriendly to the Presbyterian cause.[19]

By his indecision, Beman stirred a lively controversy in the press. A subscriber wrote to the *Georgia Journal* praising the board's selection. Beman's "qualifications by nature and education—his peculiar talents at conceiving and enforcing discipline, his unwearied ardor of everything which relates to education," wrote the correspondent, "all conspire to render him among the most popular characters to watch over the interests of that neglected institution." The writer, who signed himself "Hortensius," also suggested that the main reason for the lowly status of the university was its location and recommended that it be moved from Athens to a more favorable site.[20]

Rumor quickly spread that Beman did not want to go to Athens and that he hoped to bring the state university to Mt. Zion. On 9 June, in reply, a subscriber calling himself "No Athenian" opposed relocating the school and, commenting on Beman's alleged attempt to effect a transfer, argued, "On no one man's death or life; on no one man's acceptance or refusal of the presidency at Athens depends the life of that college. . . . Let not the trustees submit to the mortifying thought"; he cautioned, "let no one man's vanity feed on the idea that he is absolutely necessary to the well being or well doing of any well-founded college." The next week a letter signed "Scriblerius" endorsed this opinion. On 30 June Hortensius replied, accusing his critics of trying to "excite a prejudice" against Mt. Zion and Beman. Having the last word in the debate, on 28 June Scriblerius reasserted the charge that Beman sought to relocate the university. Although there is no way of determining the truth of the dispute, Beman's reluctance to leave Mt. Zion probably had led him to inquire into the possibility of transferring the school to Hancock County.[21]

---

[19]Letter, Isaac Wales to Leonard Wales, 17 July 1818; Letter, Nathan S. S. Beman to the Board of Trustees of the University of Georgia, 9 November 1818, University of Georgia Library, Athens.

[20]*Georgia Journal* (Milledgeville), 12 May 1818.

[21]Ibid., 9, 30 June, 28 July 1816.

Before the controversy had run its course, Beman accepted the presidency. In the middle of June he informed the trustees of the academy that he intended to accept the offer of the university, effective the first of January. His decision aroused some resentment since funds had been spent on new dormitory facilities with the understanding that Beman would not leave. The trustees, however, agreed not to stand in his way. Late in June Beman went to Athens for the graduation exercises and on Sunday, 28 June, he delivered the commencement sermon. On the following day he appeared before the board and announced his acceptance. He was then nominated to the Senatus Academicus Georgia as president of the university for formal approval at their next meeting and named president *pro tempore* until that time.[22]

After the dispute over his appointment, the reaction to Beman's acceptance was mixed. The Athens correspondent for the *Georgia Journal,* perhaps piqued by the rumor of Beman's attempt to take the university elsewhere, wrote that although the appointee's character was not entirely pleasing to him, the college undoubtedly would flourish under his administration. "He is a man of considerable learning, especially of the literary or belles-lettre cast," he observed. "He is an elegant and eloquent preacher and very great (perhaps too much) energy in government." "In addition to this," the writer continued, "he happens at this time to be a favorite with the heads of all the principal flourishing academies of the state. . . . He has some dignity about him, his moral character perhaps not very much inferior to that of any other divine. . . . Add to all this his enthusiastic ambition for success and fame in whatever he undertakes and I think the appointment will not be considered a bad one."[23]

Beman returned to Mt. Zion and began preparations for his departure in January. However, during the autumn, Mrs. Beman's condition worsened. Although she insisted that her husband proceed with his plans, Beman decided that he could not possibly go to Athens unless she made a very sudden recovery. Finally, in November the clergyman wrote to the

---

[22]Minutes of the Board of Trustees of the University of Georgia, 2, 29 June 1818; Letter, Isaac M. Wales to Leonard Wales, 17 July 1818; *Georgia Journal* (Milledgeville), 16 June 1818.

[23]*Georgia Journal* (Milledgeville), 14 July 1818.

Senatus Academicus to ask that he not be considered for the presidency.

> Mrs. Beman is in a low and perhaps the last stages of a chronic affection
> of the liver. Her continued and increasing indisposition through the Sum-
> mer has prevented me from making the slightest preparation for occupy-
> ing the post which you have assigned me. But what is *decisive* with me on
> this subject is that Mrs. B. though reconciled to the idea of going to Ath-
> ens when in better health and with fairer prospects of life shrinks from the
> responsibility of such a station, and entreats me not to remove her enfee-
> bled and helpless as she now is, from her present home. A request from
> her sick bed, possibly her dying pillow, cannot be denied.[24]

The board accepted Beman's withdrawal.

After relinquishing the office, Beman spent the winter of 1818-1819 caring for his wife and conducting the academy and church at Mt. Zion. To assist him in handling the business of the expanding school, Beman persuaded his brother John to come and serve as treasurer. In spite of the progress of the institution, disappointment over the University of Georgia position and despondency over his wife's continued illness cast a shadow of gloom upon Beman. Throughout the winter she failed steadily. On 3 February, at the age of thirty-five, she died.

It was typical of his devotion to his work that in the following months Beman continued to direct the academy, to minister to his congregation, and to perform numerous other duties, such as serving on a committee ap-pointed by the presbytery to study the possibility of founding a theological seminary. Although the school was never established, Beman nourished the idea for several years. In the spring of 1819 he established a chapter of the American Education Society, an organization to aid theological students of all Protestant faiths.[25] At its first meeting, Beman expressed his distress over the small number of Protestant preachers in the South and West. "The whole number even of *nominal* teachers of Christian piety," he told the members, was "inadequate for the supply of those parts of the earth where the Gospel [had] already been planted." The shortage would

---

[24]Letter, Nathan S. S. Beman to the Board of Trustees of the University of Georgia, 9 November 1818.

[25]*Georgia Journal* (Milledgeville), 8 December 1818, 16, 23 February 1819.

be even greater, he predicted, as civilization spread to the more remote areas of the world.[26]

For many years Beman actively supported the society. Under his direction, the Mt. Zion chapter collected $500 during its first three years—more than enough to finance the complete college education of one minister. This accomplishment was particularly notable in view of the small population of Mt. Zion and public reluctance to give funds for some unknown person a great distance away. A recession a few years later, instead of inducing Beman to dissolve the society, prompted him to even more strenuous efforts so that, despite hard times, the society collected $65 in 1822 and $83 in 1823.[27] In the fall of 1819 the Presbytery chose Beman to serve as its next moderator, and the following April he assumed the post, preaching on the text, "Canst thou by searching find out God? Canst thou find out the Almighty unto perfection?"—Job 11:7.[28]

In his zeal to spread the word of God, Beman conceived in 1819 the idea of publishing a weekly newspaper at Mt. Zion. He believed that not only might such a journal provide spiritual inspiration, but he also saw in it a means of raising the political, literary, and educational level of the people of Georgia. Beman formed a partnership with Isaac M. Wales and Benjamin Gildersleeve and purchased a printing shop. Gildersleeve was made editor. The partners called the new weekly *The Missionary* and, under its masthead, placed the inscription, "Go Ye into All the World and Preach the Gospel to Every Creature—Jesus Christ." The subscription was set at $3 a year if paid in advance or $3.50 if paid at the end of the year.

An important feature was the weekly report on missionary activity throughout the world. Notices of religious and educational events and meetings, political news, public announcements, and advertisements of merchants in the surrounding communities were also carried. Although Gildersleeve handled the editorial duties of the enterprise for the first two years of the paper's existence, Beman was keenly interested in the venture and influenced the younger man in his editorial chores.[29]

---

[26]Beman, *Sermon . . . Before the Mt. Zion Auxiliary Education Society*, 3, 12; Hopewell Presbytery Minutes, 166.

[27]*The Missionary* (Mt. Zion, Georgia), 12 February 1822, 17 March 1823.

[28]Hopewell Presbytery Minutes, 171-72.

[29]*The Missionary* (Mt. Zion, Georgia), 29 May 1821.

In 1820, having completed his studies at Middlebury, Carlisle returned to Georgia to assist in the conduct of the academy and to begin
studying for the ministry with his brother. The young man's return marked
the beginning of his distinguished career as an educator and religious leader
in the state. When Beman left Georgia, Carlisle continued to teach and
in his third year he was named rector of the academy. He was later chosen
as the first president of Oglethorpe University. Like his brother, Carlisle
was a stern disciplinarian. One former student claimed that he never had
been able to forget Carlisle's "terrifying countenance," while another regarded him as "less man than devil."[30]

About the time of Carlisle's return, Beman made the acquaintance of
Mrs. Caroline Bird Yancey, a young widow who lived with her mother at
"The Aviary," the family plantation at the Shoals of Ogeechee. In 1817
her husband Benjamin C. Yancey, one of the most promising of the
younger members of the South Carolina bar, had died of malaria contracted on a trip through the swamps of Edisto, while riding his law cir-
cuit. The widow and her two sons, William Lowndes, who was three years
old, and Benjamin Cudworth, Jr., four months old, had returned to the
home of her childhood.

Caroline Bird Yancey was the daughter of Colonel William Bird, a
graduate of the University of Pennsylvania who had served under Washington in the Revolution, and of Catherine Dalton Bird of Alexandria,
Virginia. In 1794 Bird moved to Warren County, Georgia, where he and
Benjamin A. Hamp purchased more than one hundred acres along the
Ogeechee River. The firm of Bird and Hamp built several mills for carding
wool and making thread, which, according to tradition, were the first of
their kind in Georgia. They also made iron from ore found in the region,
which they converted into moulds, ax bars, wagon wheels, saw-mill cranks,
mill spindles, and gudgeons. In 1802 Hamp sold out to Colonel Bird. Under Bird's management, the thread and woolen mills prospered and in time
a few houses, shops, stores, and a tavern grew up around the shoals.[31]

---

[30]Tankersley, *College Life at Old Oglethorpe*, 10-12.

[31]Grace Gillam Davidson, "Colonel William Bird of the Shoals of Ogeechee," *Atlanta Journal*, 8 November 1936; Sherwood, *Gazetteer of Georgia, 1837*,
235; Knight, *Georgia's Landmarks*, 1020; *Georgia Journal* (Milledgeville), 26 January 1814.

A short distance from the river in a grove at the foot of a hill Bird built a huge manor house. There, in an atmosphere of leisurely refinement, William and Catherine Bird raised a family of six daughters and four sons. The plantation acquired the name of "The Aviary," reputedly given to it by General McComb because of the beauty and charm of the daughters: Ariana, Catherine, Louisa, Eliza, Emily, and Caroline. The home was one of the most popular households among the leading families in Warren and Hancock counties.[32]

Colonel Bird was noted for his eccentricity. Upon his death in 1813, his will bore out this impression. The document made his sons Wilson and John managers of the estate and provided for Fitzgerald's education through medical college; but in one sentence he gave his holsters and pistols to William, with no further mention of him in the entire will. To his three unmarried daughters he left a share to be given them upon their majority or marriage. But to his wife he left only his riding chair, horse, and harness, and a servant for her use "so she may visit occasionally as she does at present," provided that she remained at the Shoals; otherwise she would have to bear all of her own expenses out of her dower.[33]

The Colonel passed his individuality on to his children. Independent and strong-willed, the family members frequently were at odds with each other. At one point, differences between two of the brothers reached such a point of disaffection that Fitzgerald inserted a notice in the county newspaper in which he denied insinuations allegedly made by Wilson as being the machinations of a "malevolent mind" and a "base, malicious heart." He concluded with the statement: "I feel bound to refute, publicly, the foul slanders of his tongue; as a man, I put them at defiance; and as a brother, I spurn his relationship."[34]

Caroline inherited her full share of the Colonel's eccentricity and strength of mind. Although intelligent, well-educated, and clever, Caroline was capable of obstinacy and vindictiveness when opposed—her father reportedly once said that if he wanted to make a raid on Hell he

---

[32]Davidson, "Colonel William Bird of the Shoals"; Knight, *Georgia's Landmarks*, 1020; Benjamin F. Perry, *Reminiscences of Public Men* (Greenville SC: Shannon and Co., 1889) 52-53.

[33]Davidson, "Colonel William Bird of the Shoals."

[34]*Hancock Advertiser* (Mt. Zion, Georgia), 7 April 1828.

would make her his first lieutenant. It was Mrs. Yancey's determination and spirit—qualities which Beman himself possessed—that may have been the very traits that attracted the widower. If so, Beman was to regret the day that he had found these characteristics appealing, for in years to come he was to find Caroline's capricious perversity a constant source of irritation.

On 3 April 1821, Beman and Mrs. Yancey were married at "The Aviary" by Rev. Payson. With his marriage, a decided change was effected in Beman's private life. The huge house on his 150-acre plantation became a noisy center of activity, for Beman's new bride brought with her two small sons, seven-year-old William and four-year-old Ben. With Beman's own children, Henry and Eliza, and his brother and sister, the family numbered eight. Within eleven months Beman became the father of another son Samuel, born 11 March 1822. However, in spite of her erratic temperament, Caroline greatly eased the minister's burden of caring for his children and facilitated his pastoral labors.[35]

Beman also acquired three slaves that his bride brought as part of her dowry. This acquisition was to prove embarrassing when he became an active spokesman for emancipation. On 11 April 1822, Beman sold the black mother and her two infants for $700, thereby ending his slaveholding career of one year.[36] However, the transaction was to be used against him for many years to come.

Less than two months after his marriage, Beman assumed the editorship of The Missionary. On 30 May 1821, a notice announced the dissolution of Beman's partnership with Gildersleeve and Wales and the formation of a new firm known as N. S. S. Beman and Company, with Jacob P. Norton and Ebenezer Cooper as his partners. The group purchased the printing office and presses and selected the clergyman to serve as editor. In his first editorial, Beman discussed the difficulties of editing a weekly journal, pointing out that "the pursuits, opinions and tastes of men are so various and discordant that to please all would be a hopeless undertaking." Therefore, the first duty of the editor, as conceived by Beman, was "to secure the correctness of his own deductions and to increase

---

[35]The Missionary (Mt. Zion, Georgia), 13 April 1821, 10 March 1823.

[36]Benjamin C. Yancey Papers, Southern Historical Collection, University of North Carolina Library, Chapel Hill.

the stock of his own information and then to present to others the deep
lines and bold features of truth and propriety as they are drawn upon his
own mind." Beman deplored the press of the day as "crammed with too
many crude materials for the intellectual and moral health of the land"
and concluded with a pledge "to contribute to the virtuous and rational
gratification of the community, and especially to render ourselves their
benefactors before the kingdom of Christ."[37]

In *The Missionary* Beman found a much larger audience than he could
command in the Mt. Zion church. In addition, editing the newspaper afforded him greater freedom in discussing political and economic subjects
that were not always well suited to examination in the pulpit. Beman most
often aimed his editorial thrusts at social customs of the time. One topic
that received Beman's relentless hounding was the theatre. In a 27 August
1821 editorial, he deplored the growth of Thespian societies. "From the
recent multiplication of these little theatres," he predicted, "we have reason to believe that every country village will soon be furnished; so that
every pin-feathered actor may flap his wings and crow majestically upon
the pinnacle of his own dung hill." Even more abhorrent were the traveling companies. The people of Georgia "should treat strolling players no
better than pedlers and prohibit their peregrinations by law," he recommended. If he had his way, he would "put in every honest hand a whip,
to lash the rascals naked throughout the world."

Beman's assaults often produced protests and recrimination. A few
weeks after one attack on the theatre, Beman noted that the editorial had
created no small stir among the admirers of theatrical productions. He told
his readers, "Though we have been threatened with 'an able and learned
answer,' yet it would seem that those who feel themselves injured by these
strictures intend to rest contented with the dignified revenge of writing
insulting letters and charging us with the postage." One wag forwarded a
theatre bill to him—collect.[38]

The clergyman also editorially warred against intemperance, a battle
he continued throughout his life. In November 1821, he initiated an attack upon the "multitude of licensed grog shops which are every where
poisoning the morals of society." Beman claimed that these places were

---

[37]*The Missionary* (Mt. Zion, Georgia), 30 May 1821.

[38]Ibid., 4 July, 27 August, 1 October 1821.

the rallying points of the idle and profligate—the headquarters of a whole cohort of detestable vices: drunkenness, gambling, profanity, and riot. Although licensed as inns for the refreshment and accommodation of the public, Beman complained, "we might call in vain for refreshment when hungry, for a bed as a place of repose, or for a bundle of fodder for our horse." Instead of a decent public inn, he described the taverns as "consisting of a large room consecrated to Bacchus, the deity of the place, a piazza for loungers in the front and a gambling cell in the rear. The common area before the door . . . answers every purpose for athletick sports such as pitching dollars, shooting rifles, gouging, breaking sculls [sic], and biting off ears and noses."[39]

In an editorial on 21 January 1822, Beman claimed that the consumption of liquor in the United States cost thirty million dollars a year, more than the total expenditures of the state and federal governments. In Georgia, he said that "grog-shops" surpassed the number of schools and churches. He was particularly distressed by the practice of permitting children to taste beverages sweetened with intoxicating liquors. "In this way," he argued, "temperate and even pious parents are peopling the world with a generation of future drunkards." Cognizant of the strength of public opinion, Beman encouraged his readers to insist that legislators and enforcement officers take action. He also urged that the grog shops be closed and that the importation, manufacture, and sale of ardent spirits be so heavily taxed that purchase would be virtually prohibited. Nonetheless, even as he relentlessly assailed the consumption of alcoholic beverages in the columns of The Missionary, Beman was not averse to publishing liquor advertisements.

Beman did not restrict his labors against intemperance to the pulpit and editorial column. In October 1821, he was appointed to serve on the Hancock County Grand Jury, and the report of that body bears the unmistakable imprint of Beman's influence. Although the jurors commented briefly on roads and taxes, most of the report consisted of a list of grievances against "the existence of a multitude of dram-shops which are the seats of almost every species of vice and immorality." Six tavern-keepers were cited for operating "common, ill-governed and disorderly" houses to the "encouragement of idleness, gaming, drinking and other misbe-

---

[39]Ibid., 5 November 1821.

haviour." The jurors listed the names of several witnesses who could verify the alleged facts and recommended that prosecution of the tavern-keepers be effected without delay.[40]

Dueling, widely utilized in the backcountry as a means of settling disputes "of honor," was another custom that came under the editor's censure. As a minister, Beman found the practice intolerable. The causes, he believed, were frivolous: "a warm debate, a newspaper essay, an inadvertent and hasty remark, an omission of some empty form of etiquette, a surly look, or a sarcastick grin is deemed an offense of that deep and scarlet die [sic] which nothing but the blood of the offender has the power to explain." Beman charged the duelist with violation of the laws of state and common humanity and of God's commandment, "Thou shalt not kill." Every challenge, he claimed, was given and accepted with the expectation of killing or being killed. Rather than an affair of honor, he told his readers, "it is an affair which commenced in pride and stubbornnes [sic] and ended in revenge and murder." To halt dueling, Beman urged public condemnation and a statute expressly prohibiting participants from holding public office.[41]

The editor also sought to suppress various forms of gambling. As a member of the county grand jury, he called attention to the acts of 1816 and 1817 prohibiting gambling. In spite of these laws, according to the jury's report, gambling was common and, still worse, itinerant gamblers were permitted to "live unmolested and prsecute [sic] their dark profession" among the unwary backcountry people. Beman also strongly opposed the state lottery as a system for the disposal of Indian lands. Condemning it as immoral, he argued that the scheme enabled nonresidents who refused to support public education, roads, and internal improvements to acquire great land holdings.[42]

Beman utilized the columns of *The Missionary* to supplement his pulpit campaign against violations of the Sabbath. In one editorial he complained that many persons found trivial and frivolous excuses for missing church—some slight indisposition "sure to vanish before the light of

---

[40]Ibid., 22 October, 17 December 1821, 21 January 1822.

[41]Ibid., 11 March 1822.

[42]Ibid., 22 October, 3 December 1821.

Monday morning" or a "little cloud not bigger than a man's head." Keenly
sensitive to impiety, Beman occasionally blazed forth on this subject in
the weekly. On 29 April 1822, he lashed out at the editor of the Savannah
Museum for publishing a notice "to the Pious—A splendid copy of the Holy
Bible will be raffled for at the meeting-house this morning—the godly are
invited to take chances." "That there are persons in every community capable of penning and posting up an advertisement like the above we are
compelled to believe," Beman retorted, "but we never before supposed that
an editor of a paper could be found in the Union who would wantonly de-
scend so low as to make his gazette the vehicle of such an infamous outrage
upon the moral and religious feelings of the publick."[43]

One of the causes that Beman consistently supported was that of public education. Although his own academy was primarily a college preparatory school with emphasis on the classics, he believed that such an
education was neither necessary nor practicable for every person. Nevertheless, he was firmly convinced that every young Georgian would benefit
from instruction in reading, mathematics, composition, and other basic
subjects, and he advanced a plan to provide schools for all of the state's
children. However, if Georgia wanted good schools, Beman knew that
qualified teachers would have to be found. "The majority of the state's in-
structors," he charged, would make "better hewers of wood and drawers
of water than directors of youthful genius and morals." He asserted that
many could not teach, would not learn, were profligate, and had come to
the region to "speculate upon the ignorance and inexperience" of the pioneer settlements.[44]

Although Beman supported a variety of other causes during his editorship—including the Choctaw and Creek missions, the American Education Society, the American Society for Educating Pious Young Men
for the Ministry, and the American Society for Promoting the Civilization and General Improvement of the Indian Tribes Within the United
States—never once did he openly attack the institution of slavery. This
is especially interesting in view of his later fame as an abolitionist. In one
editorial he wrote, "With their political condition we have no wish to interfere, but barely to remark in reference to this subject that the scheme

---

[43]Ibid., 4 February, 1, 29 April 1822.

[44]Ibid., 8, 15 October 1821.

of emancipation appears to us to be wild and destructive." Explanation for this attitude probably stems, at least in part, from his ownership of slaves for a time.

However, Beman was sympathetic to the plight of the slaves. Aware that he was treading on delicate ground, he nevertheless asserted that Christians were bound to ameliorate the condition of the slaves and to provide them with religious instruction. He argued that religious training for blacks would make them better workers and would diminish the likelihood of insurrection. Although not ready to embrace emancipation schemes, Beman ardently supported the American Colonization Society. In a 4 July 1821 editorial discussing the establishment of a colony in Africa for repatriated slaves, Beman wrote, "We have not only rescued these unfortunate victims of avarice and cruelty from servitude, but we have restored them, at publick expense, to the bosom of that country from which they had been unfeelingly torn." "We have instructed them in letters and civilization," he continued, "we have imparted to their dark and pagan minds the light of revelation and taught them to build upon the ruins of a senseless idolatry the firm fabrick of Christian hope." On 20 May 1822, Beman again endorsed the society and observed, "No person who has Christian feelings but will ardently pray for its success; and no person who cherishes the principles of humanity will throw a single obstacle in its way."[45]

Beman edited *The Missionary* for exactly a year. During that time, most of the difficulties he had prophesied in his initial editorial—disagreement, anonymous letters, and a tendency by subscribers to regard the printer's bill as the last to come due—came to pass. Aspiring poets wrote him insulting letters when their verses were not published; wags sent him doggerel with unpaid postage; and individuals smarting under his editorial blasts penned vulgar rejoinders. Beman also had to cope with the vagaries of the public mails. The late arrival of exchange newspapers occasionally left him without news of events outside Georgia. Delays in the delivery of *The Missionary* sometimes cost subscribers. At times Beman's exasperation spilled onto the pages of the newspaper. On 17 December 1821 he complained that some subscribers had not received the previous issue because the mail had neglected to stop in Mt. Zion. "We understand, however,"

---

[45]Ibid., 6 June, 4 July, 22, 29 October 1821, 20 May 1822.

he noted, "that it passed within a short distance of this place on Friday morning. Whether the carrier was desirous to make up for the loss of a day by saving a few miles travel, or had forgotten his route, we are not informed."[46]

In spite of these frustrations, Beman found the position rewarding and he relinquished the editorship with reluctance. The journal had afforded him an opportunity to address a large audience on several topics dear to his heart. It also brought rewards in the form of closer contacts with ministers, editors, and readers throughout the region. Especially pleasing was the official recommendation of *The Missionary* by the presbytery as a journal "well calculated to aid the cause of religion and general knowledge."[47]

In April 1822, the Presbytery of Georgia chose Beman to serve as commissioner to the General Assembly of the Presbyterian Church and collected $140 to help defray his expenses to Philadelphia. Beman accepted and decided to combine the official trip with a visit to his family at Hampton. Since the journey necessitated an absence of several months, he persuaded Gildersleeve to edit *The Missionary* and entrusted to Carlisle the direction of the academy. After arranging for the care of his family, he set off for Philadelphia.[48]

At the General Assembly in May 1822, Beman attended the Presbyterian Church's highest ecclesiastical body for the first time. During the next thirty years he was to wield a widespread and decisive influence upon the Assembly and the church. However, as a new delegate from one of the more remote presbyteries, Beman was little known among the members. He served on a committee to fix the boundaries of Abingdon Presbytery and was named to the church's board of missions. Although he faithfully attended the meetings, he had little influence. Following adjournment, Beman continued his journey northward. He stopped to preach at Newark, where his sermon made a profound impression upon the congregation. Samuel Hanson Cox, then a nineteen-year-old youth, later recalled

---

[46]Ibid., 30 May, 4 July, 1 October, 17 December 1821, 4 February, 22 April, 27 May 1822.

[47]Ibid., 20 May 1822; Presbytery of Georgia Minutes, Presbyterian Historical Foundation Library, Montreat, North Carolina, 1:17.

[48]*The Missionary* (Mt. Zion, Georgia), 20 May, 24 June, 1 July 1822; Presbytery of Georgia Minutes.

that Beman's address and an interview had converted him from the Quaker religion to Presbyterianism.[49]

Beman spent the summer with his family near Hampton, visiting the scenes of his childhood, renewing acquaintances, and preaching at churches in the neighborhood. He also attended a meeting of the Troy Presbytery in Middle Granville and was invited to sit as a corresponding member. Once again he exerted a marked influence upon at least one member, for nearly fifty years later the Reverend Jonathon H. Noble, a young clergyman at the time, remembered the "strong impression" that Beman's prepossessing manner and bearing had made upon him.[50]

In September, Beman started his journey south. He had received an invitation to fill for one Sunday the vacant pulpit of the First Presbyterian Church in Troy, New York, and arranged his itinerary so that he could preach to that congregation on the first Sunday of the month. Greatly impressed by Beman's sermon, the members of the First Church held a hasty meeting and on the following day sent a messenger to invite him to supply the pulpit for the next several weeks. Beman remained in Troy until November. When the congregation met to vote on a proposal to invite him to fill the pulpit on a permanent basis, a few members expressed opposition because of rumors about difficulties between the minister and his wife. When interviewed, Beman assured them that the stories were entirely unfounded. Satisfied by the minister's reply, on 11 November the committee invited him to supply the pulpit permanently. Beman accepted and left immediately for Mt. Zion to spend the winter and to make arrangements for the removal of his family to Troy.[51]

---

[49]William M. Engles, ed., *Minutes of the General Assembly of the Presbyterian Church in the United States of America from 1821 to 1835* (Philadelphia: Presbyterian Board of Publications, 1835) 32, 45, 48; Letter from Samuel H. Cox, *Proceedings of the Centennial Anniversary of the First Presbyterian Church, Troy, N.Y., December 30, 31, 1891* (Troy: Troy Times, 1892).

[50]Jonathon H. Noble Memorial Sermon, in Marvin R. Vincent, *Memorial Sermon on Rev. N. S. S. Beman, D.D., LL.D., Delivered Sunday Evening, December 17, 1871 in the First Presbyterian Church, Troy, N. Y., by Rev. Marvin R. Vincent, D.D., Pastor* (Troy: A. W. Scribner Co., 1872) 30.

[51]Henry B. Nason, *Biographical Record of the Officers and Graduates of the Rens-*

In Georgia, Beman found the church, the academy, and the newspaper flourishing, but Caroline was dejected because of the recent death of her mother. Beman resumed his ministerial duties, but left editorship of The Missionary in Gildersleeve's hands and the academy in Carlisle's. In March Beman inserted an advertisement in The Missionary offering for sale his plantation, most of the household furniture, and his horse and gig. At the April meeting of the Georgia Presbytery he petitioned for and received dismissal from his church at Mt. Zion.[52]

In the spring of 1823, Beman left Georgia, where he had come more than ten years earlier for a short period of recuperation. Several important changes had occurred during those years. He had come to a distant and unfamiliar state as a stranger and had departed as a respected member of the community and a well-known leader in religious and educational affairs. He had taken over and invigorated a struggling church in a small, rural village and had turned it into a potent force in the community. He had established an academy which in ten years had graduated more students than any other preparatory school in Georgia and which had earned a reputation as the outstanding institution of its type in the state.[53] Beman had also founded a newspaper that served not only Mt. Zion and its environs, but reached into Christian homes throughout Georgia and adjoining states. Through his organization of benevolent societies, his editorial crusades, and his public service, the young clergyman had hastened reform. Reward and recognition had come through his election to the moderatorship of Hopewell Presbytery, his appointment as commissioner to the General Assembly, and the offer of the presidency of the University of Georgia.

Mt. Zion had been little more than a hope in the minds of a group of Hancock County planters at the time of Beman's arrival, and the traveler through Georgia today will find no trace of the community, but for a few

selaer Polytechnic Institute, 1824-1886 (Troy: William H. Young, 1887) 30-34; Brief Account of the Origin and Progress of the Divisions in the First Presbyterian Church in the City of Troy (Troy: Tuttle and Richards, 1827) 8-10, 31-32; The Missionary (Mt. Zion, Georgia), 7 October 1822; Noble, Memorial Sermon on Rev. N. S. S. Beman, 30.

[52]The Missionary (Mt. Zion, Georgia), 23 September, 18 November 1822, 10 March, 5 May 1823.

[53]Ibid., 9 December 1822.

years the village was well-known throughout the state. During Beman's residence, it attained its greatest prominence. "Go ye into all the world and preach the Gospel to every creature" the Bible had commanded, and during his sojourn in Georgia Beman had done so with remarkable success.

Chapter III

Emergence
as a Leader

*The kingdom of God
now cometh with great observation.*
—comment of Rev. Asahel Nettleton
on the revival methods of Beman
and Charles Grandison Finney

On Wednesday, 18 June 1823, Beman was installed as pastor of the First Presbyterian Church in Troy, with five visiting clergymen assisting in the solemnities.[1] Following Beman's installation, he and the citizens of Troy were to enjoy three years of relative peace and harmony before the new pastor plunged the city into violent religious convulsion.

Beman found that the residents of Troy differed little from the industrious people of the Poultney Valley sixty miles away. With a population of more than five thousand, Troy was known for its enterprising nature and aggressiveness. Enjoying quick growth, Troy had completely out-distanced nearby Lansingburgh and had begun to rival Albany as a commercial and industrial center. The manufacture of iron, spikes, nails, stoves, firearms, safes, and agricultural implements provided a firm base for the economy. The town was also home for flour and grist mills, breweries, cot-

---

[1] *Troy Post*, 24 June 1823.

ton and woolen mills, tanneries, saw mills, a distillery, two shoe factories, and hosiery, paper, clothing, and carriage manufacturers. A semi-weekly and two weekly newspapers served the community. Public buildings included the courthouse, jail, clerk's office, six churches, two banks, a market house, and several fire houses.[2]

Only four months after Beman's installation, the city celebrated the opening of the Erie Canal. On 8 October a huge crowd came to watch the procession of boats and the *Trojan Trader* take on a load of merchandise—the first sent down the new canal—and proceed on its way, a coup that infuriated the people of rival Albany. Within a year, more than three hundred boats arrived and departed every month. Less than a year later, the Troy and Boston Stage Line was established with offices at the Bull's Head Tavern. Three days a week stages left for Boston, thereby affording the Hudson River community another important tie with seaboard commercial centers.[3]

Troy was also known for its progressiveness in the field of education. The city supported a Lancastrian school and several academies for boys. But the feather in its pedagogical cap was Mrs. Emma Willard's Female Seminary. Beman had known Mrs. Willard (then Emma Hart) in Middlebury, where she had established the first girls' school in which the curriculum and requirements were equal to those of the prominent boys' academies. Offered $4,000 to establish such a school in Troy, Mrs. Willard had moved to the city in 1821. One of Beman's most pleasant sights every Sunday was Mrs. Willard's young ladies seated in front of the pulpit listening to his sermon. Not long after Beman's arrival, another academy, the Rensselaer School, was opened. The school, which stressed the study of science, became Rensselaer Polytechnic Institute and, thirty years later, selected Beman to serve as its president.[4]

---

[2]J. H. French, *Gazetteer of the State of New York* (Syracuse: R. Pearsall Smith, 1860) 560-61; A. J. Weise, *History of the City of Troy* (Troy: William H. Young, 1876) 100-101, 132, 134, 153.

[3]*Troy Sentinel*, 10 October 1823; Weise, *History of the City of Troy*, 132-36.

[4]Weise, *History of the City of Troy*, 100-101; Letter from Robert Aikman in *Proceedings of the Centennial Anniversary of the First Presbyterian Church, Troy, N.Y., December 30, 31, 1891* (Troy: Troy Times, 1892) 73.

The new pastor—thirty-eight years old, tall and powerfully built, with bold, striking features and a massive head of hair—presented a commanding appearance to the residents of Troy. His stern countenance made him appear somewhat forbidding upon first meeting, but longer acquaintance revealed that he was capable of friendliness and humor. Beman took special pains to cultivate the impression of authority. Believing that the Sabbath service should be deeply serious, the clergyman sought to remove anything that might impair the solemnity of the occasion. He firmly opposed levity in the pulpit and knew how to retain the attention of his listeners.

To eliminate distractions, he placed only a desk and a single chair on the platform. Several years later, when the congregation built a new meetinghouse, Beman designed a long, high, narrow pulpit that created the illusion that the speaker was far taller than his actual height. To the rear of the pulpit he placed a fresco that led the eye of the church-goer down a vista of columns to an entablature, the cornice of which appeared on a level with the neck of a man of average height. The design served to magnify Beman, who was already unusually tall, and he appeared to tower above his congregation.[5]

Members of the First Church were to grow very familiar with the sight that greeted them when Beman mounted the pulpit in the summer of 1823. He served as pastor of the church for the next forty years, and thousands of Troy Presbyterians grew to maturity knowing no other regular minister. On that first Sunday, as he was to do for many years, Beman approached the pulpit with a firm, martial step, notebook closely hugged under his arm. He turned to face the congregation and began to speak in a voice full and resonant. Without any appearance of self-consciousness, he was uniformly self-possessed.

While Beman occasionally gave free rein to his feelings, he never allowed himself to lose control of the situation. If he felt that his emotion threatened to exceed the limits of propriety, he checked it suddenly and

---

[5]Letters from William Lee, Marvin R. Vincent, and Robert Aikman in *Proceedings of the Centennial Anniversary*, 63-64, 72; Jonathan H. Noble Memorial Sermon in Marvin R. Vincent, *Memorial Sermon on Rev. N. S. S. Beman, D.D., LL.D., Delivered Sunday Evening, December 17, 1871, in the First Presbyterian Church, Troy, N.Y., by Rev. Marvin R. Vincent, D.D., Pastor* (Troy: A. W. Scribner Co., 1872) 10.

sometimes startlingly. Unusually deliberate, he spoke slowly as if he had chosen each word with care. He preferred simple Anglo-Saxon words his listeners could understand easily, although he occasionally would dwell on a sonorous phrase with evident pleasure. His style was simple, but far from barren. On one occasion after Beman had achieved national fame, an elderly and poorly educated man, upon hearing him speak, asked, "Why, is that the great Dr. Beman? I could understand every word he said myself."[6]

As a preacher, Beman was popular mainly because he succeeded in getting his auditors to think. He hoped that his clarity and the force of logic would convince them, but he urged his hearers to think for themselves. He expressed this philosophy in one sermon: "Do not accept these views because they are mine; think for yourselves—be persuaded in your own minds."[7]

By his manner of speaking, the clergyman contributed to an impression of sincerity and integrity. Rather than relying on bombast and violent gesture, he stood before his congregation calmly and confidently, stepping from behind the pulpit and bending forward occasionally in his earnestness. Although he prepared sermons with meticulous care, he spoke extemporaneously so that he might elaborate and adapt to the reactions of his listeners.[8]

The intellectual strength of Beman's discourses attracted many of the better educated citizens, particularly the lawyers, of Troy, and the church gained in membership until it became one of the largest in the state.[9] Another attraction for the educated was the clergyman's fearless discussion of pertinent issues. At Troy he continued to speak from the pulpit on controversial public questions whenever he felt their importance warranted it.

While many were impressed with Beman's preaching, only after considerable time did they begin to understand the nature and character of

---

[6]Vincent, *Memorial Sermon*, 10-12.

[7]Ibid.; Letter from William Lee in *Proceedings of the Centennial Anniversary*, 78.

[8]Vincent, *Memorial Sermon*, 13.

[9]"Living Progress," in *Proceedings of the Centennial Anniversary*, 107; Vincent, *Memorial Sermon*, 12.

their new pastor. The most prominent characteristic of his personality—
the one with which his parishioners were soon to become well acquainted—was boldness. He never hesitated to express his beliefs and to
speak plainly and strongly. As a preacher he was thoroughly convinced of
the truth of what he declared. He did not claim to be sure of everything;
of what he was uncertain, he remained silent, but those things of which
he was sure, he was very sure. Another characteristic, probably the result
of his strict upbringing and religious views, was that he was unwilling to
compromise upon principles. He was also capable of great self-control.
While quick at retort, biting in sarcasm, and at times passionate in his
partisanship, he was able to keep his head in controversy and grew cooler
and more calculating as the dispute waxed warmer.

One of Beman's associates and friends gave a candid analysis of the
clergyman's temperament:

> Those who did not know Dr. Beman well will deny that the spirit of
> love found an illustration in him. It was at this point that he was least
> understood and most frequently misrepresented. . . . That Dr. Beman was
> sometimes arbitrary, sometimes rude, . . . sometimes sparing of the little
> amenities which go so far towards social comfort, and especially toward
> facilitating the intercourse between superiors and inferiors, are facts which
> are no secret. . . . He was a man of war from his youth, and perhaps it was
> scarcely to be expected that he would not take a certain grim delight in
> launching his darts, and exhibit an unmistakable relish in handling an ad-
> versary. He liked to make men feel his power, and you felt it even when
> he played with you. Even his foils were pointed.
> This is the only side of his portrait which many have ever seen. . . .
> The picture has another side. After all that has been said, it still remains
> true that Dr. Beman had a great depth of tenderness in his nature and a
> large capacity for loving. . . . Indeed, no one could hear him preach in
> the days of his power without being impressed by his tenderness as well as
> by his strength.
> As it was, he craved more love than he received. . . . I think that he
> felt more deeply than he let anyone know the hunger for love which he
> saw others draw to themselves. He was not unaware of the unfavorable
> impression which he sometimes made upon strangers. . . . It was in truth
> a point upon which he was sensitive. Once . . . he alluded to the fact in
> a gathering of his people and said that some people had the notion that
> he was crusty and bearish; and begged them to believe that whatever ap-
> pearances might indicate no such thing was in his heart.
> Though his dignity and apparent reserve were apt to repel strangers,
> few men could be more agreeable in social intercourse. He abounded in

anecdote, was quick and happy in repartee, had a large store of interesting reminiscences at command, drawn from varied and long experience. . . . Those who took it for granted that he was accesibble [sic] and companionable, who stormed him, as it were, he liked. He did not esteem a man the less who grappled with him and struck back. Men who had no opinions or were afraid to utter them he regarded with contempt.[10]

Although apparent to a colleague of several years, these characteristics did not manifest themselves to many in his congregation during those first years in Troy; however, Beman soon impressed them with his boldness, conviction, and determination. Whatever they thought of him, the congregation of the First Church knew that in Beman they had a man of consequence.

In May 1824, after less than a year in New York, the Troy Presbytery sent Beman to represent them at the General Assembly in Philadelphia. Although his activities were undistinguished, he served on several committees and extended the range of his acquaintanceship among the Presbyterian leaders. Upon his return, he learned of his election as a trustee of Middlebury College, a position he held until his death. Still another honor came from Williams College. In recognition of his leadership in the missionary field and his growing prominence in the church, Williams conferred upon him the honorary degree of Doctor of Divinity.[11]

Another significant event in Beman's early years at Troy was an invitation from Middlebury to deliver the commencement address. On 17 August 1825, Beman spoke on this theme: "Intelligence and virtue are twin sisters; and had not man become an alien from his Maker they would have been as inseparable as are all our intellectual and moral powers." In this address, Beman made his first known reference to slavery following his departure from Georgia. "As to slavery," Beman proclaimed to the faculty, graduates, and guests, "it has its origins in theft and injustice—and in its existence and progress in the social state it is a triple curse: a curse to the master, to the slave, and to the unborn posterity of both." Later in the

---

[10]Vincent, *Memorial Sermon*, 15-18.

[11]William M. Engles, ed., *Minutes of the General Assembly of the Presbyterian Church in the United States of America from 1821 to 1835* (Philadelphia: Presbyterian Board of Publications, 1835) 96, 112; Henry B. Nason, *Biographical Record of the Officers and Graduates of the Rensselaer Polytechnic Institute, 1824-1886* (Troy: William H. Young, 1887) 30, 34.

speech, Beman condemned the institution more strongly, saying, "Upon free institutions, slavery fixes a stain which the enlightened and generous spirit of this age will not long endure."[12] Still another activity that brought recognition to Beman during this period was his publication in 1825 of the first of several collections of hymns under the title of "The Church Psalmist."[13]

Two events in 1825 started Beman on a course of action that was to shatter the harmony between him and his congregation and was to have repercussions through the entire Presbyterian Church. The first was the publication in January of a volume entitled *Four Sermons on the Atonement.* Although the sermons would not be considered radical today, at the time many Presbyterians regarded them as little short of heresy. Dismayed by the apathy of many clergymen in spreading the gospel, Beman put forward unhesitatingly the belief that when God announced that he "sent his beloved son into the world that *whosoever* believeth in Him should not perish but have everlasting life," God meant exactly what he said. Beman argued that Christianity was not for an elect or restricted group, but for everyone. Such a declaration constituted a direct attack on the searching examinations and rigid requirements for admission to the church at that time. While many clergymen shared this belief, no man in the Presbyterian Church in America had before uttered such sentiments in so pronounced a manner. The sermons immediately stirred a lively controversy.[14]

The second, and more dramatic, of these events was inspired by the success of a young minister named Charles Grandison Finney in a series of revivals in Oneida County, New York. The revivals' emphasis was on the less pious members of the communities, rather than those whose faith was strong. Finney exhorted his listeners to abandon the passivity of waiting for God to enter their hearts, to renounce their present way of life, and to deliver themselves instantly to Christ. Beman had advanced this same

---

[12]Nathan S. S. Beman, *Oration Pronounced at Middlebury before Associated Alumni of the College on the Evening of Commencement, August 17, 1825* (Troy: Tuttle and Richards, 1825) 4, 7, 9, 30-31.

[13]Nason, *Biographical Record.*

[14]Martin I. Townsend, *Proceedings of the Centennial Anniversary,* 20-21; G. Frederick Wright, *Charles Grandison Finney* (Boston: Houghton, Mifflin, 1983) 53.

point of view in his sermons on the atonement. Finney was remarkably successful, converting whole towns in some instances. Before the revivals were completed, twenty-five congregations had taken part; not a single village in Oneida County had been overlooked. Finney estimated that at least 2,500 persons were converted.[15]

In Finney, Beman recognized a kindred spirit, a man who like himself felt that the Christian world had been negligent in its duty toward the lowly and unawakened. To remedy this neglect, Beman followed Finney's example and organized a revival in Troy. But Beman was only partially satisfied with its results, so on 9 June 1826 he invited Finney to come to Troy to assist him. In the letter, which was the beginning of a long partnership in the cause of revivals, Beman wrote,

> I have but one moment to say to you that we have heard of you, and many in this city would be glad to see you here. . . . The church is cold, though the Lord has converted some sinners as we hoped. Now I wish to submit this proposition to you, that you make the question of a visit to this place a subject of special prayer, and if the Lord will let you come— then come. Perhaps now is the most favorable time to do good. Those who are anxious for a revival *hope* and *tremble*. The result we know not. . . . It is my conviction that you *ought* to come this day; and could I go into details I believe you would think so too. But pray; and may the Lord send you speedily.[16]

Although Finney was unable to visit Troy at that time, Beman proceeded with the revival. On 2 August he renewed his invitation to Finney, telling him, "There is great excitement in the church and out of the church. Some of the professors are awake—that is a few, but the great mass hang back and some oppose with great bitterness. Sinners are fighting with all their might."[17] This time Finney assented to Beman's request.

Finney was a large man, tall and imposing. He was thirty-four years old when he came to Troy. Born in Warren, Connecticut, he had obtained

---

[15]P. H. Fowler, *Historical Sketch of Presbyterianism in the Synod of Central New York* (Utica: Curtis and Childs, 1877) 260; Charles Beecher, ed., *Autobiography of Lyman Beecher, D.D.* (New York: Harper and Brothers, 1865) 89-90.

[16]Letter, Nathan S. S. Beman to Charles Grandison Finney, 9 June 1826, Charles Grandison Finney Papers, Oberlin College Library, Oberlin, Ohio.

[17]Letter, Nathan S. S. Beman to Charles Grandison Finney, 3 August 1826, Finney Papers.

an education of sorts and then, at the age of sixteen, had begun teaching school. After four years of teaching, he decided he wanted to enroll at Yale and so began a college preparatory course. At its conclusion, however, the illness of his mother and his instructor's advice that college would little benefit a man of his ability persuaded him to abandon the idea. He began to study law. After four years he again changed his mind and this time undertook the study of theology. In December 1823, he was licensed to preach, and the following autumn he began his famous Oneida County revivals.[18]

The arrival of Finney and his "holy band" of assistants provided the spark needed to make Beman's revival a success. Finney introduced Beman to several new techniques that had worked effectively for him. One innovation was the "prayer of faith," which the evangelist claimed would be answered immediately and infallibly if made in the proper frame of mind. Two other devices were the "anxious meeting" and the "anxious seat." At the former, individuals who had felt the stirrings of remorse about their sinful state met with the pastor for prayer and exhortation to hasten along the newly awakened desire for salvation. "Anxious seats" were special chairs reserved for these "hopefuls" at the revival meetings.

One of the most controversial practices was praying and speaking by women in public, but a method that greatly irritated some members of Beman's congregation was the practice of publicly praying for persons by name without their request, consent, or knowledge and, at times, by people whose relation to them excused no such liberty. Another innovation suggested by Finney was a morning prayer meeting at four o'clock for laboring men and their families. Visits to private homes and commercial establishments constituted still another means by which the evangelists sought to awaken the community.[19] These techniques, with modifications and ad-

---

[18]Fowler, *Historical Sketch*, 258-59.

[19]*Brief Account of the Origins and Progress of the Divisions in the First Presbyterian Church; Containing also Strictures upon the New Doctrines Preached by the Rev. C. G. Finney and N. S. S. Beman, with a summary Relation of the Trial of the Latter before the Troy Presbytery, By a Member of the late Church and Congregation* (Troy: Tuttle and Richards, 1827) 16-17, 21-25, 28-29. Josephus Brockway probably is the author of this pamphlet. Fowler, *Historical Sketch*, 266.

ditions, became known as "The New Measures" and their practitioners were given the name of "The New School."

In the "holy band" of assistants and apprentices who accompanied the "master" was Theodore Weld, the son of the Congregational pastor in Hampton, Beman's hometown. Weld was twenty-three years old and already a veteran public speaker. At seventeen, after a temporary failure of eyesight that forced his withdrawal from Phillips Academy, he had toured the East and South for three years lecturing on mnemonics. In 1825 Weld had entered Hamilton College, but had been there only a few weeks when he heard Finney speak, was converted, and left college to assist and study with the revivalist. The meeting of Beman and Weld marked the beginning of a long friendship that later persuaded Beman to participate actively in the abolitionist movement.[20]

While the "holy band" infused new life into Beman's revival, their activities also provoked criticism. According to one critic, Finney's preaching would have created turmoil and aroused opposition anywhere. "There was a magnificence about him in the pulpit to inspire admiration and awe, with his towering and finely proportioned person, . . . expressive and vigorous, but graceful, gestures, his penetrating voice and varied intonations, his glaring eye, and his power of reasoning. . . . But how he searched and exposed the heart—to what a vivid consciousness of themselves he brought his hearers, and how irritating it was to many in the church and to more in the world to be thus found out."[21] Following Finney's example, Beman began "infusing greater warmth into his discourses."[22]

In their zeal, both men often exceeded the bounds of discretion and good taste. Finney became imperious, intolerant, denunciatory, and even defamatory. In his head-long enthusiasm he shocked the pious sensibilities of many by his frequent use of "hell" and "damnation."[23] According to reports, Beman indulged in reckless name-calling, allegedly making statements such as, "Mrs. Dencker is an old hypocrite and an old liar and

---

[20]Benjamin P. Thomas, *Theodore Weld, Crusader for Freedom* (New Brunswick: Rutgers University Press, 1950) 8, 11-16.

[21]Fowler, *Historical Sketch*, 263.

[22]*Brief Account of the Origins and Progress of the Divisions*, 16.

[23]Fowler, *Historical Sketch*, 264.

I will have her up for it"; "Mrs. Weatherby is an old devil"; "the members of this church are going post haste to hell" and others equally inflammatory. Beman not only invoked the power of God, but to make certain that He appreciated the dire necessity of their conversion he painted a dark and dismal picture of the person's character. Since the victims of his onslaughts were "often the oldest and most respectable members of the church," resentment flared.

Another irritant was the invasion of homes and of business establishments, often those of complete strangers, to spread the gospel. Once he gained admission, the evangelist usually greeted the startled stranger with a salutation such as, "You are going to hell," "Have you an interest in Christ?" or "Are you a Christian?" and then started an embarrassingly intimate discussion of the personal life and convictions of the victim. The reaction to such an approach often was hostile and at times resulted in eviction.

When Beman attempted to visit Mrs. Weatherby, whom he had called "an old devil" in one sermon, the preacher encountered a highly indignant husband who told him to leave. When the clergyman refused, Weatherby tried to evict him by force. In the ensuing fight, Beman was thrown and pinned to the floor. Undaunted, he shouted "Murder!" until Weatherby, afraid of a public scene or possible arrest, released him.

During the revivals, the tactics of Beman and Finney became so notorious that it was common to see school children repeating and embellishing their language and mimicking their gestures on the street corners of Troy. Opposition, however, instead of deterring the evangelists merely whetted their appetites for stronger measures and more converts.[24]

Beman was quick to adopt the techniques of his younger colleague, and once the revival was well underway Finney felt it desirable to take his talents elsewhere. However, at the peak of the revival a recurrence of tuberculosis forced Beman to his bed. In a letter to Finney, he explained his illness:

> In attending an ordination a few days since I took a cold which affects my lungs, and it will be utterly impracticable for me to go on with my usual share of labor. This is an old complaint of mine; and I know when it is necessary for me to hold back. I am willing to die in the harness, but a few

---

[24]*Brief Account of the Origins and Progress of the Divisions,* 16-17, 21-25, 28-29.

sermons prostrate my system when my lungs are in this state. Much experience has instructed me.[25]

Two days later he wrote an urgent sequel, telling of letting blood and being forced to remain in bed. Regarding the revival, he reported,

> The state of things here is alarming. Something must be done. Our church has never been thoroughly awake; and I fear this week that those who have felt the most are going back. . . . Oh! do enter into our case—the Lord here—nobody to help me—opposition strong—my health and spirits down—and Christians ready to faint. If something is not done *immediately*, the revival is over![26]

Beman had secured a substitute to fill his pulpit, but he was dissatisfied with the man's lack of fire. He wrote Finney that the young preacher had just graduated from some theological seminary, apparently "on the moon or some other cold climate." "It was no doubt fine preaching," Beman continued, "so thought the wicked, and so thought their master for aught I know." Unwilling to entrust his ministerial duties to the young man again, Beman "crawled into the pulpit" and, so hoarse that he could hardly speak, had conducted the afternoon service and an anxious meeting for seventy parishioners in the evening.[27]

Moved by the pitiable condition of his friend, Finney returned to Troy and, except for occasional excursions to fill nearby pulpits, remained in the city most of the winter. As the revival continued, opposition increased. The invasions of privacy, public prayers for prominent members of the church, and incendiary preaching stirred tremendous hostility.[28]

Outside the city, opposition to the New Measures was also growing. Many clergymen were beginning to look askance at the tactics of Finney and Beman and the outbreak of emotionalism. The Reverend Dr. Spring of Durham, New York, objected to the implication in the prayer of faith that if prayers were not infallibly answered either God was not true to his

---

[25]Letter, Nathan S. S. Beman to Charles Grandison Finney, 23 September 1826, Finney Papers.

[26]Ibid.

[27]Letter, Nathan S. S. Beman to Charles Grandison Finney, 25 September 1826, Finney Papers.

[28]Charles Grandison Finney, *Memoirs* (New York: A. S. Barnes, 1876) 205.

word or the supplicant had not prayed in faith; he felt that this doctrine could lead to the wildest fanaticism. The Reverend S. C. Aiken of Utica objected to the frequent use of inflammatory language, words such as "devil" and "damnation." Others felt that public praying by women, the intrusion of the evangelists upon the parishes of settled ministers, and similar measures were both vulgar and degrading to the ministry.[29]

Asahel Nettleton, then pastor at Jamaica, Long Island, took the lead in opposing the New School. Nettleton, an eccentric bachelor with a reputation for sudden and unexplained disappearances, had for several years suffered from poor health. Much of his opposition to Beman and Finney stemmed from his illness and from jealousy over the success of the younger men in a field in which he had once excelled. Although Nettleton was famous as a revivalist, he had an almost morbid horror of fanaticism. Accordingly, his revivals were characterized by great solemnity. Parishioners mourned their backsliding and returned to God with deep contrition. Sinners were bowed down with distress. When a revival became widespread, whole communities conducted themselves like criminals under sentence of death.

The atmosphere most congenial to Nettleton was one of hushed, mysterious stillness. "I love to talk to you," he would say, "you are so still." In almost every respect, Beman and Finney were perfect antipodes to the older clergyman. Nettleton was reverential, timid, and secretive, the "holy band" bold, robust, and demonstrative. Nettleton was subdued, the New School bombastic. Where Nettleton ensnared sinners by guile, Beman and Finney stormed them. According to Nettleton, the difference between his revivals and those of the New School was: "Seven years ago about two thousand souls were hopefully born into the kingdom in this vicinity with comparative stillness. But the times have altered. The kingdom of God now cometh with great observation."[30]

What finally moved the older man to action, however, was the rumor that the New Measures men were using his methods to sanction their own procedures. In a letter Nettleton complained,

---

[29]Fowler, *Historical Sketch*, 266; Beecher, *Autobiography of Lyman Beecher*, 91.

[30]Beecher, *Autobiography of Lyman Beecher*, 94; William D. Sprague, *Annals of the American Pulpit* (New York: Robert Carter and Brothers, 1859) 2:542-52.

They have pleaded my example for many measures which, as to time and circumstances, I utterly condemn. Some of the means which I have never dared to employ except in the most interesting crisis of a powerful revival, they have caricatured in such a manner, and raised such prejudices against myself among strangers, that they have caused me much trouble. My plans have been laid to visit many towns and cities, and have been wholly defeated by these students in divinity thus running before me.[31]

Opposition to his visits in communities that had formerly welcomed him must have been highly irksome to Nettleton.

On 2 January 1827, Nettleton decided to take steps to halt the progress of the New School and composed a long, elaborate letter to Lyman Beecher, then in Boston. Although Beecher was later to become one of the most influential members of the New Measures movement, he was a staunch opponent and critic during its early years. Nettleton wove together a monumental mass of rumors and ended with an appeal to Beecher to speak to the evangelists.[32]

Ironically, Nettleton received an invitation to go to Albany to lead a revival. With hopes of dealing the New School a blow by demonstrating that a successful revival could be conducted near their stronghold without resorting to fanaticism, Nettleton accepted. The results satisfied him. Writing to Beecher, he reported that from "two to three thousand souls assemble every Sabbath evening to hear a feeble, dying man preach." A few miles away, Beman continued his revival. On 8 January, he wrote Finney, "There have been several conversions since you left. . . . The enemy rages, but all will go well if Christians do not grieve the spirit of prayer. There is a great wish to see you here, and this feeling is stronger in more than in me."[33] Upon receipt of Beman's invitation, Finney returned to Troy.

---

[31]Letter, Asahel Nettleton to S. C. Aiken, 13 January 1827, in Bennet Tyler, *Memoir of the Life and Character of Rev. Asahel Nettleton, D.D.* (Boston: Congregational Board of Publication, 1856) 244, also 226-27; Beecher, *Autobiography of Lyman Beecher,* 94-95.

[32]Tyler, *Rev. Asahel Nettleton,* 238-49; Beecher, *Autobiography of Lyman Beecher,* 95.

[33]Letter, Nathan S. S. Beman to Charles Grandison Finney, 8 January 1827, Finney Papers.

During his visit to Albany, Nettleton undertook to learn as much as he could about the activities of Beman and Finney in Troy, although he never visited the city. In a letter to Aiken, he admitted that "a work of grace" doubtlessly had occurred in Troy. "Many sinners have hopefully been born into the kingdom," he confessed, "but it has been at an awful expense." He reported that ministers who had visited the revival expressed shock over the irreverent use of the name of God. Others, who had gone to Troy expressly to catch the flame of enthusiasm, returned saying, "We do not want *such* a revival." Nettleton learned of the growing dissension in Beman's church and delightedly passed the news on to Aiken. The errors of the New School men could be corrected, he concluded, if only they were willing to listen to older, more experienced leaders. However, as was to be revealed shortly, Nettleton was unwilling to provide the needed advice.[34]

When Finney and Beman learned of Nettleton's presence in Albany, they decided that one of them should visit the older man and attempt to adjust their differences. Finney was selected to pay the visit. Accounts of this confrontation differ. According to Nettleton's biographer, Finney was unwilling to abandon the measures that Nettleton regarded as most harmful and, because of encouragement from Beman and others, was unable to see any irregularity in his methods. Finney interpreted the meeting differently:

> Soon after my arrival at Troy, I went down to Albany to see him. . . . I found that he entirely agreed with me . . . on all the points of theology upon which we conversed. Indeed, there had been no complaint by Dr. Beecher or Mr. Nettleton of our teaching in those revivals. . . . What they complained of was something that they supposed was highly objectionable in the measures that we used. . . . I observed that he avoided the subject of promoting revivals. When I told him that I intended to remain in Albany and hear him preach in the evening, he manifested uneasiness and remarked that I must not be seen with him. Hence, Judge C., who accompanied me from Troy and who had been in college with Mr. Nettleton, went with me to the meeting. . . . I saw enough to satisfy me that I could expect no advice or instruction from him, and that he was there to take a stand against me. I soon found I was not mistaken.[35]

---

[34]Tyler, *Rev. Asahel Nettleton*, 239.

[35]Finney, *Memoirs*, 202-203.

In a letter to Beecher, Nettleton elaborated upon his part in the meetings. "You may think it strange that I did not receive him and run the risk of moulding him," he wrote, "but I could not do it without sanctioning all that he had done, and joining disorganizers all over the world, for my name was already in their service at the West."[36] Although Beecher was strongly under Nettleton's influence at the time and inclined to take his part, he later concluded that the truth regarding the interview seems to have been that Nettleton's mind was made up before he visited Albany and that nothing Finney could have said or done would have softened his attitude.[37]

Before Beecher learned of Finney's conference with Nettleton, he had written a letter to Beman and Finney in response to Nettleton's plea that he interfere and attempt to halt the activities of the New School. The object of the letter, according to Beecher, "was to justify them [Beman and Finney] against the opposition of formalists and the haters of revivals of religion, and to suggest emendations where to me it seemed they might be needed, and yet without checking the ardor, and boldness, and moral momentum."[38] A copy was sent to Nettleton, who furnished an extract to the moderator of the Troy Presbytery, who lent it to a friend. The friend showed it to others and in this manner the letter soon found its way into print in the form of a handbill. Whether this was Nettleton's intention is not known. He wrote to Beecher, regretting the "surreptitious publication of that letter of yours to me. . . . Yet I am not sure but we should all have kept silence unless you had been made to speak, contrary to your own and the wishes of your friends."[39] In Troy, Beman and Finney soon began to feel the influence of Beecher's letter upon the members of Beman's church. Fomented by this outside influence, opposition to the men and their measures mounted rapidly.

At this juncture Finney issued his first printed sermon, which added fuel to the flame. The sermon, originally preached at Utica and repeated

---

[36]Letter, Asahel Nettleton to Lyman Beecher, 10 May 1837, in Beecher, *Autobiography of Lyman Beecher*, 92-93.

[37]Beecher, *Autobiography of Lyman Beecher*, 93.

[38]Ibid., 96.

[39]Ibid., 97.

at Troy on 4 March, was on the text from Amos 3:3: "Can two walk together except they be agreed?"[40] Nettleton accepted the challenge and undertook to attack the sermon—in print. Beman was of the opinion that Nettleton had made an unwise decision; he believed that the sermon would prove to "be popular and all attempts to put it down in the gross must prove ineffectual."[41]

With opposition growing, Beman sought to protect himself, Finney, and other New Measures men from censure at the approaching General Assembly. Early in May he urged Finney to go to Philadelphia prior to the Assembly and to deliver a series of sermons in the hope of converting some of the delegates before that body met. A week later he asked Finney to come to Troy to establish a plan of action.[42] In an effort to end the dispute, Finney sought another interview with Nettleton. Beman, however, was under the impression that Nettleton would not see him. "The fact is," Beman claimed, "he is getting farther and farther off." Beman felt that Nettleton had little chance of winning enough support to take action and expressed the belief that before long Beecher would forsake the man.[43]

Throughout the dispute, both Beman and Finney carefully refrained from acknowledging the correspondence and publications of Nettleton and Beecher. Beecher's letter remained unanswered and, although Beman was tempted to write a reply to Nettleton's review of Finney's sermon, he concluded that more could be gained by silence than by the ablest of pens. Thus the matter remained until June, when Beman decided that the controversy must be halted. Convinced that the continuing disharmony endangered both Christian unity and the revival movement, he went to Boston to propose to Beecher a convention for the purposes of explanation and conciliation. Beecher agreed, and a time and place were set. On

---

[40]Wright, *Charles Grandison Finney*, 80; Robert Samuel Fletcher, A *History of Oberlin College* (Oberlin OH: Oberlin College, 1943) 1:16.

[41]Letter, Nathan S. S. Beman to Charles Grandison Finney, 26 May 1827, Finney Papers.

[42]Letters, Nathan S. S. Beman to Charles Grandison Finney, 1, 8 May 1827, Finney Papers.

[43]Letter, Nathan S. S. Beman to Charles Grandison Finney, 26 May 1827, Finney Papers.

7 July Beman wrote Finney about the contemplated meeting. "You must come," he wrote. "There can be no apology received."[44]

On 18 July the convention assembled in New Lebanon, New York, a village about thirty miles southeast of Troy. The meeting was wholly unofficial, with none of the delegates representing any church or ecclesiastical body; the purpose was simply to bring together the parties to consult, to compare views, to see if anything was wrong in fact and, if so, to correct the errors. Among those present were Beman, Beecher, Nettleton, Finney, President Heman Humphrey of Amherst College, Justin Edwards of Andover, Massachusetts, and D. C. Lansing of Auburn, New York.

The convention was organized with Humphrey as moderator. As soon as the business before the group had been stated, the New Measures delegates requested the sources of Nettleton's and Beecher's information. According to Finney, "It was discovered at once that this was an embarrassing question." Beecher replied that the New England ministers had not come to be catechized and, standing on his "spiritual dignity," refused to divulge their sources. The question then turned to how the facts about the revivals were to be learned. Beecher argued that the testimony of the New School men should be excluded since they were, in a sense, parties to the question and would be testifying in their own case. But Humphrey ruled that the leaders of the revivals were the best witnesses that could be procured, that they knew best what had been done, and that their statements would be received.

Following the moderator's decision, Justin Edwards rose and proposed a series of resolutions dealing with revivals generally. The resolutions affirmed that revivals were the work of God, that greater revivals were to be desired, that the methods of conducting revivals bore on their effectiveness, that ministers should agree on which practices were to be countenanced, and other points in a similar vein. Before Edwards finished, a New School man interrupted to ask, "We approve of these resolutions, but what is their design?" Their intent, the New School argued, was solely to create the impression that they in some way disagreed with these principles, had been guilty of violating the resolutions, and that the opposition of Nettleton and others had therefore been justified. Beecher tried to reassure

---

[44]Letters, Nathan S. S. Beman to Charles Grandison Finney, 26 May, 7 June 1827, Finney Papers; Beecher, *Autobiography of Lyman Beecher*, 101.

the New School that the resolutions implied nothing of the sort, but were merely to serve as guides for future conduct. Adoption, he contended, would show that the convention agreed on general principles.

The introduction of the resolutions was a shrewd move by the Old School, for the revivalists could not in honesty vote against them. They were adopted unanimously and, thus, the Old School scored a tactical victory. Following the vote, Edwards rose again and presented a long list of additional resolutions that became increasingly specific. Late that afternoon, he offered the proposition: "In social meetings of men and women, for religious worship, females are not to pray." At this proposal the New School men were ready to rise in anger but Humphrey, recognizing the signs of frayed tempers, called for adjournment.

The next morning Beecher renewed the discussion of public prayers by women, insisting that the practice was unscriptural. Beman undertook to answer the Bostonian. In refutation, he argued that the practice was familiar to the apostles and, citing biblical sources, contended that they had not reproved praying by women but had simply admonished them to wear veils when they did so. Apparently his answer was conclusive, for no reply was attempted. Dirck C. Lansing, a New Measures man, then proposed a substitute resolution stating that "there may be circumstances in which it may be proper for a female to pray in the presence of men." When the vote was taken, eight New School ministers cast their ballots in favor of Lansing's resolution, and the Old School members declined to vote.

On the third morning, the Old School resumed its attack with a resolution condemning the practice of calling persons by name in public prayers. Again a bitter argument ensued. Edwards apparently had an unlimited supply of resolutions, for he continued to produce one after another. When he introduced a proposal to condemn ministers who called other preachers "cold, stupid, dead, unconverted or enemies to revivals," Beman appended to the list "heretics, or enthusiasts, or disorganizers, or deranged, or mad"—terms frequently applied to the New School leaders. Finally, that afternoon, the New School counterattack got underway. Beman took the floor and condemned listening to unfounded rumors and writing letters of complaint over methods employed in revivals.

The meeting continued for three more days. During its course, Nettleton became so upset that he was unable to attend for several days. However, near the close, he returned and announced that he proposed to read a "historical letter" that gave the reasons for his opposition to the new methods. The letter, fully as long as a sermon, listed each of the practices of which Nettleton complained. When he finished, Finney flatly denied the charges, adding that if any of the assembled ministers knew or believed any of the complaints to be true "let them say so now and here." Not a single member of the convention rose to meet Finney's challenge. Nettleton and Beecher, surprised, saw no reason for prolonging the meeting.

However, once he had gained the offensive, Finney had no intention of letting the matter rest and, accordingly, proposed a strongly worded resolution condemning "lukewarmness" in religion. At this point Beecher lost his temper and thundered, "I know your plan, and you know I do; you mean to come to Connecticut and carry a streak of fire to Boston. But if you attempt it, as the Lord liveth, I'll meet you at the state line and call out all the artillery-men and fight every inch of the way to Boston, and then I'll fight you there"—rather strong language for an Old School conservative.

Following Beecher's outburst, the convention adjourned *sine die*, having accomplished little except to focus attention on the growing rift, to win widespread publicity for the New School, and to widen the breach between the two factions. The meeting may also have served to warn the Old School of the mettle of the opposition, for on the way back to Boston Beecher was heard to remark, "We crossed the mountains expecting to meet a company of boys, but we found them to be full-grown men."[45]

In Troy, Beman continued to experience difficulties with his own congregation. His enemies circulated reports that Beman had declared his intention of pursuing his critics "from house to house until he had ferreted them out, . . . driven them from their lurking places, . . . stripped them of their sheep skins, . . . and exposed the teeth of the wolf." He was supposed to have accused the merchants of "over-reaching in dealings" and accumulating "ungodly gain." Another rumor accused him of censuring his congregation for failing to admire his sermons. Repeating criticisms he had heard, Beman was supposed to have said, "You wonder how I have

---

[45]Beecher, *Autobiography of Lyman Beecher*, 100-101; Finney, *Memoirs*, 211-20; Wright, *Charles Grandison Finney*, 84, 94; Charles C. Cole, Jr., "The New Lebanon Convention," *New York History* 31:4 (October 1950): 391-95; George M. Stephenson, *The Puritan Heritage* (New York: Macmillan Co., 1952) 109-10.

heard of this? Why, I will tell you. God told me."[46] While these reports probably were exaggerated, Beman's emotionalism was beginning to alienate many in his congregation. Although he still retained the support of a majority, a vocally insistent minority was determined to oust him from the pulpit. Accordingly, they drew up a petition charging Beman with conduct unbecoming his office and asking that an investigation be made. The resolution was addressed to the trustees rather than to the church session, the usual body before which a clergyman would be brought to trial. Their purpose was to avoid a trial by the congregation, where Beman had influential support. The trustees, however, did not think themselves empowered to act and declined to interfere. Because the regular session of the Troy Presbytery was to assemble in the near future, Beman's opponents decided to seek a hearing before that body.[47]

When the presbytery convened, the petition was placed before the group. A secret session was ordered, and Beman solicited the appointment of a committee to inquire into his conduct. The committee was named, and the trial was scheduled for the following morning. At the time, the constitution of the Presbyterian Church provided two modes for bringing an offense before a judicatory: either by an individual or individuals who appear as accusers or by *common fame*. The complainants took the latter course, declaring that *common fame* charged Beman with conduct prejudicial to his position.

At the start of the trial, Beman refused to contend against so slippery an adversary as *common fame* and insisted that an actual prosecutor be named. This was the first of a series of well-planned maneuvers that characterized his defense. When the presbytery concurred with Beman's request for a prosecutor, the accusers named Colonel Albert Pawling, a wealthy pewholder and regular attendant of the First Church for many years. Beman, however, claimed that Pawling was an Episcopalian and insisted that no one be permitted to prosecute unless he were a member of his church. The presbytery again concurred.

The petitioners then named two other men, both church members, who consented to serve if they could have the assistance of counsel. In preparing for the trial, Beman had made a careful study of the church con-

---

[46]*Brief Account of the Origins and Progress of the Divisions*, 29, 34-35.

[47]Ibid., 38-39.

stitution and knew that the appearance of professional counsel in any ecclesiastical council was forbidden. He objected on this ground and the request was denied. Unwilling to undertake the case without preparation, the appointed prosecutors made two further requests, one for a stenographer and another for a delay. Both were denied. Thoroughly frustrated and incapable of pleading the case without assistance and time, the two men resigned. Finally, Henry Mallory, another church member, consented to serve as prosecutor. Mallory also asked for a delay, but the presbytery insisted that the trial commence immediately.[48]

The principal charges consisted of twenty statements allegedly made by Beman from the pulpit. The clergyman was accused of saying that his parishioners were so hollow-hearted that only on communion days could they be known as church members; that their lack of faith would plunge them into hell; that if one prayed in good faith, God would grant the prayer immediately; that most parents secretly hoped that their children would not be converted; that the clerks on River Street were ungodly and damned; and other such utterances.

Each charge specified that these were *in substance* Beman's words, but the minister insisted that in order to prove their case, his accusers would have to show that the actual words included in the charge had been spoken, stating that proof of the use of similar words would not sustain the charge. The presbytery once again supported him. Beman further demanded that the petitioners show that the remarks attributed to him were, in their original context, censurable. When these demands were accepted by the presbytery, Beman's task was simple. All he had to do was prove that the witnesses could not swear that the words in the charge were the exact words used by him in a particular context. As one of Beman's accusers pointed out, "Everybody knows that there would be difficulty in finding even two in a congregation who could give the identical words of a single sentence in a discourse, although half the house could have clearly related the sentiment."

Beman's cross-examination of the witnesses consisted mainly of questions related to the exactness of the language contained in the charges and

---

[48]Ibid., 37-42; Samuel Miller, Jr., *Report of the Presbyterian Church Case: The Commonwealth of Pennsylvania vs. Ashbel Green and Others* (Philadelphia: William S. Martien, 1839) 28-29.

the dates on which he was alleged to have uttered the statements. The witnesses were reluctant to assert unqualifiedly as true that which they recalled only vaguely; they often contradicted each other as to whether Beman had said "believe" or "fear," from what particular text he had preached on a Sunday nearly a year before, and other details. On the other hand, Beman's witnesses were well-drilled and, according to one observer, demonstrated "surprising powers of memory and a knowledge of events that appeared mysterious and inexplicable." Still another tactic by which Beman confused his opponents was his claim that the accusers had misunderstood much of what he had said. Perhaps the most remarkable feature of his defense was the minister's refusal to admit that he believed in the "prayer of faith."[49]

Largely because of his skill in bewildering the prosecution's witnesses, Beman was fully acquitted. The presbytery then passed a vote of censure upon the signers of the petition and tendered a vote of thanks to Beman for his ministerial zeal and fidelity. Although the petitioners protested the censure as an insult to justice, a transgression of authority, and an outrage of common sense, the presbytery actually had acted within the limits of its authority in reprimanding the accusers.[50]

The decision, however, did not end the controversy. Dissatisfied with the verdict, the opposition took its case to a still higher ecclesiastical court, the synod. Once more Beman was obliged to prepare a defense of his conduct. The clergyman began rallying support in September. He wrote to Finney, asking him to attend the meeting in Utica, and explained,

> A question of some importance respecting me and my congregation is to come up by way of complaint from a committee of pew owners and others. You probably know something of the application made to our presbytery at their last session and its facts. Said committee now complain to the Synod and expect there to get redress. I hope the Oneida brethren and churches will all be at their posts.[51]

---

[49]Joseph Brockway, *Apology to the Rev. Nathan S. S. Beman, With the Facts in the Case* (Troy: Troy Sentinel, 1827) 5-25.

[50]*Brief Account of the Origins and Progress of the Divisions,* 47; Miller, *Report of the Presbyterian Church Case,* 28-30.

[51]Letter, Nathan S. S. Beman to Charles Grandison Finney, 13 September 1827, Finney Papers.

When the time arrived for the committee to present its charges, the synod refused to hear the appeal. Beman considered the matter closed; but his adversaries were more formidable than he supposed and were prepared to take the grievance to the highest tribunal in the church.

The first indication that the matter was not ended came in November with the publication by Josephus Brockway of an open letter to Beman, entitled *An Apology to the Rev. Nathan S. S. Beman, With the Facts in the Case.* Brockway was part of the opposition, and the pamphlet was far from an apology. In it, Brockway reviewed the trial, accused Beman of deception in his defense, challenged the minister to make public the proceedings, and attached a list of new grievances.

Although Brockway was avowedly hostile to Beman, the poll of pew-owners' attitudes toward the pastor, which he included in the publication, probably was not biased. Since he indicated by name the sentiments of each of more than one hundred members, it seems unlikely he would distort the data. According to Brockway's survey, nearly two-thirds of the owners opposed Beman's continuation as minister. Brockway claimed that the pastor had retained control only because of his ingenious interpretation of the regulations governing the congregation and the support of a few wealthy and influential persons. After his victories in the presbytery and the synod, Beman suffered a discouraging setback in Troy; even before the petition reached the General Assembly, large numbers of his congregation deserted to the Second Church, which Beman had helped to organize in 1826.[52]

In May 1828, Beman attended the General Assembly in Philadelphia where, for the last time, he defended himself. Finney was preaching in the city, and Beman held several meetings with him prior to the convening of the Assembly. The session opened on 15 May and the following day the clerk announced that the appeal had been placed in his hands. It was referred to the judicial committee and four days later the committee ordered it placed on the docket.

On the morning of 24 May the appeal was called, and Brockway appeared to prosecute the charges. The parties involved were heard once more. The next day a representative of the Synod of Albany spoke for their

---

[52]Brockway, *Apology to the Rev. Nathan S. S. Beman,* 40-45, 52; Weise, *History of the City of Troy,* 154-55.

rejection of the appeal because of lack of constitutional notice. The Assembly deliberated upon this point and finally resolved that the petition be dismissed on the ground that the Albany Synod had not been properly approached.

However, Brockway and the petitioners were not to be outmaneuvered quite so easily. They had also submitted the charges to the Committee on Overtures, and the next day the matter came up once more. After introducing the overture, the committee had completed partial reading of the evidence before the Assembly objected. Feeling that they had said all they had to say on the subject, the Assembly voted to postpone the subject indefinitely. The matter thus was finally laid to rest, at least officially. Beman had triumphed, but the victory had been costly. Many years were to pass before he fully overcame the discontent that the controversy had created within his church.[53]

In addition to defending himself at the General Assembly, Beman took part in a conference to end the New School-Old School debate. Finney, Beecher, Lansing, Aiken, Frost, and Joel Parker—but not Nettleton—also participated. At the conclusion of the talks the group published a statement announcing that after discussing the revival controversy they were of the opinion that "the general interests of religion would not be promoted by any further publications on those subjects, or personal discussions, correspondences, conversation, and conduct designed to keep those subjects before the public mind." They pledged their influence to curtail all further debate on the issue. Thus, what they had sought to accomplish at New Lebanon was in Philadelphia finally achieved. Their success was in large part due to Nettleton's absence because of ill health.[54]

Although the agreement reached by the two factions at Philadelphia had the effect of ending public controversy in the press and pulpit, it by no means settled any differences. The New School men continued to employ the same techniques in their revivals, and their successes only intensified irritation among the Old School. In Troy Beman sought to arouse the entire city, taking particular interest in the cotton-mill workers. He succeeded in awakening one young lady to the point that she "felt con-

---

[53]Engles, *Minutes of the General Assembly*, 230-43.

[54]Finney, *Memoirs*, 223; Fletcher, *History of Oberlin College*, 16; Beecher, *Autobiography of Lyman Beecher*, 103; Tyler, *Rev. Asahel Nettleton*, 177-78.

strained to converse with the females in the factory in her department, and those adjoining." When the superintendent returned, he found the looms deserted and an impromptu revival going on. "In less than an hour," reported an observer, "both factories were stopped." Beman's work among the mill workers progressed so well that he soon was required to seek a minister to organize a congregation in the vicinity.[55]

Early in 1829 Beman found a protégé and ally in Edward Norris Kirk of Albany. The capital city had long been an Old School stronghold, and New Measures men had had little success in receiving permission to use the meetinghouses of their conservative brethren for revivals. With the arrival of Kirk to care for Albany's newly organized congregation, Beman was at last able to extend his efforts to the capital city and arranged to exchange churches with the young man. He then began teaching him the new methods. "God has planted his foot in that proud city and it shakes," Beman wrote to Finney. "Oh! what a change. . . . Kirk is all alive and his church feel exactly with us," he continued. "He is learning fast." Beman could not refrain from expressing his gleeful pleasure over the invasion. "Some of *my dear brother* Weed's people have been to him and asked him to invite me into his pulpit, but he stands out. . . . Brother Weed . . . is greatly grieved that I have been permitted to preach in Albany."[56]

To the chagrin of the Old School men, Beman's growing reputation as a preacher and revivalist began to bring calls from other congregations in spite of the controversies. Efforts were made to induce him to leave Troy for New York City, Philadelphia, or some other large city, to which Beman replied, "I do expect I shall have to go to some great city; I don't know. I am at the Lord's disposal." He was unwilling to leave Troy, however, unless he was called to a well-established church.[57]

Over the years the relationship between Beman and Finney had changed. Because of his greater maturity and learning, Beman was gradually replacing Finney as the leader of the New School. No longer was Beman the eager student seeking help and instruction. Instead, he freely

---

[55]Letters, J. P. Cushman to Charles Grandison Finney, 21 February 1828, and Nathan S. S. Beman to Finney, 23 October 1829, Finney Papers.

[56]Letter, Nathan S. S. Beman to Charles Grandison Finney, 25 March 1829, Finney Papers.

[57]Ibid.

advised Finney, often with characteristic bluntness. In March 1829, he questioned Finney: "What do you deform the outside of your letters to me for by sticking on D. D.? Do you do it to insult me, or to make the Post Master think you correspond with some *great man?*" In October, Beman complained, "I was nearly *provoked* with you, that you did not come to my study and talk over New York with Brother Kirk and myself instead of that *miserable meeting* we had at Tracy's. You are a *wise man*, but make mistakes sometimes. Those subjects which came up there ought not to have been broached, at this time, to my friends. The influence has been *bad* already." In another letter he said, "A word to the wise. Remember where you are and who are around you. It is immensely important that you carry the influence of the best men with you." Although Beman and Finney remained friends and co-workers for several years, these critical observations give evidence of Beman's growing independence. With Finney's move to Oberlin, Beman assumed undisputed leadership of the New School. By 1841 the two had grown so far apart that Beman joined the Troy Presbytery in issuing a stinging rebuke to Finney.[58]

At the beginning of 1830, public controversy between the Old and New Schools and the difficulties between Beman and his church appeared resolved. Revivals were flourishing, calls to leading churches seemed in the offing, and invitations to preach were numerous. With the prospect of peaceful and happier times ahead, Beman's work was interrupted by an attack of consumption, and he remained inactive for nearly a year. In January he twice wrote to Finney refusing to consider a call to another church and asking that an assistant be found to aid him in Troy. "My health is such that I can't hold out long without help," he wrote. No one, however, was sent. After having been confined to his home for more than two weeks, Beman complained to Finney, "It seems that I, who have literally lived for *all* the churches, in my necessities can find no one to assist me." Not until late March was Beman able to attend church, but even then his health was so poor that he knew he could not continue to conduct services.

At his request, Beman was granted six-months leave in order to recuperate. In mid-May his condition remained serious. He wrote to Finney, "I have gained a *little*, but I am only the shadow of a man. . . . I can't think of doing anything this summer and in the fall, should I live, I shall

---

[58]Ibid., 23 October 1829; Wright, *Charles Grandison Finney*, 207.

probably be compelled to flee to the South." Twice Beman tried to preach, but both times found himself too feeble to complete his sermon. By autumn a supply had finally been found. Well enough to undertake a trip to the South, Beman journeyed to Georgia where he remained until early spring. He visited Carlisle at Mt. Zion, met his brother's wife, and saw old friends and former parishioners. As his health improved, he began to accept invitations to preach in churches in the vicinity as far away as Charleston and Columbia, South Carolina.[59]

In the spring of 1831 Beman made preparations to return to Troy. A few days before his departure, he received a letter from the presbytery informing him that the principal delegate to the General Assembly could not attend and asking Beman, as the alternate, to fill his place. The clergyman traveled to Philadelphia in the company of several Southern delegates. During the journey the conversation centered on the conflicting interests of the Old and New Schools. Although the controversy had engendered considerable bitterness, most of the clergymen sincerely hoped that harmony and unity might prevail. Thus, before the Southern delegation reached Philadelphia, the party had agreed to support Gardiner Spring, an Old School man, for moderator as a conciliatory move.[60]

Beman discovered that the New School delegation, confident that it had a majority, proposed to nominate him as moderator. Securing Beman's consent, the New School moved with its plan and, in a warmly contested election, the Troy clergyman was elected by a vote of 104-93. Beman's victory marked the first time that the New School had been able to gain control of the Assembly, and the remainder of the session proved stormy. In the unaccustomed position of minority, the Old School floundered helplessly. The main issue of the convention concerned a charge of heresy brought by Ashbel Green, a former moderator, against Albert Barnes. An ardent supporter of Barnes, Beman found it difficult to remain

---

[59]Letters, Nathan S. S. Beman to Charles Grandison Finney, 1, 5, 20 January, 25 March, 17 May 1830, Finney Papers; Letters, J. P. Cushman to Theodore Weld, 8 February 1830, and Serena Streeter to Weld, 16 December 1830, in *Letters of Theodore Dwight Weld, Angelina Grimké Weld and Sarah Grimké, 1822-1844*, ed. Gilbert Barnes and Dwight L. Dumond, 2 vols. (New York: D. Appleton-Century, 1934) 1:33, 37; Nathan S. S. Beman, *An Appeal to the Presbyterian Church: Review and Vindication* (New York: Daniel Appleton, 1831) 27-29.

[60]Beman, *An Appeal . . . Review and Vindication*, 41.

impartial. At one point in the dispute he became so agitated that he asked permission to leave the chair in order to speak. Although the request was denied, Green's charges fell and the New School left Philadelphia triumphantly.[61]

The following August, Green instituted a series of attacks on Beman. As editor of the *Christian Advocate*, Green had a large and ready audience. The principal charges leveled were Green's claims that Beman made his trip South to win support for the New School and that the Troy clergyman had been guilty of flagrant partiality as moderator. For several weeks each issue of the *Advocate* contained an attack on Beman. Finally, deciding that he could no longer ignore Green's charges, Beman replied in seven articles, which were later reprinted and circulated in pamphlet form.

Beman pointed out that ill health had been the fundamental reason for his trip. That he had not gone to Georgia to arouse opposition to the Old School was proved, Beman claimed, by the fact that he had turned down invitations to meet with three Southern presbyteries. "If I had been sent out by my brethren to marshall 'the measures and the men' they must have confided this embassy to a stupid messenger," Beman observed, "and if I was self-commissioned in this business, I must have greatly misapprehended my own talents." The most ridiculous of Green's accusations was based on an editorial in the Columbia (South Carolina) *Telescope* which charged that Beman's trip was part of a plot to establish a union between church and state. According to the editor, Stephen Van Rensselaer of Troy had supplied $2,000 to back the project and had instructed Beman to collect additional contributions in the South. The alleged plot included the elevation of Henry Clay to the presidency, with Daniel Webster as vice-president. All of this was to be accomplished through the Sunday School Union, according to Green. Beman explained his illness, gave an account of his activities in Georgia, and dismissed the charge as preposterous.[62]

Equally absurd, according to Beman, were Green's allegations regarding his conduct in the General Assembly. In replying to them, Beman presented a list of precedents for his actions, pointed out the lack of any

---

[61]Ibid., 43-49.

[62]Ibid., 27-30; *Christian Advocate*, August 1831, 418.

objection by the Old School at the time, and accused his attackers of bad faith and inability to accept the fact that they were in the minority.[63]

The Green exchange marked the end of Beman's first eight years in Troy. It had been a tempestuous time. Although he enjoyed a battle, Beman had adequate cause to doubt his course. Embroiled in controversy with his own congregation during most of the period or under attack from clergymen within the church, at times he felt keenly the hostility on all sides. Added to this was the discouraging recurrence of illness that put him out of action at crucial moments. In spite of obstacles, however, he continued to labor for what he believed to be right. By 1832 Beman knew that the struggle had not been in vain. Following his election to the moderatorship of the General Assembly, Beman exerted a growing influence in the councils of the Presbyterian Church. His name became known throughout the country, and his actions contributed significantly to the historic disruption of the Presbyterian Church during the next decade.

---

[63]Beman, *An Appeal . . . Review and Vindication*, 27-30, 41-49.

Chapter IV

Family Discord

> *From affection, good Lord, deliver me.*
> —excerpt of a letter from
> Nathan S. S. Beman to his wife

Beman's private life during his early years in Troy was no less turbulent than his pulpit career. Instead of the quiet, solace, and respect that he sought as relief from his clamorous public life, Beman came home to dissension, tragedy, and financial stringency.

With the birth of a daughter Louisa in 1825, Beman's family included six children: Henry and Eliza, the children by his first marriage; Samuel and Louisa, his and Caroline's children; and William Lowndes and Benjamin Cudworth Yancey, his wife's sons. The older Beman and Yancey children were away at school during most of these years, and only the two youngest, Sam and Louisa, remained at home. Although a stern disciplinarian, Beman loved children, enjoyed playing with them, and took great satisfaction in their development and progress. However, Beman's relations with his wife were severely strained.

Almost from the outset, their marriage had been beset by discord. Even before their departure from Georgia, dissension between them had led Beman to ask the church to pass a sentence of suspension upon his wife. One of the parishioners reported this version of the difficulty:

About five months after their marriage, there was some difficulty between them when Mr. Beman locked her in a room and kept her confined
from morning until afternoon, at which time she was released by a servant. She then went to another room and threw herself upon a bed. Mr.
Beman entered the room while she was in that posture and as soon as she
discovered him she looked up at him and smiled. He abruptly turned his
hell upon her, went away, but soon returned, saying that "if locks would
not hold her, he would see if nails would." He then fastened the door with
the nails and she, alarmed and agitated, raised the window and made an
outcry for help. All blame for this transaction . . . was thrown upon her
by the church session.[1]

Although the account, penned by one of Beman's enemies, may have exaggerated the quarrel, Caroline actually had been suspended by the presbytery before their departure from Georgia.

At the time of Beman's application for the pastorate at Troy, when
rumors of disharmony in his household prompted the church to investigate, Beman had informed the committee members that his wife was a pious
and intelligent woman whom he would be pleased to introduce to the ladies of Troy. He told them that only on one occasion, when he had found
it necessary to interfere with her excessive punishment of a servant, had
there been any trouble between them. However, within a year of his installation, the congregation had become somewhat agitated over their
strife. Beman is supposed to have told friends that Caroline had always
been a woman of refractory temper and that her first husband had fallen
as a sacrifice to it. Specifically, he is reported to have said, "She wore his
life out, and her father said that no man could live with her."[2] Whether
Beman actually made such a statement cannot be ascertained; even if he
did, the young woman could hardly be held responsible for her husband's
death from malaria. The charge regarding Caroline's hasty temper contained greater truth and might well have been made by her eccentric and
outspoken father.

---

[1]*Brief Account of the Origins and Progress of the Divisions in the First Presbyterian
Church in the City of Troy: Containing also Strictures upon the New Doctrines Preached
by the Rev. C. G. Finney and N. S. S. Beman, with a Summary Relation of the Trial
of the Letter before the Troy Presbytery, By a Member of the late Church and Congregation* (Troy: Tuttle and Richards, 1827) 32-35. This was probably written by Josephus Brockway.

[2]Ibid.

In 1826, relations in the Beman household became so unsatisfactory that Beman went to court in an attempt to obtain a legal separation. Before the case actually came to trial, however, members of his congregation arranged a reconciliation. In 1827 and 1828, during the attempt to remove Beman from the pulpit, Brockway and the petitioners made an effort to introduce the minister's marital problems as one of the causes for their discontent. One critic went so far as to discuss openly the dissonance in the pastor's home in a widely circulated pamphlet. In fact, congregation members lined up, took sides, and defended the claims of each party as vigorously as they debated Beman's theology.

To add to the burdens of the clergyman, in 1829 tragedy struck. Their youngest son Samuel, who was seven years old, was thrown from a horse and seriously injured. During his recuperation, he was stricken with typhoid fever. Shortly thereafter Louisa also contracted the illness. For weeks the two children remained in critical condition while the family prayed for their survival. Louisa recovered completely, but little Sam was not so fortunate; he was disfigured by curvature of the spine and by a body permanently dwarfed. During this period, the boy suffered untold tortures from the imperfect—not to say barbarous—methods employed in treating his spinal injury. In alluding to the subject in later years, he could barely retain his composure.[3]

No sooner had the children recovered than Beman suffered the recurrence of tuberculosis. It confined him to his bed during most of the first half of 1830 and forced him to return to Georgia for the winter. The costs of medical care during these months constituted a serious drain on Beman's financial position from which he was not to recover for several years.

Their mutual concern over the illnesses of the two children led Nathan and Caroline temporarily to forget their differences, but by 1832 the eccentricities of the two were again a source of friction. Beman threatened court action a second time, but another concord was reached. In 1833 contention once more jeopardized their marriage, and finally, by 1835 relations between the couple had become so tense that a separation was ar-

---

[3]"The Late Samuel S. Beman," *St. Charles* (Minnesota) *Press,* undated clipping belonging to Catharine Marston Anderson, Seattle, Washington; Letter, Nathan S. S. Beman to Charles Grandison Finney, 23 October 1829, Charles Grandison Finney Papers, Oberlin College Library, Oberlin, Ohio.

ranged. Initially Caroline went to live with friends, remaining in Troy. But some kind of separation for an extended period of time seemed desirable and, after lengthy consultations with friends, lawyers, and the family doctor, Beman agreed to pay his wife's expenses for eighteen months while she visited her family in the South.

Shortly before Caroline's departure, Beman wrote to his wife establishing the terms upon which he would consider a reconciliation. He suggested that they state their grievances before two witnesses—one to be named by him and the other by her—who would judge the merits of their complaints and determine a course of action. "Two hours will settle the whole matter if your pride of heart will only yield," Beman wrote. He promised to treat Caroline with a tenderness and kindness "which would make you much happier than you are now, or than you can be if you go to the South in your present condition." He concluded,

> You know the visitations of conscience which you have when you part with me as you often do when your dreadful temper is excited. You think or say you are correct and right at the time, but your cooler judgment tells you that you have no justification to carry before God. I will not enlarge, I will only say I have no emotion but pity for you in writing this note and I shall regret to have you compel me to act as I certainly shall if this proposal is rejected. What I do I shall do calmly, firmly, and forever. Yours with all the commiseration which I ought to feel for your present self-inflicted suffering.[4]

The meeting was held, and before Caroline left for Georgia the couple was on relatively amicable terms again.

The contention between the two continued for several years, with Caroline living apart much of the time. The letters exchanged during their separation provide information about the causes of their quarrels, although they never specifically state the heart of the matter. Much of the trouble seems to have arisen from their similarity in temperament. Both were strong-willed, outspoken, hasty, and highly independent. Although a champion of women's rights, Beman expected complete subservience and immediate obedience from his wife. He believed that the wife should live a retired and sheltered life, centered around "the domestic fireside, the

---

[4]Letter, Nathan S. S. Beman to Caroline Beman, Fall 1835, Benjamin C. Yancey Papers, Southern Historical Collection, University of North Carolina Library, Chapel Hill.

family circle, the sequestered chamber of devotion and the quietude of sweet and endeared home."[5] Caroline, however, was not prepared to acquiesce mutely to her husband's every request. To Beman, whose conception of the wife's relationship to her husband had been influenced by the conduct and solicitous subservience of his mother, his first wife, and Abigail Bayley, Caroline's attitude was almost incomprehensible.

Contributing further to the disaffection was the dissimilarity in background of the two. Beman had been reared in a rigorous climate among rugged, hardworking people where hardship was almost the rule rather than the exception. Throughout his life, very little had ever been attained without a struggle. Caroline Bird, on the other hand, had grown up in the South amid comparative luxury and ease. Attended by a household of slaves, she had not been required to work both by her affluence and by society and had spent her hours in leisure and social activity. Caroline found pleasure in the company of gay and witty people, and she quickly struck up a warm friendship with some of the socially prominent families of Troy. Beman regarded brilliance in the social world as a "glitter which dazzles for a moment, to be extinguished and then rekindled no more." The clergyman believed that under the influence of this type of activity the passions became too easily excited and the participants led a life of mere caprice, without system or object. "Not a few," he contended, "are characterized by pride and extravagance and shine everywhere except in their own appropriate sphere."[6]

Slavery was yet another point of contention. Taught to believe that slaveholding not only was perfectly compatible with Christianity but that it was a mutually salutary relationship between members of the two races, Caroline found it difficult to understand her husband's abhorrence of the institution. To reject slaveholding as sinful was to condemn her entire family and their mode of living. Although Beman was able to persuade his wife that slavery was inconsistent with the Bible, her conviction was not deep. As soon as she was subjected to pro-slavery influences she quickly reverted to her earlier beliefs.

---

[5]Nathan S. S. Beman, *The Claims of Jesus Christ on Young Women* (Troy: N. Tuttle, 1841) 10.

[6]Ibid., 9.

Soon after their separation, Beman was particularly upset when Caroline announced that she had once more changed her mind on the subject. He replied, "Just before you left home, you had settled your mind, from the Bible, as I heard you say, that *slavery was morally wrong.* Now it seems to be a most holy thing, a gift from heaven. . . . This facility at conversion is very convenient," Beman observed, "as you can thus accommodate yourself to every age and nation."[7] Although they had owned slaves briefly after their marriage, Beman's stand against the institution had been uncompromising. Drawing upon his experience in the South, he condemned slavery as "an immense evil" and became active in the works of the American Anti-Slavery Society.[8] Beman was both embarrassed and irritated to find his wife opposing him and defending the institution.

Still another source of friction was Caroline's love of gossiping. Among her closest friends in Troy were Maria Van Ness and Mrs. Albert Pawling, the wife of one of the pewowners who had sought Beman's dismissal. Beman deplored his wife's friendship with these women and condemned their gossip as malicious. When his wife entered into a correspondence with them during her stay in Georgia, Beman wrote her,

> You have scattered your stuff through the community—gone to members of other churches who hate me and joined with them to destroy my ministerial influence, endeavored to alienate the members of my own church so as to drive them into other congregations, become intimate with two of the most slanderous women in this city out of my church, Maria Van Ness and Mrs. Pawling, and they are spitting their venom all over the country. Mrs. Pawling has entertained parties in Washington County this winter with tales she has had from you respecting me, etc., etc. This I care not for. I know her.[9]

A month later, he told Caroline,

---

[7]Letter, Nathan S. S. Beman to Caroline Beman, 21 December 1835, Benjamin C. Yancey Papers.

[8]*The South Vindicated from the Treason and Fanaticism of the Northern Abolitionists* (Philadelphia: H. Manly, 1836) 168-70; Letter, Nathan S. S. Beman to Theodore Weld, 3 February 1840, in *Letters of Theodore Weld, Angelina Grimké Weld and Sarah Grimké, 1822-1844,* ed. Gilbert Barnes and Dwight L. Dumond, 2 vols. (New York: D. Appleton-Century, 1934) 2:820-22.

[9]Letter, Nathan S. S. Beman to Caroline Beman, 15 February 1836, Benjamin C. Yancey Papers.

Let the news-carriers alone. It is all over this city as reported by you to your dear friend's image Mrs. F., that your son's wife is no housekeeper. It flies well. You have always been the sport of just such women. She tells all you write and all she writes.[10]

In the midst of his difficulties with Caroline, Beman received the tragic news that his oldest son Henry had died in Rio de Janeiro. Only twenty-one years old, the young man had contracted a serious, but unexplained, illness in the South American port and a few days later, on 20 January 1836, had died.[11]

In spite of his grief over this tragedy, Beman did not relent in his attitude toward his wife. Correspondence seems to indicate that, of the two, Caroline was more desirous of a reconciliation. More than once she wrote to her husband to ask forgiveness and to plead to be allowed to return to Troy. Beman, however, was unyielding. In response to Caroline's pleas, early in 1836 he wrote,

You talk of burying the hatchet and of being willing to bear and forbear and of dividing the blame equally between us, etc., etc., etc. Now I do not wish to dwell on this subject; but I will give you in one word the true state of the case. You have for years pursued a course in the family which has destroyed my peace. It was not originally at me, but at domestics and children. When I have endeavored to pacify and quiet you, you have made it a quarrell [sic] with me. . . . I became fully convinced last fall that I could do no more to endeavor to reclaim and to bring you to act on your own voluntary stipulations often repeated and written, and I have made up my mind to let you do as you please. . . . I have come to the conclusion that you are either deranged or you have lost your moral sense, and in this case it is my duty to let the thing entirely alone.[12]

Caroline's financial inexperience and lack of understanding of her husband's pecuniary position created another irritant. In February 1836, the pastor found it necessary to explain that he could not fulfill her request for additional funds because the cost of her trip, the expense of outfitting Henry for his ill-fated voyage, and Louisa's tuition at school had left him

---

[10]Ibid., 15 March 1836.

[11]*Troy Budget*, 22 March 1836.

[12]Letter, Nathan S. S. Beman to Caroline Beman, 15 February 1836, Benjamin C. Yancey Papers.

with an income "just sufficient to meet the current expenses of [the] family." This explanation did not deter Caroline from traveling extensively and spending on a lavish scale. The bills poured in, and Beman wrote her insistently a month later, "Permit me now to tell you what I wish you to do and what I may or ought to be permitted to expect. In the first place I wish you to make with each of your friends your entire visit when you are with them so as to save the expense of going continually from place to place." He explained, "As you know, I am poor and involved in debt, principally from having two sick children who have drawn very heavily upon me for several years past."[13]

One of the pawns in the battle between Beman and his wife was their daughter. Of all his children Beman seems to have felt the greatest affection for Louisa, and he was determined to prevent Caroline from exercising any influence over the girl. One of the clergyman's reasons for agreeing to finance his wife's trip to Georgia was to remove Louisa from her control. To his shock and dismay, in March 1836 Caroline wrote that she intended to return and spend the summer at Bethlehem where Louisa was attending school. Beman's reaction was immediate and obdurate.

> You tell me you expect to spend the summer in Bethlehem. Now what mortal can tell what you intend to do, or where you are to be? . . . It is out of the question for you to come on to Bethlehem the approaching summer. It is contrary to all good calculations, to all good faith's policy. I wish you to ponder the following. 1st. It was a positive condition on my consenting to your going to the South that you shall remain eighteen months. In this way only, you know could I have consented to the expenses to and fro. Now I expect you to keep your word. . . . You know why I sent Louisa to Bethlehem and if you come there I shall instantly take her away. . . . You know it was necessary to have her from you. . . . You must stay at the South and keep quiet . . . that the disgrace and turmoil occasioned by your conduct may die away or you may rely on it, I shall never keep house with you a day while life lasts.[14]

Caroline acceded to Beman's demand and, temporarily, abandoned any attempt to see Louisa.

---

[13]Letters, Nathan S. S. Beman to Caroline Beman, 19 February, 15 March 1836, Benjamin C. Yancey Papers.

[14]Letter, Nathan S. S. Beman to Caroline Beman, 15 March 1836, Benjamin C. Yancey Papers.

Beman's letters suggest that all of the guilt was Caroline's, that she was totally neglectful of his needs and completely oblivious to his wants. His invective and condescension hint that he was dealing with a woman of little intelligence and great obstinacy. That these assumptions are false is borne out by Mrs. Beman's replies to her husband. Her letters reveal shrewd-mindedness, a clear understanding of the temper of her antagonist, and an undeniable flair for a kind of sarcasm which, if more subtle than her husband's, was equally biting. In a letter dated 26 May 1836, Caroline wrote,

> I have received your letter dated 21 of April and I hope to profit by its seeming accusations and aspersions. Feeling that you have entirely misunderstood and misconstrued my letters, I can pardon and forgive your severity of manner in ministering to me, and yet it is mysterious that a man of your acuteness of perception should have misunderstood what myself and another laid so different a construction upon. Feeling sensible from past experience of your aptness to take my expressions different from what they really meant, I have almost invariably showed them another person that I might have omitted every expression which might seem to convey a different meaning than was intended and I thought I had been genteel and courteous, but all has not answered the purpose.[15]

Caroline continued to seek an agreement. In March 1836, she wrote that time and reflection had made her more candid and just, and that instead of adding to his troubles she was determined in the future to do everything possible to make Beman happy. "Permit me now to ask and beseech you if we should ever be permitted to be," she pleaded, "that you will receive me kindly so that I may be assisted in executing these determinations and wait and see the result before you pass sentence of condemnation." "My dear Mr. Beman, notwithstanding what has passed, do you doubt my affection for you?" she asked. "You are the father of my children, which has bound that cord which can never be broken under any circumstance; there have been times when my affections have abated but never alienated, although your letters have been harsh, not expressive of one tender feeling."[16]

---

[15]Letter, Caroline Beman to Nathan S. S. Beman, 26 May 1836, Benjamin C. Yancey Papers.

[16]Ibid.

In spite of her supplications, Caroline would not accept full blame for their differences. "I never can feel that I am that guilty person you represent me," she wrote. "I must know what I have done and what I have not done when I say that I have resisted false accusations. I do not mean to insinuate that you have deliberately falsified, but that you have been falsely impressed and I know that you have accused me of things which you received from others and that I must ever solemnly [submit that] I was never guilty." "I have erred," she admitted; "I have sinned but not to that extent which you think I have; most of my acts have never been premeditated but involuntary from the impulse of too much excitement and want of reflection (which I plead no excuse for)."[17]

This apparently sincere expression of affection and regret, however, failed to mollify Beman. He replied,

> The ground on which I now stand, and on which I have always stood, is this: That I have never commenced a quarrel with you; that all our difficulties have originated with yourself; and that when I have reproved you and restrained you (or tried to do it), and employed what you deem harsh means with you, my sole object has been to save your reputation and character and standing of my family in a Christian community. As to the real causes of these difficulties I take *no part* of the blame! They have uniformly originated with you and not with me. When they existed . . . I have no doubt many a time felt wrong and done wrong; for this I have always expressed my regret. But this has nothing to do with the vital cause of our difficulties. This you and I both know. This is the ground uniformly taken in all our pacifications—in 1826—in 1832-1833. . . . You know I would have taken a legal remedy in 1826 if you had not, and as I supposed honestly and from the bottom of your heart, taken this position.

Beman concluded, "I am almost ready to smile when you ask in your last letter, with apparent gravity, if I 'can doubt your affection?' I answer, if your conduct to me as a wife has been expression of what you call 'affection'—I say 'from affection, good Lord, deliver me!' A very little more affection would actually kill me!"[18]

In the autumn of 1837 Caroline returned to Troy hopeful of resolving their differences. Upon her arrival, Beman turned her away at the door

---

[17]Ibid.

[18]Letter, Nathan S. S. Beman to Caroline Beman, 3 April 1837, Benjamin C. Yancey Papers.

and denied her admission to the house. He not only refused to permit her to live under the same roof, but also announced his decision to sever all financial assistance. In a letter to Ben, Caroline reported, "I have written three times to Mr. B. for my things and the last time for money," but to no avail. Beman had even notified stores, shops, and the post office that he would not pay his wife's debts and that she should be refused credit in his name.[19] A friend took Caroline into her home where she lived for several years, hoping for a reconciliation and fearing that at any moment Beman might take the case to court.

Beman's conduct incensed the Bird family, who implored Caroline to sue for divorce. Her brother William wrote to Ben condemning Beman as a "brute of a husband" and advising,

> This man has spent many dollars of your father's estate for his children. . . . If she [Caroline] would be firm and take the steps she ought, it is improbable in any civilized country he would be permitted to act thus. . . . When he went South your mother supplied him with funds—when he sent his daughters to our house, Pa, Uncle Beene, and then Fitzgerald had to pay his expenses. . . . It would be his dearest gratification if he can be exempted from contributing to her support. . . . That man has been your mother's bitterest foe.[20]

Ben, who was studying law in Georgia at the time, became so angered that he began a collection of Beman's letters and other pertinent documents to assist his mother in prosecuting her husband. Although the members of her family insisted that she take the case to court, Caroline remained adamant in her refusal to sue. If she would not sue, Ben urged that she publish her side of the grievance in a pamphlet, but this too was refused.

While Beman may have had reason to be exasperated with Caroline, his unwillingness to contribute to her support and his refusal to attempt a reconciliation certainly seem lacking in the charity and forgiveness that a minister of the gospel preaches. However, in the same letter in which he proclaimed his poverty and indebtedness, Beman announced that he probably would spend the next year in Europe. Two years later, he again

---

[19]Letter, Caroline Beman to Benjamin C. Yancey, September 1837, Benjamin C. Yancey Papers.

[20]Letter, William Bird to Benjamin C. Yancey, 2 October 1837, Benjamin C. Yancey Papers.

contemplated a trip abroad, a prospect that caused Caroline to express fear that her allowance might be reduced or altogether cancelled. In 1839 Beman actually did embark for England. By that time Caroline was taking in sewing to provide for herself.[21]

In spite of Beman's treatment and her financial straits, Caroline remained in Troy for several years, specifically to be near her children. Samuel and Louisa were still in Troy and, even though she was forbidden entrance to her own home, she did not want to be far from them. However, upon his wife's return to Troy, Beman issued an ultimatum, telling Louisa that she was not to see her mother.[22]

As time passed, Louisa gradually grew farther and farther from Caroline, as well as from most of the rest of the family. Her father's influence and the instability of family relations during her childhood turned her into an aloof, introspective, and bitter woman. She grew to despise her older half-sister Eliza. Sam confessed that Louisa was "as unlike me as though we had the blood of opposite climes in us." He later said, "We do not think alike, our temperaments are utterly dissimilar; I love her more than she can ever know, but our sympathies run in different and often opposite channels." As father and daughter grew closer together, Sam felt increasingly alienated from both. "[I would like to have] opened my heart to them but their peculiar natures always repelled me," Sam later remembered. "I never doubted their love, but we [were] unalike."[23]

During the early 1840s, with her children grown and little likelihood of a reconciliation with her husband, Caroline finally returned to the South permanently. With the aid of Ben—and perhaps the letters that he had collected—she obtained an agreement with Beman whereby he promised to pay part of her expenses. Caroline spent her remaining years boarding first with one member of her family and then another, seeing old friends, and visiting with anyone who would take her in. As the years passed she

---

[21]Letters, Nathan S. S. Beman to Caroline Beman, 15 March 1836, and Caroline Beman to Benjamin C. Yancey, 11 February 1838, Benjamin C. Yancey Papers.

[22]Letter, Caroline Beman to Benjamin C. Yancey, 30 June 1839, Benjamin C. Yancey Papers.

[23]Letters, Samuel S. Beman to Benjamin C. Yancey, 7 September 1851, 12 May, 4 April 1872, Benjamin C. Yancey Papers.

became increasingly dissatisfied and contentious. Overly sensitive and easy to take offense, extravagant and yet almost constantly worried lest Beman cut off her allowance, the once-spirited Caroline wandered from place to place, bitter, alone, and homeless. [24]

[24]Letters, Caroline Beman to Benjamin C. Yancey, 22 May 1853, and William L. Yancey to Benjamin C. Yancey, 1853, Benjamin C. Yancey Papers.

Chapter V

The Education
of a Fire-Eater

Come and see what a Yankee I am.
—William Lowndes Yancey

Nathan Beman's marriage to Caroline Bird Yancey marked the beginning of an unusual relationship with still another member of the family, William Lowndes Yancey, the older of Caroline's two sons and the future secessionist. In view of Beman's indefatigable opposition to slavery and Yancey's later defense of the institution and bold defiance of the Union, the nature of their association during the years following the family's removal from Georgia poses an intriguing question. Unfortunately, most small boys do not keep diaries in which they record impressions of their stepfathers, and neither Beman nor Yancey set forth in later years their recollections of this period in their lives. However, a careful examination of Yancey's education and subsequent attitudes and convictions sheds some light on the peculiar relationship.

With Beman's ordination as pastor of the First Presbyterian Church in Troy, the young William Yancey began a ten-year residence in the heart of abolitionism and under the very roof of one of slavery's staunchest foes. During this period Yancey received all of his formal education. The forces influencing him during these formative years were often contradictory: on one side were his stepfather, the Northern academies, and Williams College; aligned against them were his mother, the Bird family, and the memory of his father. On one hand, he was subjected to the forces of discipline, hardship, abolitionism, and republicanism, while on the other, these factors were contradicted by the privileges, wealth, aristocracy, and belief in slavery of his Southern heritage.

According to Yancey's biographer, his mother exerted a decided influence upon the boy. Intelligent and well-educated, Caroline sought to inspire her sons with the ideals exemplified by their deceased father. She told them of his sense of duty and his gifts as an advocate. Caroline frequently summoned the boys to recite speeches and declamations, complimenting them on their skill and making suggestions for improvement. She taught the boys propriety in manners, conduct, and dress. Perhaps most important, she passed on to them an appreciation of their Southern origin and background through descriptions of life at The Aviary and explanations of Southern institutions. These influences, however, were at least partially offset by her difficulties with her husband. Unfortunately, the almost perpetual conflict that characterized relations between Caroline and Beman during the boys' childhood was not without its effect, although subsequent events suggest that Ben was more seriously distressed by it than was William.[1]

William's future as a political leader was also influenced by Beman. His sermons, his zeal in conducting revivals, his actions in the New School controversy, and his opinions on education, slavery, temperance, politics, and a host of other matters all played a part in shaping the character, habits, and attitudes of Yancey.

Temperamentally, Beman and Yancey were much alike. Although in the course of his life Yancey earned the sobriquet "fire-eater"—a hot-tempered person always ready to quarrel or fight—and his stepfather was often guilty of hasty action, both were essentially men of determination and deep conviction. As a child, Yancey was high-spirited, "always a social rebel among his playmates, ever commanding and generally accustomed to repel any attempts to subordinate him with the stern logic and arbitrament

---

[1]John Witherspoon DuBose, *Life and Times of William Lowndes Yancey*, 2 vols. (New York: Peter Smith, 1942) 1:32; Letters, Caroline Beman to Benjamin C. Yancey, 22 May 1853, and William L. Yancey to Benjamin C. Yancey, 1853, in Benjamin C. Yancey Papers, Southern Historical Collection, University of North Carolina Library, Chapel Hill.

of the fist." At nineteen, he was described by his law teacher as a young man of "impulse and deep feeling," but still "good and regular" in his habits. An aunt noted that her young nephew was as "lively as ever," but cautioned Ben not to be influenced by "William's wild notions."[2] Unlike Beman, Yancey was charming and at ease in social gatherings; when alone, however, like his stepfather he was inclined to melancholy and meditation.[3]

The masthead of *The Missionary*, "Go Ye into All the World and Preach the Gospel to Every Creature," might be applied equally well to explain the conduct of both Beman and Yancey. Basically, both were crusaders. When in later years he was denounced as an agitator, Yancey accepted the appellation and replied, "Agitation, incentives to exertion, inducements which impel inquiry are sources of knowledge and wisdom." In words which he might have first heard from his stepfather's lips, Yancey elaborated, "The prophets of old were agitators. . . . The Divine Martyr, dying, died amidst convulsions of nature which shook the earth in its foundations. His last injunction to His disciples was to go forth to proclaim His words until every heresy should yield. . . . If we have the right on our side it is our bounden duty to agitate," Yancey replied to his critics. "If we are in the wrong, agitation will prove the truth. No good cause has ever been delayed by agitation, and every error has trembled before it." Yancey apparently learned his lesson well from his stepfather.[4]

Yancey also possessed a sense of duty and moral obligation that led him to refuse compromise for the sake of expediency. In a speech on 8 January 1856, he declared, "I thank God that I have had the courage to obey the dictates of my reason and to abide by the restraints of my conscience, even at the sacrifice of the favors of the Democratic party!" Throughout his career, Yancey demonstrated his willingness to forsake political rewards, public office, and popularity for principle.[5]

---

[2]*New York Herald*, 29 November 1861; DuBose, *William Lowndes Yancey*, 1:33; Letters, Louisa Cunningham to Benjamin C. Yancey, 20 July, 6 August 1833, Benjamin C. Yancey Papers.

[3]DuBose, *William Lowndes Yancey*, 1:33.

[4]Ibid., 1:339-40, 362.

[5]Ibid., 1:151, 220, 319, 362; 2:439-40, 492, 497.

Although he was denounced over the years as a demagogue, traitor, and disunionist, Yancey never shirked a battle. Echoing Beman, he frequently deplored partisan opposition but never let it prevent him from crusading with evangelical fervor for what he thought was best for his state and people.[6]

Perhaps Yancey benefited most from his stepfather's example in his development as an eloquent and masterful orator. Although the establishment of a causal relationship depends on circumstantial evidence, Beman's influence on Yancey is shown not only in the similarity of their speech methods and philosophies but by the development of both Ben Yancey and Samuel Beman as speakers of unusual prowess. If it were possible to describe Yancey's oratory in a single sentence, the observation by one of his contemporaries that "he was all directness, all earnestness, all determination, all fire" would probably come closest to providing an accurate description. Except during the New School revivals, Beman impressed his hearers in much the same way. He was "calm, dignified, earnest—oftentimes intensely earnest; but never nervously impassioned—always keeping control of himself and his audience."[7]

Contemporaries, whether friend or foe, agreed that Yancey's power lay in his ability to simplify complicated issues and to marshal facts to support his position. A typical press reaction was the report of the St. Louis *Bulletin*: "His power over the people lies in the fact that his speeches are masterpieces of argument; that his logic is irresistible. . . . The argument, too, is done up, not in showy and sparkling dress, but in pure, simple and massive English."[8] The Mobile *Tribune* called one of Yancey's speeches "the simplest speech that we have heard this season, but full of the severest logic, expressed in the most appropriate language, the words falling exactly in the place the orator chose to marshal them. This is the beauty of Yancey's speeches."[9]

---

[6]Ibid., 1:113, 205-206, 216; 2:404.

[7]W. C. Richardson, "Hillard and Yancey—a Parallel," *Montgomery Advertiser*, 8 November 1908; Henry B. Nason, *Biographical Record of the Officers and Graduates of Rensselaer Polytechnic Institute, 1824-1886* (Troy: William H. Young, 1887) 30-34.

[8]*St. Louis Bulletin*, 25 October 1860.

[9]*Mobile Tribune*, 2 November 1860.

Beman was noted for the simplicity of his speeches and the logic of his analyses, and Yancey may well have imbibed some of his stepfather's theories of style and persuasion. In his famous sermon to the General Assembly in 1832 Beman explained his reasons for favoring simplicity of style and manner in preaching. He believed that when too much attention was given to style and method, "admiration may be excited, but the conscience is untouched. . . . The delighted audience praise the speaker, but never condemn themselves."[10]

The similarity of the two men does not end there, for they were markedly alike in their action and movements when addressing an audience. Both were self-possessed and employed easy, appropriate, and emphatic gestures. Like Beman, Yancey exercised restraint in the use of emotion, although he was capable of rousing his audience to heights of feeling when it suited his ends.[11]

A final similarity that should be noted is that both spoke extemporaneously, although each carefully thought through and outlined his speeches in advance. Their notes were almost identical in form. Main headings were listed with a few clues as reminders and wide margins to permit last-minute adaptations. When called upon to furnish copies of speeches for publication, both men found it necessary to rewrite the addresses from memory and their notes.[12]

Several of Yancey's attitudes toward public institutions and customs also seem to have been influenced by his stepfather. The religious instruc-

---

[10]Nathan S. S. Beman, "A Discourse Delivered at the Opening of the General Assembly of the Presbyterian Church, on the 17th of May, 1832," *Cincinnati Journal*, 22 June 1832.

[11]Nason, *Biographical Record*; Richardson, "Hillard and Yancey"; Jonathan H. Noble Memorial Sermon, in Marvin R. Vincent, *Memorial Sermon on Rev. N. S. S. Beman, D.D., LL.D., Delivered Sunday Evening, December 17, 1871 in the First Presbyterian Church, Troy, N.Y., by Rev. Marvin R. Vincent, D.D., Pastor* (Troy: A. W. Scribner Co., 1872) 10; Henry S. Foote, *The Bench and Bar of the South and Southwest* (St. Louis: Soule, Thomas and Wentworth, 1876) 238.

[12]Nason, *Biographical Record*; Vincent, *Memorial Sermon*, 13; Letter in Robert Aikman, *Proceedings of the Centennial Anniversary of the First Presbyterian Church, Troy, N.Y., December 30, 31, 1891* (Troy: Troy Times, 1892) 72; Manuscripts in William Lowndes Yancey Papers, Alabama State Department of Archives and History, Montgomery.

tion received in the Beman household is apparent in almost all of Yancey's major speeches. Frequent reference to Christian precepts and biblical parables indicates a close familiarity with the Bible. "The essential element of all our liberties," Yancey once wrote, "is freedom of conscience—in religious and temporal affairs." A regular attendant of the Presbyterian Church, Yancey also led his family in daily worship in his home, morning and evening.

Yancey also found himself in accord with his stepfather on the importance of public education. During his campaign for the Alabama legislature in 1841 he pledged to labor for that cause "until the means of acquiring this right was within the reach of every child" and, upon election, one of his first efforts was to seek funds for the schools of Alabama.

Although he was not a total abstainer, Yancey learned moderation in the consumption of alcoholic beverages from Beman. Benjamin Perry noted that he had never known Yancey to engage in any kind of dissipation, and it seems Yancey's temperance in the use of liquor was never broken.[13]

While Beman seems to have exercised considerable influence on the young Yancey, on the questions of slavery and dueling the Alabamian came to differ sharply with his stepfather. What opinions Yancey held while still living in the North are not known; however, before he had spent many years in the South, custom and tradition prevailed over Northern preaching and example. As a youth Yancey must have found it difficult to arrive at a clear-cut opinion on slavery since his mother vacillated between approval and disapproval. Even Beman seems to have been uncertain of his position on slavery during his years in Georgia. Other contradictory influences were the support of slavery by Yancey's Southern relatives and the strong antislavery sentiment at Williams College. The Troy years were formative ones in Yancey's life, but these conflicting attitudes probably left the boy undecided.[14]

In time Yancey also renounced Beman's attitude toward dueling. In spite of his stepfather's contempt for the practice, twelve years after Yancey departed from the North he participated in a duel with Representative

---

[13]DuBose, *William Lowndes Yancey*, 1:70, 76, 102, 135, 296, 400-401.

[14]*The Missionary* (Mt. Zion, Georgia), 6 June 1821; Letter, Nathan S. S. Beman to Caroline Beman, 21 December 1835, Benjamin C. Yancey Papers.

Thomas L. Clingman of North Carolina as a result of the Alabamian's maiden speech in Congress. While this was Yancey's only duel, the instance reveals that Beman's arguments were not strong enough to withstand the pressures of local custom and public opinion.[15]

The precise degree of responsibility attributable to Beman in moulding the character and attitudes of Yancey is a matter of speculation. Certainly Beman always maintained a close interest in the education and progress of his own children and, presumably, also his stepsons. On the other hand, several factors suggest that William and Ben Yancey were not so carefully supervised by the minister as were the other children. First, Beman's differences with their mother probably diminished his influence. Second, responsibility for the education of the Yancey boys had been assumed by the Bird family; thus, the choice of schools for the two was Caroline's decision rather than Beman's. Finally, during most of the family's residence in Troy, Yancey was at school several months out of each year.

However, even in his formal education, Yancey did not entirely escape Beman's influence; DuBose reports that the boy began his education under Beman's tutelage at Mt. Zion Academy.[16] After the family moved to Troy, Yancey attended schools at Chittenango, Troy, Bennington, and Lenox.[17] Of these, little is known of the academies at Chittenango and Troy. Founded in 1824 by John B. Yates, who served as president of the school until 1832, the Chittenango academy was called Yates Polytechny Institute and attracted students from all parts of the country. Seven professors taught the classes, and the school was widely known for the liberality of its program.[18] Concerning his education in Troy, all that is known is that Yancey attended one of the small academies in the town.

More is known about the Brick Academy in Bennington. Founded in 1821, the two-story brick building with its white steeple was the pride of Bennington. Under the headship of George W. Yates, the school pursued

---

[15]*The Missionary* (Mt. Zion, Georgia), 11 March 1822; DuBose, *William Lowndes Yancey*, 140-45.

[16]DuBose, *William Lowndes Yancey*, 32.

[17]Ibid.

[18]L. M. Hammond, *History of Madison County, State of New York* (Syracuse: Truair, Smith and Co., 1872); *New York Observer*, 29 March 1834.

the typical college preparatory curriculum. A significant aspect of the future orator's education at the Brick Academy was the Friday afternoon recitations in which the students declaimed, orated, and took part in disputations.[19]

William completed his college preparatory training at Lenox Academy in Lenox, Massachusetts. Founded in 1803 "for the instruction of youth in piety, morality and the liberal arts," the academy was one of the most illustrious in New England. The curriculum included languages, mathematics, philosophy, and the "common branches of English study." As at Bennington, each student was required to participate weekly in exercises in composition and declamation.[20]

Enrollment at Lenox Academy in 1830, Yancey's final year, was 127 students: 99 boys and 28 girls. Yancey was one of 21 students in the Greek and Latin languages. The public examinations at Lenox were famous for their severity and usually attracted a sizable crowd of visitors, many traveling a considerable distance. The annual commencement program also attracted many guests. Where Yancey stood in his class is not known, but his admission to Williams College the following year as a sophomore suggests that he ranked high.[21]

That Yancey did not attend any of the new manual labor academies is interesting and may be significant. Beman and many of the New School Presbyterians were strong advocates of this type of education. However, the fact that the Bird family defrayed most of the costs of his education probably accounts for Yancey's disregard of his stepfather's enthusiasm for the new schools. Another interesting aspect of Yancey's preparatory education is his enrollment in four different academies in seven years. Certainly the reason does not seem to have been scholastic difficulty, for his college entrance examination indicates achievement far beyond that of the average preparatory-school graduate. The explanation lies in the youth's

---

[19]John V. D. S. Merrill and Caroline R. Merrill, *Sketches of Historic Bennington* (Cambridge MA: Riverside Press, 1898) 51-52.

[20]R. DeWitt Mallary, *Lenox and the Berkshire Highlands* (New York: G.P. Putnam's Sons, 1903) 2, 20; *One Hundredth Anniversary of the Founding of Lenox Academy* (Pittsfield MA: Sun Printing, 1905) 7-8.

[21]Mallary, *Lenox and the Berkshire Highlands*, 2; *Catalog of Officers and Students of the Lenox Academy, March, 1830.*

restlessness. This conclusion is suggested by a letter written by Yancey's Aunt Louisa Cunningham to Ben. In it, she cautioned the younger brother "not to be led astray by William's wild notions, who never could rest in one place two months at a time."[22]

In spite of his frequent transfers, Yancey acquired an excellent education. Except for his training in Troy, he attended academies that were among the most distinguished in the Northeast. He received training that was not only scholarly, but eminently practical; in addition to the acquisition of a broad understanding of the classics and literature, he developed skill in writing, speaking, and mathematics, all essential to the tasks of daily life and to participation in public affairs.

Following his graduation from Lenox, Yancey entered Williams College in the autumn of 1830. The transition to college probably was not difficult since Williams differed little from Lenox Academy, being similar in size and curriculum, with courses at Williams essentially a continuation of the studies at Lenox. Located on the main street of Williamstown, the college campus consisted of three red-brick buildings: West College, the original building in which freshmen and sophomores were housed; East College, in which juniors and seniors lived; and the new chapel, the largest and most impressive of the buildings. The handsome campus seemed somewhat incongruous in the midst of the town's clapboard dwellings and places of business, among which pigs and cows roamed at will.[23]

Williams College in 1830 was a poor, struggling institution. Isolated by two ranges of mountains—the Taconic to the west and Hoosac five miles to the east—the school existed primarily to serve the farm and mountain boys of the region. The students were unsophisticated, but eager. One professor, at the opening of a new term, observed, "Students are coming in, old and new, fellows that you can tell as far as you can see them for having come out of the mountains. . . . There is no use in grumbling that we don't make gentlemen in colleges," he continued. "If people could see

---

[22]Letters, Louisa Cunningham to Benjamin C. Yancey, 20 July, 6 August 1833, Benjamin C. Yancey Papers.

[23]Frederick Rudolph, *Mark Hopkins and the Log* (New Haven: Yale University Press, 1956) 10, 14-15; Calvin Durfee, *History of Williams College* (Boston: A. Williams and Co., 1860) 345-47.

the quality of the wool we get I think they would give us credit for pretty fair cloth."[24]

Partly from necessity and partly the result of tradition, students lived plainly and simply during Yancey's years at Williams. Furniture and furnishings consisted of the barest essentials. The boys carried their own firewood and drew their own water from the college well, with the result, according to one student, that "there was no excessive use of that element of comfort and neatness." Consistent with the tradition of frugality, once a year the president suspended classes on "Gravel Day" so the students might regravel the college walks.[25]

The momentous words, "Chum, God is here!" uttered by an undergraduate in 1825 to welcome back his roommate summarize the prevailing attitude toward religion at Williams. The aim of the school was to make men and, in the pursuit of that objective, the faculty was convinced that a Christian influence transcended in importance both scholarship and curriculum. Thus, each day began with a sunrise prayer service; vespers came in the afternoon; and on Sunday three religious services were held, with attendance required at two. The school had acquired a reputation as a seat of vigorous revivalism as a result of revivals in 1806, 1812, and 1826.[26]

The battle with Satan for the souls of Williams students was not an easy one. The mountain and farm boys were boisterous, high-spirited, and uncommonly fond of drink. Before Yancey's matriculation much had been done to stamp out intemperance by two campus temperance societies. However, their efforts had by no means been entirely successful. The school also boasted the first antislavery organization in Massachusetts—the Williams Anti-Slavery Society—and a majority of the students were members. However, in spite of these promising signs, the school was compelled to enforce a lengthy list of regulations governing attendance at chapel,

---

[24]Letter, Mark Hopkins to Albert Hopkins, 3 September 1832, in Rudolph, *Hopkins and the Log*, 66.

[25]Durfee, *Williams College*, 23, 303.

[26]Rudolph, *Hopkins and the Log*, 11, 14, 45, 89, 127; Leverett Wilson Spring, *A History of Williams College* (Boston and New York: Houghton and Mifflin, 1917) 134-35.

conduct in classes, studying, and pranks in order to maintain decorum and promote piety.[27]

Because of the advanced nature of his study at Lenox, Yancey was permitted to enter Williams as a sophomore. Tutors—young college graduates with little teaching experience—supervised the work of the two lower classes. This system placed Yancey under the instruction of Mark Hopkins, who was perhaps the most influential figure at Williams during the nineteenth century and who served as the college's president after 1836.

Hopkins, a Williams graduate and a physician, joined the faculty at the beginning of Yancey's first term. Although hired to teach moral and intellectual philosophy, Hopkins was not trained in this field and he was never much of a scholar. In later years, he admitted, "I don't read books; in fact, I never did read books." He freely confessed that he did not understand metaphysics and that he was unable to make "head, tail or body" of Immanuel Kant. So, instead of beginning his lectures with a philosophical abstraction, Hopkins drew upon his experience as a physician and began with a study of the human body—an approach that must have surprised his students—and proceeded to outline to the class the organs of the body and their function. After weeks of anatomy, he finally made the transition to the mind, thereby justifying the lectures' title.

His intellectual inadequacy never embarrassed Hopkins. For him, Christian salvation was the object of human endeavor and a young man's attitude toward intemperance, reading novels, and slavery was far more important than his understanding abstract philosophy. Accordingly, he discoursed to his classes about marriage, voting, cleanliness, exercise, property ownership, and sundry practical topics. While Yancey did not study under the professor during Hopkins's mature years, he was subjected to his example of Christian morality and his inspired guidance.[28]

One of the most significant features of Yancey's first year at Williams was a prolonged religious revival that began in January. Beman was indirectly responsible for the event, for President Edward Dorr Griffin was

---

[27]Arthur Latham Perry, *Williamstown and Williams College* (published by the author, 1899) 509; Spring, *A History of Williams College*, 136, 138-43; Durfee, *Williams College*, 24, 283-95, 323.

[28]Perry, *Williamstown and Williams College*, 495, 504, 510-11; Rudolph, *Hopkins and the Log*, 27-28, 32-33, 43-47, 52-53.

so impressed with one of Beman's revival meetings he had attended that he preached a sermon on the effort at Williams. The account reportedly made so profound an impression that the students scheduled a four-day meeting. The fervor spread quickly and, by the end of April, twenty men— more than one-fifth of the student body—had professed a religious experience.[29]

During Yancey's junior year Beman figured prominently in another revival at Williams. Just before the revival, the students demonstrated that they differed little from undergraduates everywhere. Eager for a few extra vacation days, several scratched themselves with corn cobs to induce an itch, claimed that a small-pox epidemic was sweeping the campus, and petitioned for immediate adjournment. To the collegians' chagrin, the faculty detected the ruse and refused the petition. A few days later the revival began with Beman as the principal speaker. Unlike his Troy revivals, the meetings were free from noisiness, public professions of faith, and other exhibitions. Nevertheless, he had a tremendous effect on the student body, and several conversions occurred among the students shortly after his first lectures. Beman remained in Williamstown for several weeks and, according to Professor Albert Hopkins, the revival marked a turning point in the religious history of the college.[30]

Although Yancey learned a great deal about public speaking from his stepfather, in his development as an orator he was perhaps even more deeply indebted to Williams' President Griffin, who was also Beman's friend and associate. Griffin was inclined to be pretentious and, as a result, was regarded by some students as pompous. He further irritated many by demanding close attention to his sermons and by insisting that students doff their hats to him along the streets of Williamstown.

Griffin, nevertheless, had a salutary effort on the collegians because of his rhetorical powers and skill as a teacher. His huge size—full six feet, three inches in height and weighing 240 pounds—white hair, and expressive countenance gave him an appearance of venerable benignity, yet dominating personal power. Griffin's voice was described as "capable of every modulation from the thunder of denunciation to the softest tones of

---

[29]Perry, *Williamstown and Williams College*, 428-29.

[30]Letter, Mark Hopkins to Harry Hopkins, 25 December 1831, in Rudolph, *Hopkins and the Log*, 63; Perry, *Williamstown and Williams College*, 429, 488.

persuasion." Never a profound theologian, the president relied heavily on great dynamism and solemnity for effect in his preaching. A few critics deplored Griffin's stentorian manner, complaining that even when he asked to have a window raised or lowered he was wont to rise to his full height, point a sweeping gesture, and employ his richest oratorical tones. Most students, however, were impressed with the president's sermons and found them models for imitation and emulation.

Griffin's forte was teaching rhetoric; one colleague observed, "I should not suppose it possible for any one to take young men of the talents and attainments of those composing our Senior class, and prepare them to write and speak with so much power." Griffin's method was to call upon one of the seniors to read an original essay or to recite a declamation while the rest of the class took notes. After the performance, he called upon each student to deliver a critique. Griffin then criticized both the performer and critics, sparing nothing with students who had offered trifling commentaries. He also spent much time assisting students individually on matters of style, structure, and delivery. Fortunately, in spite of his own full-blown speaking, Griffin deplored bombast in the efforts of his students.[31]

The near-unanimity of opinion on Griffin's power as a speaker and his effectiveness as a teacher suggests that young Yancey probably benefited from his guidance. Although Yancey had heard such outstanding preachers as Beman, Finney, and Weld, his study with Griffin provided a sound theoretical basis and valuable practice for his own almost unsurpassed ability in manipulating audiences in later life.

Another important aspect of Yancey's speech training resulted from his membership in the Philotechnian Literary Society. The organization had its own library, met regularly, and sponsored debates, orations, and criticism on national, international, and local questions, as well as philosophy, manners, literature, and the Bible. During Yancey's senior year the society became keenly interested in the presidential campaign and decided to sponsor a debate on the topic "Would the election of General Jackson tend to destroy the Union?" Beman's preference for the Whig party and his dislike of Jackson apparently had not influenced the young man, for at the 17 October meeting Yancey argued the negative. Although he

---

[31]Durfee, *Williams College*, 176-77, 182; Spring, *A History of Williams College*, 148-53; Perry, *Williamstown and Williams College*, 417-18, 430, 437, 444-46.

lost the debate, his ability as a speaker attracted the attention of local politicians who asked him to stump the region in behalf of Jackson and the Democrats.

Yancey's interest in the election had been further stimulated by the candidacy for the state legislature of Professor Ebenezer Emmons of Williams. Yancey accepted the invitation to campaign and, although the Philotechnians had rejected his arguments, both Jackson and Emmons triumphed in the general election. This brief political stumping experience, the kind of campaigning at which Yancey was to excell in later years, afforded him an opportunity to test the principles elucidated by Beman and Griffin and gave him his first taste of political campaigning.[32]

In addition to his interest in politics and the Philotechnian Society, Yancey assisted in the publication of *The Adelphi*, a literary magazine. During his final year he was named Senior Orator at an exhibition of his class and First Orator at a program at the Adelphic Union. Yancey finished his work six weeks before commencement and, although eligible for a degree, he did not remain to take it, probably because of financial reasons. Most of the expense of his education had been borne by the Bird family, and conscious of the cost, the young man probably was eager to begin earning his own way as soon as possible. Whatever the reason, in July Yancey left for South Carolina to begin studying law under Benjamin Perry.[33]

On one occasion many years after his return to the South, Yancey told a Northern audience, "Twelve years of my life spent among New England farms were not thrown away. Come and see what a Yankee I am. . . . " The influence of his sojourn in Yankee territory was not limited to rural values; his education in the academies of New York and New England, the years at Williams College, and the Calvinism of his stepfather and teachers all left their impress on the young man. Counteracting these forces were the influences of his mother and his Southern heritage. In the Beman household, the marital difficulties of his mother and stepfather, the incendiarism of the revivals, and Beman's prolonged controversies with

---

[32]Spring, *A History of Williams College*, 137, 145-46, 169-70; Perry, *Williamstown and Williams College*, 520-21.

[33]Spring, *A History of Williams College*, 145; Benjamin Franklin Perry, *Reminiscences of Public Men* (Greenville SC: Shannon and Co., 1889) 52.

his parishioners and fellow clergyman provided a climate of emotionalism and uncertainty for the youth.

In spite of these conflicts, Beman's example probably was beneficial in several respects. The clergyman's conviction that each man was obligated to agitate for reform, his sense of duty and refusal to compromise on principles, and his courage and willingness to stand alone if necessary impressed themselves deeply on Yancey's mind. Perhaps most important to him was his stepfather's example in oratory, for through this medium Yancey gained his greatest prominence and exerted his most forceful impact upon American history. That these skills were to be employed in opposition to one of Beman's most cherished reforms—the abolition of slavery—must have been a bitter disappointment to the minister.

Chapter VI

A Decade
of Dissent and Division

> God gird us to do all valiantly
> for the helpless and innocent.
> —Theodore Dwight Weld

It was during the decade of 1830-1840, a period when his marital relations were most tempestuous, that Beman wielded his greatest influence as a reformer. Within the Presbyterian Church he pressed the New School revolt against the conservatives to a dramatic and far-reaching climax in 1838. Significantly, the final disruption resulted from his insistence that the church take a stand on slavery. Outside the pulpit, Beman also advocated a variety of reforms designed to suppress intemperance, prostitution, and other forms of vice and licentiousness.

The foremost goal toward which Beman's mind and labors were aimed throughout this period was the drive to infuse the Presbyterian Church with new vigor. Following his election as moderator in 1831 and the ascendancy of the New School, Beman and his supporters made no attempt to mollify their opponents or to reach a compromise. Instead, in his opening sermon at the General Assembly of 1832, Beman delivered a thinly veiled attack on the Old School by condemning the inefficiency of modern preaching as compared to that of the Apostles. After beginning by lauding the remarkable success of the Apostles, Beman contended that their superiority was attributable not to inspiration, to miraculous intervention, or to the age in which they lived, but to their more extensive and exhaustive labor. Although disclaiming any intention of bringing a charge of indolence against the ministers, Beman contended, "That there are many in the sacred office against whom the charge might be sustained in its full force there can be no doubt."[1]

Beman argued that the Apostles' preaching had been characterized by greater simplicity and directness than was to be found in the sermons of his day; too many preachers had lost sight of the principal object of preaching—the salvation of souls. In defense of the methods of the New School, Beman tried to show that the successes of the Apostles were largely the result of appeals to the heart and conscience. "They preached *to* men," he asserted, "and not *about* them. . . . Their object was to make a deep and saving impression upon their hearers." Defending another of the New Measures, Beman argued that the Apostles aimed for immediate success: "They were so confident that God *would* grant His influence that they hardly commenced an enterprise but they saw it already accomplished. In every undertaking, whether secular or spiritual, an *expectation* of success is one of the necessary elements of successful action." The Apostles never sent a man home to think, he claimed, but urged repentance and salvation while the impression of the sermon was still fresh upon his mind.[2] Such an obvious attack would hardly heal the rift between the two factions. The New School continued to press its advantage and widen the breach until the issue was finally resolved in the historic division of 1838.

Among the reforms to which Beman, as well as most of the New School clergy, lent active support during these years was the movement to eradicate intemperance. As early as 1821 Beman had spoken against alcoholism. In Troy he organized a temperance society to which he spoke frequently.[3] He joined the American Temperance Society and traveled about the state preaching against the "monster." Armed with a battery of statistics, Beman treated intemperance both as a social problem and as a

---

[1] Nathan S. S. Beman, "A Discourse Delivered at the Opening of the General Assembly of the Presbyterian Church, on the 17th of May, 1832," *Cincinnati Journal*, 22 June 1832.

[2] Ibid., 9-13.

[3] *Troy Budget*, 6 January, 7 July 1829.

moral issue. He presented statistics to show the cost to the consumer and the taxpayer, estimating that with the indirect costs of absenteeism, the support of paupers, and treatment of diseases incurred through alcoholism, the total cost of liquor was $127,000,000 a year, or enough to pay off the national debt in five months. Applying the estimate to Troy alone, Beman set the cost at $25,000, or "one handsome estate poured down every year in the form of liquid poison."[4]

Beman painted a gloomy picture of intemperance, calling it a "disease which is performing the work of death with a more desolating vengeance than the yellow fever or the plague." He said, "Look at the drunkard. . . . He is already a naked skeleton or a bloated corpse: a walking mummy—when he can walk—a mass of semi-animated putrefaction." Beman declared, "In his cups, the drunkard is generally a temporary fool or madman. His very horse exhibits the external symbols of mortification for the load he carried and his dog is ashamed to keep his master company."[5]

For a man of Beman's conviction, the remedy for intemperance seemed easy enough: simply adopt the principle of complete abstinence. He advised the temperate to refuse liquor in any form, even as a medicine, and never to offer it as an item of hospitality. He pleaded with women to form temperance societies, to proscribe all ardent spirits in their homes, and to avoid association with men who regularly paid their respects to their hostesses' sideboards.[6]

When cholera gripped the East in 1832 Beman believed intemperance to be one of the primary causes. In an effort to prove this hypothesis, he undertook a study of the relationship between the two. He claimed that he had not found a single instance where cholera commenced among the temperate, that dissipation lessened resistance to the disease, and that alcohol generated "from five-sixths to nine-tenths of the destructive power of the cholera." Furthermore, he marshaled statistical data to prove that nearly all of those who contracted cholera were intemperate. In light of these sweeping claims, Beman must have been somewhat embarrassed later

---

[4]Nathan S. S. Beman, *A Discourse Delivered in Stephentown, December 25, 1828, and in Troy, January 11, 1829, before the Temperance Societies of Those Towns* (New York: John P. Haven, 1829) 2-5.

[5]Ibid., 6-18.

[6]Ibid.

in the year when his friend and associate, Charles Finney, was stricken with the disease.[7] In Troy, Beman succeeded in getting all twenty-five physicians to subscribe to a declaration against the use of liquor. He also supported the New York Young Men's Temperance Society, delivering in December 1833 the principal lecture at their fifth anniversary meeting in New York City.[8]

In 1834, Beman was instrumental in the formation of the United States Temperance Union, which united the activities of a host of societies in the field. At its meeting in Philadelphia in May, the American Temperance Society endorsed the recommendation of forming a national group and appointed fifty-four leading temperance workers to carry out the project. Meeting a week later, the group organized the United States Temperance Union. Beman's appointment to a five-man committee to nominate the officers of the new society and to prepare the business of the meeting attests to his eminence in the field at that time.[9]

Beman was also interested in the manual labor system of education under which students spent part of each day working on a farm or in a shop operated by the school. The alleged benefits of vigorous exercise and reduced costs of education were regarded as particularly desirable for theological students. The Oneida Presbytery in upper New York established Oneida Institute, the first such school in this country. Several other theological schools and a few colleges soon adopted the plan. Under this system, students lived rigorously, rising as early as 4:00 A.M., performing their chores, attending devotions, going to classes, and then returning to the farm or shop for additional work. They existed on a frugal diet and every attempt was made to prevent a single moment of idle occupation.

The New School coterie, especially Charles Finney and Theodore Weld, was particularly active in the support of this system of education. In 1831 Finney enlisted the aid of Arthur and Lewis Tappan, two brothers

---

[7]Nathan S. S. Beman, *The Influence of Ardent Spirits in the Production of the Cholera* (Troy: n.p., 1832) 2, 5; Charles G. Cole, Jr., *The Social Ideas of the Northern Evangelists, 1826-1860* (New York: Columbia University Press, 1954) 122-23.

[8]*New York Observer*, 14 December 1833, 15 February 1834.

[9]Ibid., 24, 31 May 1834; "Seventh Report of the American Temperance Society," *Permanent Temperance Documents of the American Temperance Society* (Boston: Seth Bliss and Perkins and Marvin and Co., 1835) 1:451.

who were wealthy merchants interested in reform and philanthropy. With their help, he organized the Society for Promoting Manual Labor in Literary Institutions and appointed Weld as general agent. Beman supported the society, and early in 1831 the theological seminaries at Oneida and Auburn sought him as a teacher; but because of ill health and a reluctance to leave Troy, he refused both invitations.[10]

Beman began to consider the possibility of establishing a manual labor school in Troy, while Edward Kirk, his revival associate, contemplated a similar project in Albany. For several years Beman and Kirk each had trained two or three theological students, giving the young men instruction at their homes and making available to them their private libraries. In the fall of 1832, Beman, Kirk, and Rev. Marcus T. Smith decided to amalgamate their classes and open a manual labor theological seminary in the vicinity of Albany and Troy.[11] Beman wrote to Finney for advice on how to operate the school and how to raise money. Finney forwarded the letter to Weld, appending the note, "Now [that] such men have taken hold . . . it is infinitely important that they have all the necessary help at once. Brs. Beman and Kirk are the right men as you know. But they must have you with them to start this thing by a few lectures and a few hours conversation upon the means, etc."[12]

Whether Weld visited Troy is not known. However, by the end of the year, the Troy and Albany School of Theology had been established at Fort Schuyler near Albany. In November 1835, it was moved to Troy and expanded. Smith resigned and William Larned was appointed professor of sacred literature. Beman held the post of professor of theology, and Kirk served as professor of sacred rhetoric and pastoral theology.

---

[10]Benjamin P. Thomas, *Theodore Weld, Crusader for Freedom* (New Brunswick: Rutgers University Press, 1950) 18-26; Letters, Theodore Weld to Charles Grandison Finney in *Letters of Theodore Dwight Weld, Angelina Grimké Weld and Sarah Grimké, 1822-1844*, ed. Gilbert Barnes and Dwight L. Dumond, 2 vols. (New York: D. Appleton-Century, 1934) 1:44.

[11]Cole, *Social Ideas of the Northern Evangelists*, 76; Letter, Nathan S. S. Beman to Charles Grandison Finney, 25 March 1829, Charles Grandison Finney Papers, Oberlin College Library, Oberlin, Ohio; David O. Mears, *Life of Edward Norris Kirk* (Boston: Lockwood, Brooks and Co., 1877) 86.

[12]Barnes and Dumond, *Letters of Theodore Weld, Angeline Grimké Weld and Sarah Grimké*, 1:91.

The manual labor aspect of the school proved a dismal failure, for Beman and Kirk found that sharp businessmen frequently overcharged them for materials for the workshop. Many of their purchases were unnecessary, and the inexperienced seminarians broke and damaged tools and equipment. When the completed products were taken to the market for sale, the commercially naive pastors again found themselves at the mercy of the merchants. Kirk reported, "We found, thus, that neither the sanitary nor the financial results justified our expectations; and we contented ourselves with the mental without the manual labor."[13]

Perhaps the most curious reform movement with which Beman was associated during these years was one that aimed to eradicate "the world's oldest profession." In 1830 John R. McDowall, a young graduate of Princeton Theological Seminary, organized in New York a society "for the moral and religious improvement of the Five Points." He obtained financial support from Arthur Tappan and others interested in benevolent schemes and opened the Asylum for Females Who Have Deviated from the Paths of Virtue. Two years later, McDowall brought out a lurid account of prostitution in New York, *The Magdalen Report*. Its sensational style and clinical details immediately attracted widespread attention, with the result that several other organizations were quickly constituted to fight prostitution.

The New School Presbyterians supported an organization called the American Society for Promoting the Observance of the Seventh Commandment, formed in January 1834. Beman collected a donation of $27 from "a few females" and sent it to the society; from Albany, Edward Kirk sent "encouragement"; and it is reported that Finney sent a mattress! The American Female Moral Reform Society, the most influential of the several organizations in the field, had 20,000 members, 361 chapters, and a subscription list for their paper of over 16,000 by 1838.[14]

While the activities of Beman and the New School in behalf of temperance, manual labor education, and the eradication of prostitution were conducted with zeal, not until the abolition movement caught their fancy

---

[13]*New York Observer*, 14 November 1835; Mears, *Edward Norris Kirk*, 86-87; Thomas, *Theodore Weld*, 38; Barnes and Dumond, *Letters of Theodore Weld, Angelina Grimké Weld and Sarah Grimké*, 1:91.

[14]Cole, *Social Ideas of the Northern Evangelists*, 125-28.

was the mettle of the Northern evangelists truly tested. Prior to the 1830s, the American Colonization Society was generally accepted as a glorious Christian venture. Almost every church in the country set aside at least one Sunday each year to praise the society and to collect donations to resettle free blacks in Africa.

At Mt. Zion Beman had endorsed the organization, but by 1833, he, Weld, Finney, and others had begun to question the society's aims. The reformers were disturbed by the omission of any statement in its constitution condemning slavery. Contending that members could, without inconsistency, be Christians or infidels, friends or foes of slavery, they claimed that some supporters of the organization hoped only to increase the value of slave property by sending free blacks to Africa.[15]

The society's failure to respond to pressure advocating a statement favoring abolition, or at least one disapproving slavery, prompted a group of reformers to organize the American Anti-Slavery Society in Philadelphia on 4 December 1833. Article two of its constitution explicitly stated that "the objects of this Society are the entire abolition of slavery in the United States." The society also proclaimed its intention of trying to influence Congress to end the domestic slave trade, to abolish slavery in the District of Columbia, and to prevent the extension of slavery into any new state admitted to the Union. Philanthropist Arthur Tappan was elected president and William Lloyd Garrison was named secretary of foreign correspondence.[16]

Although he had attacked slavery from the pulpit and had included free blacks in his congregation, Beman did not actively associate himself with the American Anti-Slavery Society until the spring of 1835 when he attended the meeting of the General Assembly in Pittsburgh and saw the work Theodore Weld was doing. Weld had been hired as an agent for the society and was in the city to learn the sentiments of the ministers and elders on the subject of abolition. Although he had been urged to try to force the slavery issue onto the floor, even at the risk of disrupting the As-

---

[15]Thomas, *Theodore Weld*, 67-68; William Jay, An *Inquiry into the Character of Tendency of the American Colonization and American Anti-Slavery Societies* (New York: Leavitt, Lord and Co., 1835) 127.

[16]Thomas, *Theodore Weld*, 51-53; Jay, *American Colonization and American Anti-Slavery Societies*, 127.

sembly, Weld demurred and worked behind the scenes. He estimated that forty-eight, or one-fourth, of the delegates—in contrast to just two abolitionists who had attended the 1834 meeting—were favorably disposed toward the antislavery cause.[17]

At an antislavery meeting organized by Weld, Beman delivered one of his most widely publicized speeches. Pointing out that he was no stranger to slavery, having resided in the South for several years, he asserted that "It is an immense evil." Attacking the "hands off" attitude of some clergymen, Beman argued, "Slavery will never cure itself—this let-alone policy . . . is moral heresy." He contended that the question was of concern to all citizens, for everyone shared in the government of the District of Columbia, "the central mart of the traffic in human flesh." "Yes, sir, we at the north do govern slave shambles," he claimed; "our hands are not quite so clean as we have supposed." Referring to the acquiescence of the General Assembly to Southern demands not to act on the issue, Beman asked, "Are our Southern brethren infallible?" He then made his famous accusations: "They are very kind-hearted brethren, yet some of them sell the image of Jesus in their slaves! Are they competent judges in the case? The wise man says, 'A gift blindeth the eyes.' They judge with the price of human flesh in their hands." When Beman's critics later learned that he had once owned and sold slaves himself, they were to cite this passage as evidence of hypocrisy.[18]

Beman's attack on the apologists for slavery, even though made outside the Assembly, did not endear him to the clergy who wished to ignore the vexatious issue. The Troy minister indicated in debate on another matter that he was fully aware of the unpopularity and suspicions that his remarks had induced.[19] Although both Beman and Weld refrained from bringing the issue to the floor of the Assembly, a delegate from Illinois attempted to introduce the subject. The Assembly, although refusing to act, did name a committee—the majority of whom were known to be op-

---

[17]Thomas, *Theodore Weld*, 95; A. J. Wise, *Troy's One Hundred Years* (Troy: William H. Young, 1891) 131.

[18]*Anti-Slavery Record* 1:7 (July 1835): 81.

[19]*New York Observer*, 20 June 1835.

posed to any action—to report at the next session. Beman was one of the members appointed.[20]

The introduction of the slavery issue in 1835 further complicated already existing doctrinal disagreements between the Old and New Schools and threatened to bring about a new division along strictly regional lines. The Old School was particularly frightened by this prospect, for should the Southern delegates—most of whom were Old School in their ties—decide to withdraw, the New School would have a commanding majority. Consequently, the Old School quickly took advantage of the slavery controversy to win the support of the Southern forces. This was not difficult, for the Southerners realized that they might be denied membership if the Assembly should decide that slaveholding was a sin.

Shortly after adjournment of the General Assembly of 1835, the Philadelphia *Presbyterian*, a conservative organ, sounded the alarm. It urged that the Assembly refrain from any agitation or discussion of slavery and cautioned the clergy to be "alive to the approaching crisis." The *Presbyterian* continued to proclaim impending disaster and early in 1836 charged the New School with planning to introduce the slavery question in the next Assembly in order to force the Southern churches to secede. The journal was successful in rousing several Southern synods to issue statements denying the authority of the General Assembly to legislate on slavery and threatening to withdraw if the subject were raised. Beman must have been dismayed to find the name of his former pupil, Benjamin Gildersleeve, attached to the statement of the Charleston Presbytery.[21]

In the interim between the Assemblies of 1835 and 1836, Theodore Weld made a historic visit to Troy. Weld's lecture tours as an agent for the American Anti-Slavery Society had been a succession of triumphs. During the years since his association with Finney, from whom he had learned to excite and then control a crowd, Weld had become a stirring and powerful speaker. Tall, handsome, imaginative, and bold, in 1835 he had yet to taste defeat. Weld arrived in Troy fresh from a successful tour

---

[20]Thomas, *Theodore Weld*, 95.

[21]C. Bruce Staiger, "Abolitionism and the Presbyterian Schism of 1837-1838," *Mississippi Valley Historical Review* 36:3 (December 1949): 393-99; *Philadelphia Presbyterian*, 13 August 1835, 10 March 1836; *Religious Monitor* 12 (December 1835): 382.

of Ohio, Pennsylvania, and western New York. Aware of his reputation as a rabble-rouser and his ability to provoke a crowd to mob violence, many in the city strongly opposed Weld's appearance in Troy, and the city was aroused to a feverish pitch of antagonism toward the man and his cause even before his arrival. The mayor publicly expressed regret that he did not have the authority to prevent Weld from entering the city.[22]

Arriving in Troy in his shag overcoat, linsey-woolsey suit, and cowhide boots, Weld immediately conferred with Beman, Rev. Fayette Shipard of the Congregational Church, and other leaders of the Troy Anti-Slavery Society. He began lecturing 22 May in Bethel Church, the Congregational meetinghouse. After three lectures, attendance increased so greatly that a larger meeting place was needed. Upon Beman's application, the trustees of the First Presbyterian Church granted Weld permission to use their church. However, after the abolitionist had spoken twice to packed houses, the objections of some congregation members led the trustees to rescind their earlier action.

Weld and Beman were not informed of the action until they reached the church, where a large crowd had assembled. After being told of the trustees' decision, the two men started to dissolve the meeting. Weld gave a lengthy speech explaining the decision, expressed his regrets at the cancellation, and announced that the meeting would adjourn following a prayer by Beman who then embarked on a long prayer. A hostile crowd outside set up a cry of protest at the length of Weld's explanation and Beman's prayer. As the two men left the church, the mob surged forward, taunting the speakers, and threatening violence. A small band of members of the antislavery society kept the rioters from the men until they reached Beman's home. Shortly after the pair had retired safely within the parsonage, the mayor of the city arrived. He told Weld that he considered him a "dangerous citizen" and warned against continuing his antislavery speaking in Troy.

Neither Beman nor Weld could be easily intimidated. Meeting the following day with the managers of the Troy Anti-Slavery Society, they decided in the interests of free speech and Christian principle to continue the meetings. Beman suggested that a committee approach the mayor to learn the course he intended to adopt in the crisis "where the great ques-

---

[22]Thomas, *Theodore Weld*, 100-101, 113-15.

tion must be solved whether the mob or law are [sic] to bear rule." After adopting the resolution and naming a committee, a date was set for Weld's next speech. The committee met with little success in its interview with the mayor. He agreed to try to protect Weld, provided the abolitionist restricted his lectures to the daytime, but said that he could not promise that he would be able to control the mob.

On Monday evening, 7 June, Weld returned to Bethel Church. Throughout the day, his opponents had been at work posting handbills that invited all those opposed to the lectures to meet in front of the courthouse. Earlier that evening a public crier had gone about the streets, ringing his bell and calling to all who would listen: "All you who are opposed to amalgamation meet in front of the courthouse!" As a result, Bethel Church was packed; some there to hear the lecture, others present for the sole purpose of disrupting the meeting.

Opening, Weld read those parts of the state constitution guaranteeing the rights of free discussion and free assembly. When he turned to the subject of slavery, the anti-abolition faction broke into stomping, hissing, clapping, and shouting. In vain Weld tried to raise his voice above the roar, only to be met with a shower of eggs. When Weld resumed speaking, the rioters surged through the doors and up the aisles. Three times they attempted to seize and drag Weld from the platform, but each time the preachers and a bodyguard of young men from the antislavery society repulsed them. The attackers then hurled brickbats. Finally, after nearly two hours of combat, the mayor appeared and ordered the church emptied. The city attorney, a man of great strength, seized the ringleader of the mob and held him by the throat while several deputies escorted Weld and Beman to their lodging. The crowd followed close behind, shouting epithets and pelting the speakers and officials with sundry objects.

The next day, a committee of the antislavery society met with the Common Council in an effort to obtain assurances that Weld would be protected from attack at future meetings. The mayor, however, expressed the opinion that law and order could not be maintained if Weld insisted on lecturing again. The abolitionist had serious misgivings about remaining in Troy after hearing of the mayor's statement. "Anti-abolition fury . . . is breaking out anew," he wrote to a friend, "and with deadlier hate than ever." In the following days, whenever he appeared on the streets, he did so with a bodyguard of young men as he had become the target of insults, threats, and assorted missiles.[23]

Although friends urged him to leave for his own safety and city authorities harrassed him, Weld remained in Troy and tried to wear down the opposition. No less determined, Beman continued to participate in the meetings, but with the protection of a revolver. Resigned to martyrdom, Weld wrote to a friend, "Let every abolitionist debate the matter once and for all . . . whether he can stand at the post of duty, and having done all and suffered all, . . . fall and die a martyr not accepting deliverance. . . . God gird us to do all valiantly for the helpless and innocent. Blessed are they who die in the harness and are buried on the field or bleach there."[24]

Weld did not die in the harness at Troy, but he was twice seriously injured in riots. Seemingly, the battle could have waged indefinitely, but the mayor and city authorities finally declared that, law or no law, Weld would be ejected forcibly if he refused to leave. Realizing the futility of further attempts to overcome the hostility, both Beman and Weld agreed that it would be better if he went peaceably.[25]

The event influenced Beman in several ways. Irritated by the opposition and determined to see the conflict carried to a successful conclusion, he took a more active part in the antislavery crusade. The combat also strengthened his friendship with Weld, and Beman became one of the lecturer's most loyal supporters. Finally, the publicity given to the events in Troy stamped Beman as an abolitionist in the public mind and brought him requests to speak throughout the East.

------

[23]*Friend of Man*, 14 July 1836; Thomas, *Theodore Weld*, 115; Gilbert H. Barnes, *The Antislavery Impulse, 1830-1844* (New York: D. Appleton-Century, 1933) 85; Jonathan H. Noble Memorial Sermon in Marvin Vincent, *Memorial Sermon on Rev. N. S. S. Beman, D.D., LL.D., Delivered Sunday Evening, December 17, 1871, in the First Presbyterian Church, Troy, N.Y., by Rev. Marvin R. Vincent, D.D., Pastor* (Troy: A. W. Scribner Co., 1872); A. J. Weise, *History of the City of Troy* (Troy: William H. Young, 1876) 172.

[24]Barnes and Dumond, *Letters of Theodore Weld, Angelina Grimké Weld and Sarah Grimké*, 1:309-10.

[25]Thomas, *Theodore Weld*, 115-17; Barnes, *Antislavery Impulse*, 85; Vincent, *Memorial Sermon*, 6.

Beman's next clash with the anti-abolition forces came on the ecclesiastical front. In May he again attended the General Assembly, where the delegates, aroused by *The Presbyterian,* gathered with every expectation of an attempt by the New School to read the Southern synods out of the church. The meeting proceeded smoothly until the committee on slavery reported. The majority of the committee submitted a resolution declaring that "the subject of slavery is inseparably connected with the laws of many of the States of this Union with which it is by no means proper for an ecclesiastical body to interfere." According to them, any action by the Assembly would only tend to divide the churches and was, therefore, inexpedient.

In collaboration with another member of the committee, Beman prepared a minority report which he insisted upon submitting as a substitute for the majority resolution. The minority report asserted:

1. That the buying, selling, or holding [of] a human being as property, is in the sight of God, a heinous sin, and ought to subject the doer to the censures of the church.

2. That it is the duty of every one, and especially of every Christian, who may be involved in this sin, to free himself from its entanglement without delay.

3. That it is the duty of everyone, especially of every Christian, in the meekness and firmness of the gospel, to plead the cause of the poor and needy by testifying against the principle and practice of slaveholding; and to use his best endeavors to deliver the church of God from the evil; and to bring about the emancipation of the slaves in these United States and throughout the world.

The Southerners were prepared for this tactic; prior to convening they had agreed that if any such action was taken, they would refuse to submit to the decision. Armed with this threat, the Southern members attacked Beman's resolution. After a long and heated debate, a coalition of Old School and Southern delegates succeeded in indefinitely postponing the subject by a vote of 154 to 87.

Although the postponement carried by a large majority, the solution was not entirely satisfactory to either the Southerners or the abolitionists, for many in both camps wanted the subject settled finally and immediately. The size of the vote against postponement further distressed the Southern delegates, for they knew that the issue would rise again. The Old School, however, had laid the groundwork for an alliance with the South which two years later would enable them to force a separation. Before the Assembly adjourned, the two groups met secretly and arranged for a committee of correspondence to keep them informed of any moves of the antislavery forces.[26]

During these crucial years, the New School turned increasingly to Beman for leadership. Since the moves of Finney to Oberlin College and Lyman Beecher to Lane Seminary in Cincinnati, Beman had carried the major responsibility for the course of the movement. Although eminently successful as an antislavery speaker, Theodore Weld had neither the reputation nor the stature within the church to undertake the role.

This new prominence was not without drawbacks. Because of his zealous agitation, the clergyman came under increasing attack in both the popular and the religious presses. It was also during this time that Caroline was proving to be a source of irritation and embarrassment. Shortly before the Weld riots in Troy, she decided that slavery was not inconsistent with Christianity and wrote her husband of her change of mind. Beman was incensed. Guarded references to his "personal situation" and "other things which I need not name" in subsequent correspondence with Weld reveal Beman's concern over Caroline's attitude.[27] The marriage of William Yancey in August 1835 necessitated further explanations, for Yancey's wife brought with her thirty-five slaves as part of her dowry. With a wife convinced of the morality of slavery and a stepson who was a large slaveholder, other men might have hesitated to denounce slavery and slaveholding, but not Beman.[28]

---

[26]William Goodell, *Slavery and Anti-Slavery* (New York: William Goodell, 1853) 153-55; James G. Birney, *The American Churches, the Bulwarks of American Slavery* (Concord NH: Parker Pillsbury, 1885) 35; Staiger, "Abolitionism and the Presbyterian Schism," 400-402; Ezra H. Gillett, *History of the Presbyterian Church in the United States of America* (Philadelphia: Presbyterian Publications Committee, 1864) 2:469n.

[27]Letter, Nathan S. S. Beman to Caroline Beman, 21 December 1835, Benjamin C. Yancey Papers, Southern Historical Collection, University of North Carolina Library, Chapel Hill; Letters, Nathan S. S. Beman to Theodore Weld, 10 May 1837, February 1840, in Barnes and Dumond, *Letters of Theodore Weld, Angelina Grimké Weld and Sarah Grimké,* 1:383, 2:820.

[28]John Witherspoon DuBose, *Life and Times of William Lowndes Yancey,* 2 vols. (New York: Peter Smith, 1942) 1:70.

Beman's major embarrassment was that he had once owned slaves himself. Increasingly distressed by Beman's influence upon the General Assembly, the Southerners made a careful investigation of his past. They, of course, discovered that he had both held and sold slaves while living in Georgia. By 1836 rumor of this was widespread. In January 1837, Sarah Grimké wrote to Weld that she had received a letter from a theological student in Tennessee inquiring whether Beman had sold his slaves when he moved to the North. "Art thou able to tell me?" she asked. "I remember something was published in the Emancipator about it, but I do not recollect distinctly."[29]

The proslavery forces publicized Beman's former slaveholding in a pamphlet, *The South Vindicated from the Treason and Fanaticism of the Northern Abolitionists*, published anonymously in 1837. The author observed, "It is unnecessary to describe the Reverend Dr. Beman of Troy, one of the most noisy and violent of the canting supporters of abolition, who *first sold out his slaves*, and then denounced those 'who sell the image of Jesus.' " To this dismissal, the writer appended a copy of the bill of sale executed by Beman in 1822 when he sold for $700 three slaves, a mother and her two infant children, acquired as part of Caroline's dowry.[30] This

---

[29]Barnes and Dumond, *Letters of Theodore Weld, Angelina Grimké Weld and Sarah Grimké*, 1:383.

[30]*The South Vindicated from the Treason and Fanaticism of the Northern Evangelists* (Philadelphia: H. Manly, 1837) 168-70. The bill of sale reads as follows:

"State of Georgia, Hancock County

"Know all men by these presents, that I, Nathan S.S. Beman, of the county and State aforesaid, have this day bargained and sold to Jacob Wilcox of Savannah, of the said state, three negro slaves, viz. Cloe, a negro woman, about thirty-four years of age, her son George, four years of age, and her daughter, Cuyline, an infant, for and in consideration of the sum of seven hundred dollars, to me in hand paid, the receipt and payment of which sum in full are hereby acknowledged; and I, the said Nathan S.S. Beman, do agree to warrant and defend the right of the aforesaid negroes to him, the said Jacob Wilcox, his heirs and assigns, forever, against all claims whatever.

"In witness whereof, I have hereunto set my hand and affixed my seal, this 11th day of April, 1822.

Nathan S.S. Beman

"Signed, sealed and delivered in presence of Leavitt Thaxter, Wm. Greene Macon, I.I. C. Register the 15th June, 1822, Phil L. Simms, Clerk Sup'r Court."

A copy of the bill of sale is also to be found in the Benjamin C. Yancey Papers.

attempt by the proslavery forces to silence Beman proved a failure. Willing to admit past errors, Beman took the stand that everyone, and especially every Christian, was obligated to free himself from involvement with slavery. This he had done. Furthermore, he believed that Christians were duty-bound to speak out against the institution. This, too, he was prepared to do.

Beman became so deeply imbued with the spirit of abolitionism that he seriously considered leaving his pastorate in Troy to work exclusively for the antislavery cause. Late in 1836 the American Anti-Slavery Society announced that they were sending Beman on a mission to Europe.[31] Although he was unable to make the trip, Beman did not relinquish the idea. In 1837, shortly before departing for Philadelphia to attend the General Assembly, he wrote a confidential letter to Weld, seeking to arrange a meeting in order to consult with him about strategy for the session and "some other things which may induce me to engage permanently in the cause of the oppressed." Referring to his difficulties with his wife, Beman confided that "there are some things in my *personal* situation which you can *guess* which render it peculiarly necessary for me to see you." Although Beman was not to leave his pastorate in Troy, he did not wholly abandon the idea of becoming an agent for the American Anti-Slavery Society for several years.[32]

The General Assembly of 1837 was one of the most significant in the annals of the Presbyterian Church, for at this meeting the action was initiated that would result in disruption a year later. Almost immediately following the adjournment of the Assembly of 1836, the Old School faction had intensified its campaign to secure the support of the South. *The Presbyterian* continued to charge the New School with agitating the slavery question for the purpose of driving the South from the church, and thereby gaining control of the Northern orthodox.[33] The South accepted the invitation to join in a united conservative front. All that remained was to

---

[31]*Religious Monitor*, December 1836, 335.

[32]Letters, Nathan S. S. Beman to Theodore Weld, 10 May 1837, 3 February 1840, in Barnes and Dumond, *Letters of Theodore Weld, Angelina Grimké Weld and Sarah Grimké*, 1:383, 2:820-22.

[33]Philadelphia *Presbyterian*, 23 July 1836.

determine the best means of ridding the church of the antislavery agitators.

The Old School decided that the most effective method would be to abrogate the 1801 Plan of Union and to excise the most offensive antislavery synods on doctrinal, rather than abolitionist, grounds. The Plan of Union, an arrangement between the Presbyterians and Congregationalists adopted to cope with the problem of administering to the religious needs of scattered western settlements, provided that ministers of either denomination might serve in their churches regardless of the form of government of individual congregations. In the course of time, many Congregational preachers had come to embrace the "radical" innovations of the New School. Thus, the Old School decided to be rid of these agitators and chose to excise the four synods of Western Reserve, Utica, Genessee, and Geneva—all on record in favor of abolition.[34]

Leaders of both camps gathered in Philadelphia prior to the General Assembly to formulate strategy for the coming conflict. Claiming that the objectionable judicatories had never been organized as Presbyterian bodies, the Old School drew up a memorial that outlined the steps necessary to purify the denomination. Nowhere in the document was the subject of slavery so much as mentioned. The New School prepared an attack on the proposed excise based on the constitution of the church.

On 18 May the Assembly convened in the Central Presbyterian Church. The Reverend Dr. John Witherspoon, one of the most active conspirators in the Old School plot, delivered the opening sermon on the text "Now I beseech you, brethren, by the name of our Lord Jesus Christ, that ye all speak the same thing, and that there be no divisions among you." The two factions were ably represented with Witherspoon, Jefferson Breckinridge, and Ashbel Green heading the Old School contingent and Beman, George Duffield, John P. Cleaveland, and Baxter Dickinson at the forefront among the New Measures men. The respective strength of the parties was revealed on the ballot for a new moderator, with the Old School-Southern coalition candidate winning 137 to 106.[35]

As a member of the Committee on Bills and Overtures, to which the Old School memorial was referred, Beman sought to halt the excising be-

[34]Staiger, "Abolitionism and the Presbyterian Schism," 393, 405-407.

[35]Gillett, *History of the Presbyterian Church*, 2:505-507.

fore it reached the floor, but to no avail. However, he did prevent the Old School committee members from carrying out a plan to increase the number of "errors" committed by the accused synods.

On the floor, debate on the report continued throughout most of a week. Beman led the New School attack, arguing that the resolutions were impracticable and unconstitutional and that both presbyteries and churches throughout the country would resist the move. Beman's arguments are reported to have made a decided impression on the body, but they were not sufficient to prevent defeat. In spite of a defection in the Old South ranks, on the final vote 128 delegates voted for excision measures against 122 opposed to the action. Following the memorial's adoption, the Old School offered a resolution excising the Synod of Western Reserve. The motion was sustained, and the Assembly then proceeded to rid itself of Utica, Geneva, and Genessee as well. Although the final disruption of the the church did not occur until the following General Assembly, the division was already a reality.[36]

While the Old School clearly had out-maneuvered its adversaries and regained control of the church, its ascendancy was short-lived. During the next twelve months the New Schoolers embarked upon a campaign to regain their power. In August they met in Auburn, New York, to outline their procedure and decided that the four synods and presbyteries involved were neither to abandon the Plan of Union and the churches formed under it, nor to recognize the action of the Assembly as having any validity. They were ordered to send delegations to the Assembly of 1838 and to claim their seats by constitutional rights. In addition, the group issued what came to be known as the Auburn Declaration, a statement in which the charges of doctrinal irregularity made by the Old School were contrasted point by point with teachings and practices of the New School men.

In the spring of 1838, Beman, Lyman Beecher, Cleaveland, Samuel H. Cox, and several other New School leaders published a call for a meeting of all commissioners in Philadelphia. Noting that "the measures adopted at the last Assembly . . . [gave] reason to apprehend unhappy collisions at the opening of the Assembly as well as subsequently," the call asked the delegates to meet three days before the Assembly convened. At the caucus, New School representatives reaffirmed their plan to press for

---

[36]Ibid.; Staiger, "Abolitionism and the Presbyterian Church," 409-11.

readmission of the excised synods and worked out final details for the presentation of their case.

On the eve of the grave struggle, Theodore Weld—ever practical—filled an hour between meetings by exchanging marriage vows with Angelina Grimké and then set off for a public lecture. Forewarned of the abolitionist's incendiary views, the city of brotherly love welcomed Weld with a stirring riot that lasted far into the night. Thus, the stage was set for one of the most consequential battles in the history of the Presbyterian Church.[37]

When the General Assembly met on Thursday, 17 May, the first question before it was the manner in which the Assembly was to be constituted. William Patton, a New School man, attempted to offer a motion that the roll be completed by adding the names of the excised delegates. The retiring moderator David Elliot refused either to entertain the motion or to recognize an appeal from his ruling. After the clerk had reported the roll, Elliot asked if any commissioners were present whose names had not been enrolled. Erskine Mason of New York then made a second motion to complete the roll by adding the commissioners from the excluded presbyteries. Declaring the motion out of order, the moderator again refused to entertain an appeal to his ruling.

At this decision, general uproar broke out upon the floor, with delegates seeking recognition, commissioners interrupting each other, and the moderator vainly trying to restore order. John P. Cleaveland of the Presbytery of Detroit sought to read a paper proclaiming the violation of the rights of the excised delegates. He argued that since the moderator had been negligent in his duty to readmit these delegates, the election of a new moderator was necessary. Cleaveland moved that Beman take over the chair as temporary moderator and, after seconding, took the vote on his own motion. The Old School, caught unaware by the coup, sat silently while the New School members proceeded to elect Beman.

Upon completion of the voting, Beman made no attempt to take possession of the chair but, instead, arose in the aisle and asked for motions

---

[37]Robert Ellis Thompson, A *History of the Presbyterian Church in the United States* (New York: Charles Scribner's Sons, 1895) 116-19; Samuel Miller, Jr., *Report of the Presbyterian Church Case: Commonwealth of Pennsylvania vs. Ashbel Green and Others* (Philadelphia: William S. Martien, 1839) 56; *New York Observer*, 26 May 1838.

to organize the Assembly. With only the New School taking part, the delegates elected officers and then voted to adjourn to the First Church. There, in succeeding meetings, they repealed the excising acts, elected replacements for the Old School trustees, and carried out the business of the Assembly. The separation was a fact. For the next thirty-three years, the two factions operated as separate churches. With them in their revolt, the New School carried 533 churches and more than 100,000 communicants, or about four-ninths of the ministry and membership of the Presbyterian Church.[38]

The responsibility for the division must rest with both factions. Although the Old School took the initiative in bringing about the final disruption, for more than a decade Beman, Finney, and other New Measures men had relentlessly pushed reforms and pressed innovations that could only alienate the more conservative element within the church. Perseveringly, they had sought to introduce a new gospel and, with it, a new system of moral relations and a new scale of human rights. The threat to the Old School lay in the rapid growth of the movement and the increasingly dominant role played by the New School in the councils of the church.

To the Southern clergy the danger lay in the application of the new philosophies to the institution of slavery and the implications to all judicatories tolerating slaveholding within their bounds. Certainly Beman's censorious reprimand of the Old School in his opening sermon of 1832, his relentless aggressiveness in succeeding Assemblies, and his close association with the American Anti-Slavery Society hastened the disruption. Whether the schism could have been averted through a more conciliatory approach by the New School seems unlikely, for once abolitionism had been incorporated into the theology of the new movement dissension became inevitable. The question became simply whether the church would divide along theological or geographical lines.

---

[38]Thompson, *A History of the Presbyterian Church*, 116-19; Miller, *Report of the Presbyterian Church Case*, 55; Gillett, *History of the Presbyterian Church*, 2:528-30; *New York Observer*, 26 May 1838.

Chapter VII

Temperance
and Travel

*The splendid gin palaces of London
stand in bold defiance
with their doors wide open.*
—Nathan S. S. Beman

Following his participation in the battles over slavery and Presbyterian
theology, for most of 1839 Beman diverted his enthusiasm for agitation to
the temperance movement and shifted his scene of operation to the British Isles. Although Beman spoke on other matters while in England, he
devoted the bulk of his speaking and public activity to the New British
and Foreign Temperance Society. Organized temperance activity in the
United States antedated the English effort by more than ten years. Because the American Temperance Union had made great strides in that
time, the British societies were highly interested in the accounts of the
methods and successes of their American allies as related by Beman and
other visitors.

Beman sailed for England in January 1839, only eight months after the
climactic events in Philadelphia that led to the Presbyterian schism. For
some time he had wanted to visit Britain and the continent and had had
two previous opportunities. As early as 1835 the General Assembly had
elected him to represent the church at the annual meeting of the Con-

gregational Union of England and Wales, and in 1836 the American Anti-Slavery Society had announced that he would serve as their agent on a mission to Europe.[1] Although he was unable to carry out either of these assignments, Beman's correspondence for the next two years indicates that he had not abandoned the idea.[2] However, his difficulties with Caroline, the expense of her visit to the South, Henry's death, and financial losses during the panic of 1837 thwarted his aspirations.

One reason for his long-cherished journey was his poor health. Troubled by a recurrence of tuberculosis Beman decided to seek restoration abroad and at the same time visit those places he had longed to see. He arranged to serve as a representative of the American Temperance Union and the Young Men's Temperance Association of New York at the annual meeting of the New British and Foreign Temperance Society and as a delegate from the New School to the sessions of the Congregational Union of England and Wales. Presumably, financial assistance from these organizations enabled him to make the trip.

During his voyage, Beman maintained a diary, and shortly after his arrival in London he sent the New York *Evangelist* a series of lengthy letters. This correspondence gives a more detailed account of Beman's day-to-day activities than is available from extant papers for any other period of his life. They also provide insight into customs of the period and a visitor's first impressions of England.

In his first letter, mailed from London in February, Beman recounted the events of his departure on the morning of 11 January 1839, a few minutes before noon. He sailed on the *Montreal*, captained by Seth B. Griffing. A few friends had accompanied Beman to the docks and "expressed

---

[1]William M. Engles, *Minutes of the General Assembly of the Presbyterian Church in the United States of America from 1821 to 1835* (Philadelphia: Presbyterian Board of Publication, 1835) 479; *Religious Monitor*, December 1836, O. 335.

[2]Letters, Nathan S. S. Beman to Caroline Beman, 15 March 1836, and Caroline Beman to Benjamin C. Yancey, 11 February 1838, Benjamin C. Yancey Papers, Southern Historical Collection, University of North Carolina Library, Chapel Hill; Letter, Nathan S. S. Beman to Theodore Weld, 10 May 1837, in *Letters of Theodore Dwight Weld, Angelina Grimké Weld and Sarah Grimké, 1822-1844*, ed. Gilbert H. Barnes and Dwight L. Dumond, 2 vols. (New York: D. Appleton-Century, 1934) 1:383.

their wishes for my safety upon the mighty deep and for a return with invigorated health, and then bade farewell."

To Beman, it was a moment of intense interest: "In feeble health and with spirits far from buoyant, I was bidding farewell, perhaps forever, to my native shores and skies," he wrote. "I might be gazing upon these familiar objects—the receding city, the shortening spires, the calm and peaceful bay, with its beautiful islands, for the last time. There was not a person on board with whom I had the slightest acquaintance." The place and circumstances also forced upon him a sad recollection. He was reminded that about three years earlier "a darling son, a youth of lovely spirit—himself a stranger and alone on board the vessel—sailed from this port, and never returned. His bones sleep far from kindred and friends, while his spirit, I trust, lives in heaven." As night closed around the ship, Beman went to his stateroom feeling doubtful about leaving home, friends, and country, and committing himself to an uncertain adventure.

The morning rose with favorable prospects. Beman strolled the deck to inspect the packet and pronounced it a fine ship: "550 tons, coppered and copper fastened; the cabin neatly finished, the staterooms commodious (one of which it was my good fortune to occupy alone); and sea stores in great variety and abundance strewn or hung around in all directions." Beman felt that, while affliction had compelled him to enter upon the expedition, Providence had been very kind in the arrangements that attended it.

At noon they were about 140 miles from the Hook when the wind rose and the ship began to rock. Notwithstanding a determined resistance on his part, Beman's dire anticipation was speedily realized when the first symptoms of "that most annoying, and least commiserated of all diseases—sea sickness"—appeared. He summoned every mental and physical resource, he walked about, sat up, and lay down, but all to no avail. He finally was compelled to "settle up the whole score." If this had been the end of it, Beman would have had good reason to congratulate himself. But for him it was to be repeated over and over again on his trip across the Atlantic.

By the fourth day, his seasickness had subsided and he began to take some interest in the others around him, both crew members and passengers. "When upon land they [the sailors] have but few associates, and those too of the baser sort, whose only interest is to corrupt and plunder them.

And yet they are fragments of Christian nations; they are Americans and Britons."[3]

As he became acquainted with his fellow passengers, Beman was surprised to find that they were all English; except for some members of the crew, Beman was the only American on board. While the English and Americans were essentially alike in Beman's opinion, they were emphatically intolerant of each other's peculiarities, each frequently condemning the other for the very thing of which the condemnor was a prime offender. If the subject was government, an Englishman could not endure a system where liberty was carried to licentiousness, even though in Beman's opinion there was probably no country where such violent attacks were made upon the government, both in public speeches and the press, than England. Although Beman believed that Americans also had a great talent for such inconsistency, "the daughter was not the mother country yet in that peculiar gift."

On two subjects Beman was always happy to agree with his new English friends—slavery and the interference of Americans in the affairs of Canada. He believed that the steps taken by Britain to end slavery and the slave trade would "cover her name with glory among the nations to the end of time," but he feared that the United States was weaving for itself a "robe of infamy" equally conspicuous and lasting. Regarding relations between Britain and Canada, Beman was convinced that no point was more self-evident than that the United States should not intervene.

On 16 January, the *Montreal* found itself in the Gulf Stream with a strong northwest wind, and the next three days brought head winds, cold weather, and seasickness. Sunday morning, 20 January, Beman conducted a worship service attended by most of the passengers. But it was a melancholy reflection for him that few of the officers or sailors were present and that generally they seemed to have little interest for such.

To Beman's intense displeasure, the cabin of the ship was invaded a few days later by an "evil": "a multitude of little black and red apparitions . . . commonly called cards." He accused the English of being "passionately fond of communing with this kind of spirits" and speculated on whether this was because they think more intensely than other people and need relaxation or the reverse; or whether this addiction was intended to

---

[3]New York *Evangelist*, 1 June 1839.

remedy a certain taciturnity to be found among them. Whatever the cause, Beman was not hesitant in admonishing his fellow passengers. He informed them that such games had been invented to amuse an old fool who happened to be the king of France and, not very subtly, implied that history had shown that their appeal was to persons of similar intelligence. His admonishments were in vain. He was particularly distressed by one young Englishman who slept most of the day so that he might be wide awake and alert for the evening card games.

On their twenty-second day at sea, the passengers were pleased to find themselves in the neighborhood of three other vessels under full canvas and a vast number of seagulls which appeared to have come out to convey the ship into port. "We were now in soundings and the first specimen brought up by the lead taught us that we were in the Channel near the coast of France."[4]

About ten o'clock on Sunday, 3 February, in spite of thick fog, they caught their first glimpse of land. It was Start Point on the coast of Devonshire, but it was not until the next morning that they had a full view of the coast. Without a pilot to guide them, the ship had sailed past the Needles, the usual entrance to Portsmouth, during the night. Morning found them on the south side of the Isle of Wight, but a few miles from land. Beman described the area as one of the most charming and garden-like spots in England: "One of the first things that attracts the eye and fixes the attention of a stranger on approaching this part of England is its bold and bluff coast. I believe there is nothing like it in our country. In some places, the tall, chalky cliffs rose almost perpendicularly from the very margin of the ocean; in others, the slope which conducted to the neighboring heights was gradual and gentle."

At nine o'clock on the morning of 4 February, a pilot came alongside and, after completing some diplomatic etiquette, was received on board. The pilot, "a regular John Bull," saluted with "A fine morning, captain," although the fog and mist were so thick that they quickly penetrated anything but an India-rubber overcoat. Stepping aboard, the pilot peremptorily issued an order to the crew respecting the ship, to which the captain promptly replied, "I can manage my own vessel, sir. I need no help."

"It makes no difference to me," the pilot coolly responded.

----

[4]Ibid., 8 June 1839.

"But it does to me, sir, for I choose to keep the command of my ship as long as I can. I don't need a pilot at all, except to answer the law."

At that point, both parties fell silent; the packet continued on its course under the direction of the captain. Portsmouth and Gosport, with their extensive fortification and many warships, soon appeared in full view. Beman was so relieved to arrive in sight of land that even though he was a staunch believer in republican government it would have taken very little at that moment to make him quite loyal to the young Queen Victoria. As it was, he swore to obey all of the laws of England if only he might be permitted to set foot on terra firma once more.

The last official on board before the ship was permitted to land was the health officer. Assured by the captain's responses to his questions, he hoisted a small copper box upon a rod. The box contained a Bible, which the captain kissed, as required by law. To Beman's dismay, the health officer then "regaled himself with a glass or two of Port." The ship soon was at anchor at the Mother Bank off Portsmouth. In a few minutes the passengers and their effects were on board the *Navarin*, a cutter belonging to the line, and "with feelings of gratitude to God for his guardian care upon the ocean and with those high and novel sensations peculiar to the bosom of a stranger on his visit to a foreign land," Beman planted his feet for the first time on British soil at three o'clock, 4 February 1839.

In his fourth letter to the *Evangelist*,[5] Beman continued the account of his travels, giving his first impressions of England.

> Portsmouth is situated on the island of Portsea, and in connection with the town of Portsea (for they may be considered as forming one town) contains between forty-five and fifty thousand inhabitants. . . . The town itself is not very imposing in appearance, its streets being for the most part narrow and dirty. I saw no buildings which were remarkable for the beauty or elegance of their architecture. To an adventurer from the new world, the principal attractions will be found in its venerable antiquity and the great extent and strength of its fortifications. . . . The streets, the shops, and the public and private buildings differed in so many features from those in the large towns of my own country as to assure me that I was indeed *abroad* and yet even so much like them in other particulars as to make me feel quite at home.

---

[5]Ibid.

Beman was impressed with the gentlemanly manner in which everything was conducted at the Customs House, experiencing none of the insolence he often observed in officials with a "little brief authority" and "no prying into little matters such as the extent or poverty of a man's wardrobe—no examination of a single traveller's threadcase to see whether his silk and needles are of British manufacture or not."

After his visit to the Customs House, Beman strolled the streets of Portsmouth. All of the passengers, including the captain, dined at the Quebec at five o'clock. The only difficulty occurred when, upon receiving his bill, Beman found he had been charged six pence for ale. He handed the bill to Captain Griffing who, familiar with the clergyman's stand against alcoholic beverages, crossed out the charge and wrote "no go" in pencil against the item. Beman saved the document to defend himself should he later be accused of trans-Atlantic deviation from the temperance doctrines he preached and practiced at home.

At eleven o'clock on the morning of Tuesday, 5 February, Beman took his seat on the box with the coachman for the trip to London. To be on solid ground was something, but to be in England was more, and Beman thought he had begun to understand what an Englishman means when he says, " 'A fine morning, sir,' when, for your life, you cannot tell what there is fine about it, except that it is not as dark, by a few shades, as Egypt."

In his fifth letter,[6] Beman described the trip from Portsmouth to London. Based on his experiences and observations during this trip, Beman decided that coach travel in England was much finer than in the United States. Everything, in his judgment, was nearly perfect: the roads were smooth and hard; the coaches, although not large or very elegant, were generally well made and fleet; they traveled at about ten miles per hour; and there were few delays on the road. One minute was enough time to discharge one team and take on another, and the changes were entirely free of the furious, hurried "hurricane manner" he had observed elsewhere and found very annoying. He was also pleased that on the trip to London he witnessed "none of that important swaggering, none of those low and limping attempts at wit, nothing of that downright profane and broad vulgarity which, I am sorry to say, characterizes too many of the public conveyances in our own country."

---

[6]Ibid.

Nearly two months elapsed before Beman again addressed the readers of the *Evangelist*. The reasons for the delay were illness and, upon recovery, his participation in a series of meetings in London and the provinces. Although available records do not reveal the nature of his indisposition, on 23 March the *Journal of the New British and Foreign Temperance Society* announced that Beman had arrived in England, but that ill health had "rendered it necessary for the Rev. Doctor to visit the Continent for a season."[7] Beman crossed the channel to France and Belgium. Upon visiting Paris he was impressed with the wealth, talent, and taste of the capital. In the city, he noted, one could find everything that is "intellectual, accomplished and brilliant in the kingdom." The French provinces he found less attractive; the villages were dirty and poverty-stricken. "The country, for the most part," he observed, "presents one vast extended common—cultivated to be sure—without wall or fence, hedge or ditch, interspersed here and there with the solitary village or hamlet . . . which is anything but an oasis in the midst of the surrounding desert."[8]

In April Beman returned to England. Early that month he delivered his first speech to a British audience at the Third Annual Festival of the Bristol Temperance Society. The meeting was held in the town hall and, although the proceedings had been "considerably shortened" because of interest in hearing the American visitor, Beman was preceded by five other speakers. Finally, the Reverend James Edwards, the leading figure in the temperance movement in Brighton, introduced Beman, reminding the assembly that the American was in "feeble health, and had consented to say but little."

Beman spoke primarily on the history of the American Temperance Union. In relating the American experience, he mentioned that in the United States physicians generally agreed that liquor had few, if any, medicinal values. Upon arrival in England, however, he said that he had been astounded to discover that most Englishmen believed that a few drinks a day were essential to good health. When he questioned this idea on the *Montreal*, he related, the English passengers considered him a fanatic and

---

[7]*Journal of the New British and Foreign Temperance Society* (London) 1:12 (23 March 1839): 1.

[8]Nathan S. S. Beman, *The Intellectual Position of Our Country* (Troy: N. Tuttle, 1839) 13; New York *Evangelist*, 28 August 1845.

laughed in his face. In London, he said, the attitude was, "Lor, bless your soul, we can't live in England without beer!" Beman presented a lengthy rebuttal of this point of view, concluded with a plea to abstain, and sat down to loud applause.[9]

From Bristol Beman went to Great Harwood in Buckinghamshire, where he spent a week at the home of the dissenting minister of the village. Hoping that the air would improve his physical condition, he took daily walks and frequently saddled the parson's horse for a ride into the surrounding countryside. He also delivered two temperance lectures, one in Great Harwood and the other in nearby Fenny Stratford.[10] Upon his return to London, Beman embarked upon a period of strenuous activity during which he participated in the annual conventions of several organizations and delivered a large number of addresses and sermons. He gave his first speech in the city upon the anniversary of the Wesleyan-Methodist Missionary Society on 29 April.[11]

On Tuesday, 7 May, Beman attended the annual assembly of the Congregational Union of England and Wales held in Exeter Hall. Located in the Strand, Exeter Hall had been built only eight years before, but already it had become the site for the annual "May meetings" of religious and reform organizations. The great hall could seat 3,000 people, but only about 275 persons were present on this occasion. Most were ministers, but some lay delegates, visitors, and theological students were also in the audience. The Reverend Dr. Thomas Raffles of Liverpool took the chair at nine o'clock and the meeting opened with hymns and a prayer. Following a short address by the chairman, Rev. John Blackburn introduced the American guests, Beman and Rev. William Patton of New York.[12]

After speeches by several delegates, Beman addressed the assemblage. In his opening remarks he stressed his affection for England and the com-

---

[9]*Journal of the New British and Foreign Temperance Society* (London), 1:15 (13 April 1839): 121-23.

[10]Ibid., 1:19 (11 May 1839): 159.

[11]*Report of the Wesleyan-Methodist Missionary Society for the Year Ending April, 1839* (London: Wesleyan-Methodist Missionary Society, 1839) vi.

[12]*The Congregational Magazine* (London), (June 1839): 373; Henry B. Wheately, *London Past and Present* (London: John Murray, 1891) 2:26.

mon bond between the United States and that country. "I was in the ministry when preparations were making for the last war," he said, "and I lifted up my voice in the pulpit against it." His assertion that England and America should stand together for the purpose of enlightening, purifying, and saving the world brought cheers of approval. After pointing out that he and Patton represented the Presbyterian Church, Beman emphasized the similarities between that sect and the Congregationalists of England and Wales. He concluded with a denunciation of slavery and remarks upon the importance of revivals and missionary work. The speech apparently was a success, for he was interrupted many times by cheers and applause.[13]

Two days later, Beman participated in the forty-fifth annual meeting of the London Missionary Society, also held in Exeter Hall. This session proved to be unusually important in the society's history, and Beman was accorded the privilege of introducing the most significant resolution of the proceedings. Sir Cullen Eardley Smith served as chairman. After several resolutions, he introduced Beman. As a delegate from the American Board of Missions, Beman pointed out that he had been an active member of the Board of Missions for thirteen of its twenty-six years and then gave a history of American missionary work. Digressing briefly to commend the British on the emancipation of their slaves, he stated, "I venerate your first of August, and it is saying a great deal, when I tell you that I venerate it as I do the fourth of July." Beman then made the history-making resolution, which was that the society raise the unprecedented sum of one hundred thousand pounds during the next year to expand its missionary work in Asia and Africa. Although several years passed before the organization attained this amount, the 1839 meeting so reinvigorated the society that the following year it sharply increased its income to a total of £91,119.[14]

For five days beginning on 17 May Beman participated in a series of temperance meetings. At these, he once again became involved in controversy. Although not so deeply implicated as usual, Beman and his American colleagues—E. C. Delavan and William Patton—undoubtedly

[13]New York *Evangelist*, 10 August 1839.

[14]*The Missionary Magazine and Chronicle* (London) 3:37 (June 1839): 82-93; Richard Lovett, *The History of the London Missionary Society, 1795-1895*, 2 vols. (London: Henry Frowde, 1899) 2:657-60.

contributed to the rupture that followed the dispute. Patton and Delavan were well-known to Beman: the former was a Presbyterian minister with whom he had been associated in various benevolent enterprises; and the latter was a wealthy Albany landowner who had made his fortune as a wine dealer. About ten years earlier, he had become convinced of the evil of intemperance and became a leading figure in the United States' temperance movement. In 1835 he had achieved notoriety by publishing an article accusing Albany brewers of using filthy water in making beer. The brewers brought a suit for libel, asking for damages amounting to $300,000. Because of the widespread publicity given to the suit, Delavan's name was well-known in English temperance circles. At the time of his visit, the case was still pending.[15]

The scene of the controversy was the third annual meeting of the New British and Foreign Temperance Society and the issue was the pledge required for membership. During the first three years of the society's existence, members had been permitted to sign either of two pledges. The first required members merely to abstain from drinking anything intoxicating; under the second, members not only agreed to abstain themselves, but also promised not to give or offer liquor to others.[16] The 1839 dispute resulted from a proposal to require all members to sign the second pledge. The American Temperance Union had resolved the same issue early in its history in favor of the second pledge. Consequently, this position was generally known as "the American pledge."[17]

In March 1839, a majority of the central committee of the British Temperance Society resolved to seek adoption of the American pledge. In late April, the official publication of the organization endorsed the proposal.[18] By the annual meeting in May, most of the local auxiliaries and

---

[15]Allen Johnson and Dumas Malone, eds., *Dictionary of American Biography* (New York: Scribner's Sons, 1930) 5:221; *National Cyclopedia of American Biography* (New York: James T. White, 1901) 11:207.

[16]*First Report of the New British and Foreign Society for the Suppression of Intemperance* (London: J. Pasco, 1837) 29.

[17]Dawson Burns, *Temperance in the Victorian Age* (London: Ideal Publishing Union, 1897) 27, 30.

[18]*Journal of the New British and Foreign Temperance Society* (London) 1:17 (April 1839): 1.

branches had taken a stand on the question.[19] Whether Beman, Delavan, and Patton had attempted to influence the local groups is not known; however, all three strongly favored the American pledge and in the weeks preceding the convention they met several British temperance leaders and most likely discussed the issue with them.

Before any change in the rules of the society could be effected, the proposal had to be submitted to two groups: the Delegates and the Members. The proposal to alter the pledge was first officially made at the meeting of the Delegates at the Crown and Anchor Tavern. The Crown and Anchor had a rich and illustrious past, one ill-suited to prepare it for a temperance tempest. There Sir Joshua Reynolds had maintained the advantage of wine in assisting conversation. Samuel Johnson and James Bowwell had frequently been its patrons. William Pitt, Thomas Erskine, and John Curran were members of clubs that met there for talk and refreshment.[20] Nevertheless, on the afternoon of Friday, 17 May, sixty Delegates of the New British and Foreign Temperance Society and seventeen visitors assembled at the historic tavern to debate means of curbing intemperance.

The meeting opened with a prayer by James Edwards of Brighton. John Dunlop, president of the Scottish Temperance Union, was then called upon to preside; he was to play an important role in the turbulent struggle. A quiet, dignified, and middle-aged Scotsman, Dunlop had ten years before organized the National Temperance Reformation in Scotland and had since become one of the most influential temperance figures in Britain.[21]

Dunlop's first act upon assuming the chair was to introduce the three members of the American delegation. Each spoke briefly. Beman assured the Delegates of his cordial interest in the cause, disclaimed any right to vote in the proceedings, and expressed hope that at some future time he might again address the group. Patton and Delavan expressed similar sentiments. A resolution to substitute the American pledge for the two pledges

---

[19]Samuel Couling, *History of the Temperance Movement in Great Britain and Ireland* (London: William Tweedie, 1862) 103-104.

[20]Wheately, *London Past and Present*, 1:480.

[21]*Journal of the New British and Foreign Temperance Society* (London) 1:22 (1 June 1839): 194; Dawson Burns, *Pen Pictures of Some Temperance Notables* (London: National Temperance Publication, 1895) 10-11.

was then introduced. After a long and angry discussion, the motion to adopt was defeated, 33 to 27.[22]

That evening, Beman met with the Members, the society's other governing body. Again a motion of substitution was defeated, 337 to 236. When the assembly reconvened on Saturday morning, the Americans took a more active part in the proceedings. Delavan requested that the assembly reconsider its decision, but the chair ruled that since many Delegates had departed with the understanding that the question was settled the proposal could not be revived. The Americans, however, persisted, and finally another ballot was taken. When the decision of the previous day was reconfirmed, several who advocated adoption of the American pledge refused to participate further in the proceedings and signified their intention of forming a separate society.[23] The attempt to secure adoption of the American pledge had not, however, been abandoned, and the society was to hear more of the proposed amendment.

No business was transacted on Sunday. Beman had been invited to deliver a special lecture to the Delegates and Members. Accepting, he presented his sermon on "The Old Ministry," the address in defense of the New Measures which he had delivered to the General Assembly in 1832.[24]

On Monday the annual procession of the New British and Foreign Temperance Society took place. At nine o'clock, groups from the London branches and auxiliaries began to arrive at Lincoln's Inn Field. By eleven o'clock, the field was densely packed with marchers, bands, and carriages. A little before noon, the procession began to move in the direction of the Strand. The parade was headed by four soldiers wearing the uniforms of the Blues and their temperance medals. Immediately following was the South London Auxiliary with several carriages in which rode the officers, Beman, and the other American guests. Members of other associations followed, walking four abreast and wearing blue and white satin rosettes.

---

[22]*Journal of the New British and Foreign Temperance Society* (London) 1:22 (1 June 1839): 194-95; Couling, *History of the Temperance Movement in Great Britain and Ireland,* 114.

[23]Couling, *History of the Temperance Movement in Great Britain and Ireland,* 115-16.

[24]Nathan S. S. Beman, *The Old Ministry: Being a Lecture Delivered in London,* 19 May 1839 (London: John Snow, 1839).

The branches carried banners with inscriptions such as, "Woe unto him who giveth his neighbour drink" and "Let us unite to banish poverty, disease, and crime." Crowds lined the streets to watch the entire procession, which was about a mile-and-a-half in length.

The marchers reached Kennington Common about four o'clock in the afternoon. Approximately 25,000 persons were assembled in the common, and according to the official report, "with the exception of here and there a drunken person attempting to interrupt the proceedings, the whole was a scene of order and peace." After the addresses, the groups adjourned to Horn's Tavern, Mariners' Church, and Exeter Hall for tea, refreshments, and more speeches.[25]

Beman accompanied the South London Auxiliary to Horn's Tavern in Kennington for their annual festival where more than six hundred members sat down to tea. After refreshments, the Earl of Stanhope took the chair and speeches were delivered. Late in the evening, Beman addressed the gathering. Again he gave a history of the temperance movement in the United States. After expressing hope that the United States would follow Britain in the abolition of slavery and that the British would follow the Americans in temperance reformation, he contended that the principal obstacles to temperance in England were the laws, the ministry, and the women. With regard to the latter, he claimed that he had never seen such a disposition to drink among women as in Britain. Contending that liquor was more dangerous to women than to men, he argued that he had known thousands of men who had overcome intemperance but had never known an intemperate woman who had succeeded in overcoming the curse.[26]

The following morning, Tuesday, 21 May, the controversy over the American pledge reached its climax at the final meeting of the Members in Exeter Hall. One historian characterized that session as "the most extraordinary and most tumultuous meeting ever held within the walls of that building."[27] After calling the meeting to order, the Earl of Stanhope, who

---

[25]*Journal of the New British and Foreign Temperance Society* (London) 1:22 (1 June 1839): 185-86.

[26]Ibid., 186-87.

[27]Couling, *History of the Temperance Movement in Great Britain and Ireland,* 117.

was in the chair, addressed the Members. He stated that he would not adopt the American pledge, that he could not recommend it to others, and that he would resign from the society if it decided in favor of this pledge.

Following Stanhope's speech, Beman, Delavan, and Patton spoke; each strongly endorsed the American pledge. When Beman's turn came, he told the assembly that he had made up his mind to remain silent, but because of the opposition to the remarks of his American colleagues he had concluded that it was his duty to speak out. After saying that he represented two temperance groups that required the American pledge but had refused to serve as a delegate of another because it endorsed only the short pledge, he presented a lengthy argument to show that alcoholism could not be curtailed with half-measures. Although he refrained from explicit instructions to his British associates, Beman clearly indicated his support of the proposed amendment.[28]

When the Americans had concluded, Jabez Burns moved a resolution calling for "nothing less than an unflinching and uncompromising course of action." Burns's resolution was the signal for disorder. Stanhope tried to maintain control, but dozens of Members sought to address the group. A vivid description is provided by Samuel Couling:

> At this period the meeting presented an appearance of vast confusion and anarchy—the mass of the more eager disputants crowded densely around the chair—they debated across the front of the president, so that Lord Stanhope was concealed frequently from the audience. Lady Sarah Somerset, who sat on his lordship's left hand, was evidently alarmed, and a Quaker female forced herself through the ring apparently with an intent to render her ladyship any assistance that might be necessary. The confusion increased, the cross-fire of the debates became more fierce, and one person from the body of the house shouted out something about the chairman vacating his place. In a few seconds we saw the noble earl slowly rise from the chair and retire, attended by several individuals. The chairman having retired, a vote of thanks was put and carried amidst the clapping of hands and waving of handkerchiefs and hats.[29]

Following Stanhope's withdrawal, the body sought to select a new chairman. Delavan declined. A Mr. Heyworth accepted, but was unable to re-

---

[28]Ibid.; New York *Evangelist*, 31 August 1839.

[29]Couling, *History of the Temperance Movement in Great Britain and Ireland*, 118-19.

store order. Finally, Dunlop took possession of the chair and succeeded in bringing the meeting to order. After a vote on the motion, he declared the American pledge adopted by a large majority. Although the insurgents had triumphed, less than a month later the organization was torn asunder with the withdrawal of Lord Stanhope and other prominent members who formed a new society. [30]

After the meeting, a "grand Soiree" was held at the Crown and Anchor in honor of the Earl of Stanhope and the American deputation. The Earl, however, was conspicuously absent. The committee must have been disappointed, for elaborate pains had been taken to arrange an occasion suited to the tastes of the aristocracy. The journal of the society described the arrangements:

> As the occasion was peculiar, it was thought proper to endeavor to arrange this festival in such a manner, as to be in accordance with the habits of the distinguished guests; and also, so as to suit the comfort of those individuals of the upper classes, who, after the fatigue of the multitude in the forenoon, might be desirous of enjoying a select evening party, free from crowd or heat, and furnished with all the elegancies as well as the comforts of life.
>
> An excellent musical band was therefore in attendance; the price of the tickets was raised; and fruit, ices, and dried fruit, as well as tea and coffee, formed part of the entertainment; this was not partaken all at once, but services of the fruit took place during the intervals of the speeches. This had an uncommonly good effect; and the room being large and lofty, the ladies and gentlemen enjoyed the pleasure of an occasional promenade to the sound of the music, besides the relish of the entertainment and the delight of intellectual excitement. [31]

Dunlop occupied the chair, with Beman and Patton seated on his right.

After a speech by Dunlop, Beman was introduced. He stated that he had spoken so often and so long at their meetings that he was almost tired of hearing his own voice. However, in view of the events of the day, he felt he should say a few words as an American to a British audience. He then stressed the many common ties between the two countries. An allusion by Dunlop to the upper and lower classes of society served as an ex-

---

[30]Ibid., 119-20.

[31]*Journal of the New British and Foreign Temperance Society* (London) 1:22 (1 June 1839): 190.

cuse for Beman to make a poorly disguised attack on the aristocracy and, indirectly, on the Earl of Stanhope. In America, he said, *all men* were considered princes. He was glad that the English temperance movement had begun among the people because "the great ones of the earth were too happy to think about being reformed, were too fond of their pleasures to think about relinquishing earth for heaven." Although he stated that he questioned whether it would be courteous for him at that time to refer to the subject of the American pledge, Beman nevertheless congratulated them on "the advance they had made" and warned "You must not go back." The band struck up "Yankee Doodle" as he sat down amid cheers. [32]

Shortly after this meeting Beman sent to the *Evangelist* a letter in which he presented his observations on intemperance in England.

> Drunkenness is the curse of Britain. The temperance reformation has but just begun. It can hardly be said to have formed a character or gained a standing in the country. The old moderation societies are still making war very pacifically against distilled liquors and they keep up their own courage, and their muscular vigor too as they think, for this crusade by a free and liberal use of the whole tribe of fermented liquors. A more Utopian scheme was never dreamed of in any country than the attempt to cure drunkenness by potations of the most subtle and agreeable of all intoxicating liquors; but in England, where the land is literally deluged with the fermentation of wine and beer, it is an enterprise which can excite nothing but contempt. The splendid gin palaces of London stand in bold defiance with their doors wide open seven days in the week and blaze as many nights in the week with their brilliant gaslights and smile at such puny efforts to purify the land from the contamination of intemperance. . . .
>
> Almost the whole nation, if we except the 900,000 tee-totalers who are now to be found in the United Kingdom, . . . are in the habitual and daily use of fermented liquors. All the operations of life—labor, pleasure, rest, sleep—are carried on by this kind of steam power. It is thought by many to be as necessary to existence as bread or meat; and in the successful treatment of disease it stands first on the list in the whole materia medica. It is this advantage over every other medicine—that it is equally adapted to every disease, and that, too, at every stage and in every form, and any man can be his own physician, and appetite is an admirable substitute for medical skill. Hence it happens that we have almost an entire nation exhibiting the finest appearance of health, taking medicine from morning till night; and what is truly marvelous is that it is pronounced the best medicine in the world and yet it never effects a cure. . . .

---

[32]Ibid., 190-92.

I have often been amused to observe with what gravity and particularity my brethren in the ministry appeal to the [medical] faculty in vindication for their practice of taking a little wine. The family physician is the end of all controversy in this matter. My gravity (great as it is) was rather disturbed by an incident which occurred at a little dinner party composed entirely of ministers one day in London during the anniversaries. The wine had come on and with it, as usual on such occasions, a discussion of the practical influences of its use, particularly by ministers of the gospel and especially in this day of overwhelming intemperance. One young brother, with his wine glass in his hand, took shelter as usual under the wing of the faculty; but in order to show that his case was an exempted one and that his physician was certainly right, he remarked that his adviser had assured him that in eighteen cases in twenty wine was injurious. My reverend colleague from the United States said to him, "Sir, can you tell me how the two cases which form the exception to the general rule always happen to get into the ministry?" Silence ensued and this knotty question has not yet been answered.[33]

Following his participation in the meetings of the New British and Foreign Temperance Society in London, Beman spent most of his remaining two months in Britain touring the provinces to visit the clergy, to deliver sermons, and to participate in temperance activities. Typical of his work in the latter were his visits to Bristol and Bath. At Bristol the occasion was the fourth anniversary celebration of the local total-abstinence society. The meeting was held on the evening of 17 June in the Assembly Rooms in Prince's Street. After the opening exercises, Beman addressed the society in a vein similar to his Brighton and London speeches, including a statement congratulating the British on abolishing slavery.[34] The next day Beman traveled to Bath to participate in the third anniversary of the Bath Temperance Association. In the afternoon a procession, complete with bands, banners, carriages, and marchers, passed through the streets. That night more than eight hundred persons gathered at the Assembly Rooms for a tea party and speechmaking. Both Beman and Pat-

---

[33]New York *Evangelist*, 24 August 1839.

[34]*Journal of the New British and Foreign Temperance Society* (London) 1:28 (13 July 1839): 242; *Bristol Mercury*, 22 June 1839; *Bristol Times*, 22 June 1839; *Felix Farley's Bristol Journal*, 22 June 1839.

ton, who also attended the meeting, addressed the gathering amid enthusiastic applause and cheering.[35]

Beman sailed for the United States on 24 August. Two days before his departure, the Congregational Union sponsored a valedictory service in his honor at Castle Green chapel in Bristol. John Blackburn, one of the secretaries of the Union, delivered the principal address to the large audience, which unanimously adopted a resolution expressing appreciation to Beman for his visit and labors. Responding in an appropriate speech, Beman told the gathering of his friendship for England and said that he anxiously looked forward to the day when the United States would follow her example in abolishing slavery. He then bade farewell to the congregation. The service was concluded with several hymns written especially for the occasion.[36]

The New British and Foreign Temperance Society also expressed its appreciation to Beman and to Patton for their work. "These gentlemen, on various occasions, both in the metropolis and the provinces," the society acknowledged, "devoted themselves to the advocacy of our principles; and there can be no doubt that they will be long associated with the most pleasing recollections of many who were privileged to hear them."[37]

On Saturday, 24 August, Beman and 115 other passengers boarded the *Great Western* steamer at its moorings in Kingroad in Bristol. At seven o'clock the ship left its dock. Exactly what Beman felt at the moment is impossible to determine. However, not long after his return to the United States, he expressed a desire to attend an antislavery meeting to be held in England the following May. He also proposed that the American Anti-Slavery Society send an agent abroad for eighteen months or two years to obtain information on slavery throughout the world. "I should like to be

---

[35]*Journal of the New British and Foreign Temperance Society* (London) 1:28 (6 July 1839): 233-34; *Bath Chronicle*, 20 June 1839; *Bath and Chiltenham Gazette*, 25 June 1839; *Bath Herald*, 22 June 1839; *Bath Journal and General Advertiser*, 24 June 1839.

[36]*Bristol Mercury*, 24 August 1839; *Congregational Magazine* (September 1839) 600, 604.

[37]*Third Report of the New British and Foreign Society for the Suppression of Intemperance* (London: J. Pasco, 1839) 97-98.

sent on such a mission," Beman declared, "and I would give my whole soul to it." Apparently, Beman found his visit to England rewarding and, excited by his travel in foreign lands, wished to venture abroad once more.[38]

[38]*Bristol Mercury*, 31 August 1839; Letter, Nathan S. S. Beman to Theodore Weld, 3 February 1840, in Barnes and Dumond, *Letters of Theodore Weld, Angelina Grimké Weld and Sarah Grimké*, 820-22.

Chapter VIII

For a Protestant America

This is papacy
on the banks of the Mississippi.
—Nathan S. S. Beman

The *Great Western* arrived in New York on 10 September 1839, seventeen days after leaving Bristol. Beman disembarked and immediately began the trip upriver to Troy to attend the opening session of the annual meeting of the American Board of Commissioners for Foreign Missions, convening that same day in his own church. He knew that many of his congregation, most of his close associates in the ministry, and some of his dearest friends would attend the sessions. When he reached the First Presbyterian Church, he was not disappointed, for more than two hundred ministers had assembled—the largest attendance in the board's history. The following night Beman reported on his visit to England and on the feelings of the British toward America. One observer said of the meeting, "If the First Presbyterian Church can hold two thousand people by packing, they were there."[1]

After the excitement of his return had subsided, Beman slipped back into his familiar routine. Unfortunately, this included dealing with the

---

[1]*New York Observer*, 21 September 1839.

personal difficulties that had distressed him before his departure. Caroline, capricious and strong-willed as ever, had taken rooms only a few doors away from his own residence. And although she still sought a reconciliation, Beman refused to consider such a possibility. In retaliation, she attended his church services every Sunday, making a special point to sit in the front pew. To add to his displeasure, Beman learned that in spite of having strictly forbidden her to see Louisa, Caroline had been visiting the girl during his absence.[2]

In addition to his marital problems, Beman discovered that the routine of his clerical duties seemed dull after the adventure of foreign travel. Within five months he had become so discontented that he wrote Theodore Weld to offer his services in the antislavery movement. Beman explained,

> Since my return, my health is much improved, but still not as vigorous as formerly. I now do my usual amount of preaching and other labor. There are some reasons, such as the age at which I have arrived, the protracted period of my efforts in Troy, and my wish to have a little more leisure than I now can command for writing which induce me to indulge some speculation of changing my position and manner of life. There are other things which I need not name, which bear upon the same point. I should like to become in some way connected with the great movements which are making, in this country, for the universal freedom of man. . . . I should be willing at some period not distant to retire from my pastoral charge to a farm in Washington County, which I have purchased of my aged father who is still living, and which is only partly paid for, if I could get of your Society an appointment of an agency for Vermont and the Northern part of this State, and receive such a compensation as would enable me to sustain myself and pay off some not very heavy debts.[3]

Nothing came of Beman's suggestion to Weld, but later that year he was offered the presidency of Middlebury College, an offer he declined. He did

---

[2]Letters, Caroline Beman to Benjamin C. Yancey, 30 June, 8 September 1839, Benjamin C. Yancey Papers, Southern Historical Collection, University of North Carolina Library, Chapel Hill; Letter, Theodore Lesley to the author, 16 April 1957; *Troy Directory, 1839* (Troy: N. Tuttle, 1839).

[3]Letter, Nathan S. S. Beman to Theodore Weld, 3 February 1840, in *Letters of Theodore Dwight Weld, Angelina Grimké Weld and Sarah Grimké, 1822-1844*, ed. Gilbert H. Barnes and Dwight L. Dumond, 2 vols. (New York: D. Appleton-Century, 1934) 2:820-22.

agree to withhold public announcement of his refusal until after the August commencement, at which he presided and conferred the diplomas, enjoying, in his words, "a very short and a very happy presidency." In view of Beman's high regard for Middlebury and his dissatisfaction in Troy, his refusal initially seems surprising. However, the resolution of his difficulties with his wife clarifies this decision. In 1840 the two finally reached an understanding whereby Caroline agreed to return south permanently and the minister promised to send her a regular allowance. Perhaps the prospect of being spared the awkwardness of her presence made his pastoral chores seem less onerous.[4]

Having resolved this one difficulty, Beman was yet plagued by his financial problems. Although he was able to secure funds to attend an antislavery convention in nearby Albany in April 1840 and the September meeting of the Board of Commissioners for Foreign Missions in Providence, Beman was increasingly concerned about his straitened circumstances. He detested indebtedness and regarded failure to meet financial obligations as a sin; only a few years earlier he had preached a sermon on just this particular sin. With debts from his family's illnesses still unpaid, the necessity of contributing to Caroline's support, and his obligation to meet payments on the Hampton farm, Beman found his situation growing steadily worse. By the spring of 1841, he was so poor that he confessed to a colleague that he would be unable to attend the annual meeting of the Home Missionary Society. "I have suffered much embarrassment of purse and feeling," he wrote, and urged his friend to aid him in securing payment of funds owed him by the church so that he might attend the meeting.[5]

A year later, still not completely free from debt, Beman had improved his position sufficiently that he was able to attend the annual meeting of

---

[4]Letter, Nathan S. S. Beman to L. S. Cist, 18 January 1862, Pennsylvania Historical Society, Philadelphia; *Troy Directory, 1840* (Troy: N. Tuttle, 1840).

[5]Mary Theophane Geary, *A History of Third Parties in Pennsylvania* (Washington: Catholic University Press, 1938) 39; *New York Observer*, 19 September 1840; Nathan S. S. Beman, *The Gospel Adapted to the Wants of the World* (Boston: Crocker and Brewster, 1840); Letter, Nathan S. S. Beman to Samuel H. Cox, 22 May 1841, Pennsylvania Historical Society; Nathan S. S. Beman, "Punctuality in the Payment of Debts," *American National Preacher* 11:11 (April 1837): 165-74.

the General Assembly's Interim Committee and the yearly session of the Foreign Missions' Board of Commissioners in Philadelphia in May. In October, he addressed the Young Men's Education Society of New York and Brooklyn.[6] During his impecuniosity, Beman devoted considerable time to the preparation of *The Church Psalmist*, a collection of hymns published early in 1843. The hymnal received a highly enthusiastic reception from the ministry, although Beman was criticized for his promotional efforts on behalf of the volume.[7]

Compared to his usual zeal in the promotion of reforms, Beman led a relatively quiet life between 1840 and 1845. No doubt his inaction was in part because of insufficient funds, but he also had no cause that fired his imagination. However, Beman was never able to restrain his inclination to agitate for long, and events were transpiring that soon would propel him into controversy once more.

The issue that aroused the clergyman was the doctrine of American nativism, a movement that failed, but even as a rejected political program contributed to a better understanding of the nature of American democracy. Throughout the history of the country, a host of such influences have gradually modified, altered, and subtly transformed the Founding Fathers' original concept of the United States. In every age, new philosophies and ideals have challenged existing attitudes and institutions. Some of these doctrines found public acceptance and were incorporated into the image of America. A great many others stirred men profoundly for a time, only to be rejected and ultimately discarded. Yet, as they disappeared they stimulated insight and firmer faith in American ideals. Such an influence was the nativist movement.

Nativism was a conservative movement born out of a desire to preserve the United States as it was at the time of its founding: a predominantly Protestant, Anglo-Saxon nation. Two factors contributed to Beman's growing fear of foreign ideas and customs and led him to support the nativist movement: his long-standing interest in education and the rapid expansion of immigration into the territories and new states of the West. In 1841 Beman's interest in education was further stimulated by his appointment as a vice president and lecturer at Rensselaer Polytechnic In-

---

[6]*New York Observer*, 28 May, 19 November 1842.

[7]Ibid., 8 April, 3 June 1843, 23, 30 August, 1, 8 November 1845.

stitute, an association which was to last for more than twenty years.[8] Through his lectures at Rensselaer, Beman became acquainted with the ideas and attitudes of the current generation of collegians. He found many of their beliefs disturbing.

More influential on Beman's growing nativism was the rising tide of immigration and the settlement of these foreigners in the West. Although Beman and many other Americans had long doubted the wisdom of permitting a large European population to enter the country, they became more fearful and suspicious when they heard reports that western schools were not teaching American concepts and ways to the newcomers.

Since colonial days, the Protestant Anglo-Saxon population had displayed distrust and jealousy of foreign influence on American politics and public affairs. The feeling was most pronounced among the descendants of the Puritans in New England. Men who had fought in the Revolution and their direct descendants still constituted a large part of the population of the country; many regarded both the settlement of New England and the war as part of a holy mission. Because of his own religious background and Revolutionary forebears, Beman viewed the founding of America as divinely inspired. "I have long believed," he once said, "that God directed our forefathers to the bleak coast of New England and planted their feet on the rock of Plymouth and, after having deeply schooled them in the lessons of adversity, made them a prosperous and happy people that they may bear a prominent part in the conversion of the world to Christ."[9]

Venerating the institutions created by the Puritans, these nativists objected to foreign customs and manners. They thought that the immigrants too often spoke only their native languages and exerted little effort to learn English, tended to be clannish, observed old-world traditions, and resisted Americanization in general. Another reason for antagonism—and an important one—was the attitude of the native-born toward intemper-

---

[8]Palmer C. Ricketts, *History of Rensselaer Polytechnic Institute* (New York: John Wiley and Sons, 1934) 92, 108.

[9]Nathan S. S. Beman, *The Influence of Freedom on Popular and National Education* (Troy: Young and Hartt, 1846) 71.

ance. The New Englanders, especially, deplored the use of intoxicants and often condemned the foreign-born on that score.[10]

Another source of exacerbation was the immigrants' political support of the Democratic party. This feeling was more pronounced among the wealthy and conservative native-born, most of whom were Whigs. This group also tended to be Presbyterian and Episcopalian, two denominations that leaned toward the Whig point of view on matters affecting foreigners.[11]

Probably the most frightening of this aspect to Protestants was the large number of Catholics coming into the country. Between 1808 and 1844 the number of dioceses in the United States expanded from 1 to 21, Catholic churches grew in number from 80 to 611, and priests from 68 to 617. Many descendants of colonists who had come to America seeking religious freedom nursed a fear that the Catholic Church might aspire to temporal power in the United States, and thereby regarded the influx of Catholics with alarm.[12]

Of more direct influence on Beman were political developments within New York State. In 1834 the vague antagonism against the foreign-born was transformed into open hostility with the publication of a series of letters in the New York *Observer*, a religious weekly. Samuel F. B. Morse, inventor of the telegraph, wrote twelve letters that purported to show that the Leopold Foundation, a Catholic organization in Vienna, sought to subvert American liberty through church expansion. He contended that the papacy had organized the society to build power so that, in time, the Catholic Church could gain control of the government. The letters at-

---

[10]John P. Senning, "The Know-Nothing Movement in Illinois," *Journal of the Illinois State Historical Society* 7:1 (April 1914): 10; Louis Dow Scisco, *Political Nativism in New York State* (New York: Macmillan Co., 1901) 21; M. Evangeline Thomas, *Nativism in the Old Northwest, 1850-1860* (Washington: Catholic University Press, 1936) 123.

[11]Floyd Benjamin Streeter, *Political Parties in Michigan, 1837-1860* (Lansing: Michigan Historical Commission, 1918) 164, 212; Scisco, *Political Nativism in New York State*, 23.

[12]Streeter, *Political Parties in Michigan*, 164, 213; Senning, "The Know-Nothing Movement," 11; Geary, *Third Parties in Pennsylvania*, 61.

tracted attention throughout the country, and one result was the formation of the New York Protestant Association.[13]

Although he probably was familiar with Morse's letters, Beman refrained from any discussion of the issue in his sermons and correspondence
until 1840 when he was stirred to action. Heretofore, the public schools
had been under the control of the Public School Society, a Protestant
dominated organization that apportioned the state's educational funds;
however, it gave monies only to those schools it deemed worthy of support. That year Governor William Seward stated that the children of foreigners often were denied the advantages of public education because of
prejudice and recommended "the establishment of schools in which they
may be instructed by teachers speaking the same language with themselves and professing the same faith."[14]

Although the Catholics had maintained schools without public aid for
many years, as soon as the governor issued his pronouncement they demanded a share of the school moneys for their own institutions. The Public School Society refused, and at once it became a political issue. To
counteract Catholic demands, opponents formed the American Protestant Union in 1841 and elected Morse as their president. Calling itself a
"national defensive society," the organization stated as its goal, "to preserve for ourselves and to secure for posterity the religious, civil, and political principles of our country, according to the spirit of our ancestors."[15]
Faced with defeat because of the political activity of the Protestant group,
the Catholics turned to Bishop John Hughes, a man who came to sym-
bolize Catholic expansionism to American Protestants and in whom Beman found one of his most formidable adversaries.[16]

Hughes was a native of Ireland who had come to Pennsylvania as a
young man. His employment as a gardener at Mount Saint Mary's College
led him to study Latin and, later, to enter the college as a seminarian. He
was ordained as a priest in 1826. After serving several congregations in
Pennsylvania, he went to New York. There he found an apologetic people

---

[13]Scisco, *Political Nativism in New York State*, 21-25.

[14]Ibid., 32.

[15]*New York Observer*, 12 June 1841.

[16]Scisco, *Political Nativism in New York State*, 32-35.

interested in citizenship and a better social condition but unfamiliar with the means to attain their goals. Hughes seized control of the diocese and, a fighter himself, challenged the Catholic foreign-born to insist on their rights.[17]

Although he had been in New York for only a short time when the Public School Society controversy erupted, Hughes was not a novice in politico-religious debate, having entered the lists more than once with prominent Protestants while in Pennsylvania. Confronted with impending defeat on the schools issue in the fall elections of 1841, the bishop surprised the opposition by calling an Irish-Catholic meeting to nominate a separate ticket. The Protestant clergy and the daily press, almost without exception, condemned the priest for meddling in politics. But the vote forcibly demonstrated to the Democratic party their dependence on the Catholic vote, for every Democratic nominee who did not received the bishop's endorsement went down in defeat. The subsequent destruction of the Public School Society, under Seward's sympathetic eye, chagrined the Protestants. The religious riots in New York in 1842 further intensified nativist sentiment.[18]

In view of his background and religious beliefs, Beman not surprisingly was infected by the wave of anti-foreign and anti-Catholic feeling. An Anglo-Saxon heritage, Revolutionary ancestry, a New England boyhood, a strict Calvinist education, fierce patriotism, an abhorrence of intemperance, and a Protestant theology cinched his involvement in the nativistic movement. That he did not become active earlier in the movement is remarkable, for not until 1843 did open attacks on Catholics and foreigners begin to appear in his speeches. In July of that year, in an address to the Union and Phoenix societies of Hamilton College, Beman said of the foreign population,

> They feel no natural sympathy with our soil and our institutions. In politics, they often bring with them a strong tincture of monarchy . . . or are converted into furious radicals; and in either case they make bad republicans. . . . But we have more to dread from a foreign religion than even from foreign politics. The only type of Christianity adapted to this

---

[17]*Dictionary of American Biography* (New York: Charles Scribner's Sons, 1932) 9:352-55.

[18]Ibid.; Scisco, *Political Nativism in New York State*, 35-37, 46.

country is that which was brought over by our pilgrim fathers—a Christianity which forever abjures all amalgamation with the government, and which asks no other favor of the State than to be let alone. . . . We have, at this juncture, more to dread from the Papacy than from any other source.

Later in the speech, Beman stated his opinion of the activities of Bishop Hughes, saying,

> The understanding which seems to exist between the Romanists and the politicians has already created a sort of virtual establishment of the Papal religion among us. What other denomination called Christian ever go to the polls in a body? With what church, but the Roman Catholic, have politicians ever dared to tamper in connection with elections? Who but the Romanists have interfered with the system of public education, and desired as a church to lay their hands on the school fund? . . . We should keep a keen, jealous eye upon them. . . . The movement of this ecclesiastico-political machine, as its burning wheels roll through any country, is fearful and desolating.[19]

With an increasing number of influential men voicing similar sentiments, the nativist movement spread rapidly in both the political and clerical realms. By March 1844, nativist political organizations existed in New York City, Albany, and most of the state's southeastern counties. With each successive election, the movement gained strength until, at the beginning of 1845, the nativists counted one state senator, fifteen assemblymen, and four United States congressmen among their representatives. On 4 July 1845, the national Native American Party was officially organized.[20]

In the churches, the strongest organization was the American Protestant Society. Formed in 1843 for the purpose of converting Roman Catholics to Protestantism, the society distributed tracts in several languages and employed foreign-speaking agents to promote its cause. Beman joined the organization and, at its anniversary meeting in 1845, introduced a resolution stating "that the present state of Romanism in this Country demands the entire efforts of Protestantism." In a supporting address, he argued that the peculiar nature of American institutions neces-

---

[19]Nathan S. S. Beman, *The Claims of Our Country on Young Men* (Troy: N. Tuttle, 1843) 19-21, 22.

[20]Scisco, *Political Nativism in New York State*, 22, 34, 47-49; *New York Observer*, 12 June 1841, 21 January, 11 February, 16 March 1843.

sitated careful vigilance, an intelligent population, and a religion founded in Protestantism. He condemned the Catholic Church as "the most perfect work of Satan."[21]

In addition to nativist influences from New York City, Beman for several years had been subjected to anti-Catholic propaganda from the West. One of the most notable opponents of Catholicism in the western states was Lyman Beecher. Following his move to Cincinnati in 1832, Beecher embarked upon a campaign to alert the Protestant clergy to the supposed danger of Catholicism in the Mississippi Valley. In 1835 Beecher toured the East delivering his famous *Plea for the West,* in which he argued that the western territory was rapidly being filled with foreign emigrants "unacquainted with our institutions, unaccustomed to self-government, inaccessible to education, and easily accessible to prepossession and inveterate credulity and intrigue . . . and sinister design." Foreign immigrants had increased, according to Beecher, from five to thirty-seven percent of the population and would soon outnumber the native element.[22]

Newspapers, missionary publications, the religious press, and sermons and letters of western ministers intensified the fear that the West was becoming a Catholic stronghold. As early as 1835, one Michigan newspaper declared that the foreigners and Catholics were "the chosen instruments of the demagogues to strengthen and perpetuate their ruinous influence over the people of this country."[23] Almost every issue of the *Home Missionary* contained some reference to the Catholic "threat." In May 1842, it reported,

> Already the foundations are laid for social institutions such as our fathers knew not. Foreign Papists are planting our fairest territories thick with their schools. Colony after colony of men of a strange tongue and stranger association are possessing themselves of our soil and gathering around our ballot boxes. In Missouri, Illinois, and Arkansas there are seventy-four priests with literary institutions of every grade in which, at least, a thousand youths are now training.[24]

---

[21]*New York Observer,* 24 May 1845.

[22]Lyman Beecher, *A Plea for the West* (Cincinnati: Truman and Smith, 1835) 11.

[23]*Detroit Journal and Courier,* 19 August 1835.

[24]Thomas, *Nativism in the Old Northwest,* 56.

The *New York Observer* was particularly active in attacking the purported plan of the Catholic Church to capture the West.[25]

Four days after Beman spoke at Hamilton College, a group of Protestants in New York established The Society for the Promotion of Collegiate and Theological Education at the West to assist western Protestant colleges and thereby offset Catholic influences.[26] The idea for the organization originated in 1842 when several western schools found themselves threatened with extinction because of financial difficulties. Eastern philanthropists had become reluctant to support them, and even the ministry began to exclude their agents from their pulpits. Suspicion of western schools was common. Many Easterners believed that the West had too many colleges and that many of them were little more than schemes for speculation staffed by swindlers, quacks, and radicals. To overcome these attitudes, the western colleges consolidated their fund-raising efforts and took their proposals east where they found the support that led to the formation of the society.[27]

Although he was not present at the organizational meeting, Beman was enthusiastic about the society and was named to its first board of directors. Benjamin F. Butler, former Attorney General and Secretary of War, was elected president. Beman attended the first annual meeting in New York on 25 September 1844. Speakers at that session and subsequent meetings made it abundantly clear—if, indeed, anyone had exercised any doubt—that the organization was not wholly altruistic, for from the beginning they repeatedly proclaimed the threat of Catholic control of the West.[28]

---

[25]*New York Observer*, 9, 16 April, 5 November, 10 December 1842, 14, 21 January, 11 February, 16 March, 1, 15, 22 April, 22 July, 12, 20 August, 9 September, and 2 December 1843, 18 May 1844.

[26]Ibid., 8 July 1843; *First Report of the Society for the Promotion of Collegiate and Theological Education at the West* (New York: J. F. Trow, 1844) 4.

[27]*New York Observer*, 12 August 1843; *First Report of the Society for . . . Education at the West*, 6-8.

[28]*Annual Reports of the Society for . . . Education at the West, 1844, 1845, 1846* (New York: J. F. Trow, 1844, 1845, 1846).

Interest in western expansion, curiosity about the territories and the newly created states, and growing concern over reports of Catholic influence prompted Beman to arrange a trip to the Mississippi Valley in the summer of 1845. Just before his departure, he attended in New York City the meetings of two organizations that were active in the West. At the annual conference of the American Home Missionary Society he delivered a speech in which he complimented the organization on its western accomplishments, but warned that the Catholics had spent large sums of money in the West in recent years and contended that the society should accelerate its activities to offset these gains. At the meeting of the board of directors of the Society for the Promotion of Collegiate and Theological Education at the West, Beman agreed to investigate the colleges being aided by the society. He started west late in the spring and returned three-and-a-half months later. Most of his time was spent in Michigan, Illinois, Indiana, and Ohio, although his itinerary also included the territories of Iowa and Wisconsin. He mentions briefly visiting two other states, Kentucky and probably Missouri.[29]

A series of letters written to the New York *Evangelist* gives a fairly complete itinerary of his trip. On 13 June Beman left Troy by train. He spent Sunday, 15 June, in Buffalo and on Monday evening he boarded the steamer *Empire* for the trip down Lake Erie. When he awoke Tuesday, the steamer was following the coastline of Ohio. That morning the boat reached Cleveland, where it remained for eight hours. Beman took advantage of the delay to tour the city.

On 18 June Beman reached Detroit, where he was to attend a convention of Presbyterian and Congregational ministers. During his visit, he was the guest of Lewis Cass, newly elected senator and recent ambassador to France. The two had much in common. From the time of his settlement in the frontier community, Cass had promoted a variety of religious and educational schemes. In 1816 he was instrumental in bringing a settled minister to Detroit; the following year he served as president of a newly organized Bible society; and in 1821 he was one of the incorporators of the First Protestant Society. In 1830 he became president of the Society for

---

[29]*New York Observer*, 17, 24 May 1845, 25 April 1846; Nathan S. S. Beman, *The Influence of Sunday-Schools at the West* (Philadelphia: American Sunday School Union, 1846) 3.

Promotion of Female Education. In addition, the governor and statesman was a total abstainer and had served as the first president of the Congregational Temperance Society. His wife, a devout Presbyterian, was generally admired for her charitable enterprises. The Casses were warm hosts and, upon his departure, Beman expressed his appreciation of his treatment by the "truly kind and hospitable family of Governor Cass." "My associations with this excellent family," he said, "will continue with me . . . and shed a fragrant influence upon my mind through the future journey of life."[30]

Beman remained in Detroit for five weeks, during which time he made short excursions to Pontiac and Monroe where he preached at the local churches. In Pontiac, as in many of the communities he visited, the clergyman met several former members of his congregation. "This is one advantage," he observed, "which a pastor has over almost every other man in traveling through the Western country."[31]

On 5 July, Beman journeyed further westward, visiting Ypsilanti, Ann Arbor, Jackson, Marshall, Battle Creek, and Kalamazoo. At Ann Arbor, he toured the struggling new University of Michigan and commented favorably upon its faculty and buildings. In Marshall and Battle Creek he delivered sermons to the Presbyterian congregations.[32]

Leaving Michigan, he traveled to Chicago and then along the shores of Lake Michigan into Wisconsin. In late July he was in Milwaukee. From there he crossed the state to the Mississippi River and on into Iowa and then boarded a steamer for a trip downriver to Missouri and central Illinois. In August he visited Illinois College in Jacksonville, one of the schools being aided by the Society for the Promotion of Collegiate and Theological Education at the West, and by the end of the month he was in Springfield. Early in September, he stopped at Wabash College in Crawfordsville, Indiana, another society-aided school, and then continued his trip to Indianapolis. From there he moved southward to Madison, Indiana, on the Ohio River, on into Kentucky, then up the Ohio to Elyria

---

[30]New York *Evangelist*, 26 June, 3 July, 21 August 1845; Frank B. Woodford, *Lewis Cass, the Last Jeffersonian* (New Brunswick: Rutgers University Press, 1950) 165-68, 192, 218, 230, 296.

[31]New York *Evangelist*, 28 August, 23 October 1845.

[32]Ibid., 6, 13, 20, 27 November 1845.

and a meeting of the Western Reserve Synod. On 5 October he boarded a steamer at Cleveland to return to New York.[33]

Although Beman did not keep a journal, accounts of his trip in letters, speeches, and reports indicate that he was unprepared for the grandeur of the West. The sheer size of the territory surprised him; between the Rockies and the Alleghenies lay "room for another Assyrian empire, or for a second Roman."[34] The natural splendor of the region also made a vivid impression on Beman. "All is on a grand scale," he noted, "but it is the magnificence of nature and not of art." The stands of unbroken forest, the Mississippi and Ohio rivers, and the Great Lakes inspired his awe. Nevertheless, he seemed even more impressed with his first vision of the prairie—that vast, silent green land, virtually uninhabited; a grassy seascape studded here and there with oases of oak, maple, walnut, and pecan, and fringed with the sassafrass, the persimmon, and the sumac. He discovered that the country was not only vast, but "as rich in resources as it is broad and boundless; never did the mortal eye rest in silent rapture upon a finer soil or upon more luxuriant productions."[35] Of the resources of the region, Beman noted,

> It is true that a small proportion of it only is yet under cultivation. We have the almost boundless prairie, with its sod yet unbroken—the dense, primeval forest, which has never echoed to the sound of the axe-man—the oak opening, though in appearance like cultivated parks, untouched by the hand of art. . . . [If] I have ever rejoiced in looking at the products of agriculture, it was while crossing some of those vast prairies or other fertile portions of the west and seeing a single field of waving wheat, already white to the harvest, a mile square, owned by a single man . . . or while gazing upon an immense forest . . . of Indian corn.[36]

He predicted, accurately, that the territory would become one of the rich-

---

[33]Ibid., 21, 28 August, 25 September, 30 October, 6, 13, 20, 27 November 1845; *New York Observer*, 18 October 1845.

[34]Nathan S. S. Beman, "Collegiate and Theological Education at the West," *American National Preacher* 21:3 (March 1847): 55.

[35]Nathan S. S. Beman, *Second Report of the Society for the Promotion of Collegiate and Theological Education at the West* (New York: J. F. Trow, 1845) 21; Beman, "Collegiate and Theological Education," 60.

[36]Beman, *Second Report*, 19.

est farming areas in the world. "In one word, everything necessary for converting the wilderness into smiling harvest fields and joyous and exulting cities nature [has] furnished in abundance." Beman forecasted that with the rapid population growth, soon "the people who shall spread over these broad prairies and settle along those large rivers . . . will govern the country."[37]

Because of the political future of the region, Beman took careful note of the circumstances, attitudes, and beliefs of the settlers. He sought information in rude log cabins, in the fields, and in town squares on the weekly market day. He talked with home missionaries, visited colleges, and preached at rural meetinghouses. In his words, he sought to "gain access to the hearts of the people." From his contacts Beman developed admiration and respect for the pioneers. Of their generosity, he commented, "I have experienced their hospitabilities beyond my power to repay, and which it will ever be my pleasure to acknowledge."[38]

In anticipation of the day when the West would influence national affairs, Beman proposed that "if the people of that valley are to govern this whole land, with all its growing and almost boundless resources, then they should be educated for their post of honor and trust." However, he believed that they could not do this for themselves, for they had neither "the men nor the means for it." Of necessity, "physical wants take precedence of everything," he explained; "men are employed in clearing their lands, building their houses, and obtaining the means of subsistence for themselves and families, and they have but little time or energy for anything else."[39]

Beman was particularly concerned over the influence of slavery in the area. In Kentucky and along the Ohio River Valley lived large numbers of Southern emigrants. In Indiana, Illinois, and Ohio, where settlement had been characterized by Southerners pushing the frontier north and Puritan stock working southward, strong sectional antagonism had developed. In the midst of neighbors who sympathized with the South lived New

---

[37]Ibid., 20; Beman, "Collegiate and Theological Education," 60.

[38]Beman, *Second Report*, 21.

[39]Beman, *Influence of Sunday-Schools*, 3; *New York Observer*, 25 April 1846; Beman, "Collegiate and Theological Education," 61.

Englanders opposed to slavery. Observing this cleavage, Beman feared that the proslavery element might achieve political dominance in the new states.[40] This danger was forcibly brought home to him in June at a convention of Congregational and Presbyterian ministers in Detroit, where the issue was debated at length. Taking an active part in the discussion, Beman urged the churchmen to stand firmly against slavery.[41]

Beman also inquired into the influence of the Catholic Church in the valley. As might be expected in view of the near-hysteria surrounding the subject, the advance warnings of the Beechers and others, and Beman's own inclination to distrust the Catholics, the clergyman's direst fears were confirmed. He announced after his tour that the Catholics had "long had their eyes on the country in question . . . and [were] making special efforts to repossess themselves of this territory and control it under the government of the United States." The Jesuits, he claimed, were especially active, and he regarded them as among the best politicians in the world— the only ones willing to postpone success until they could educate at least one generation. He refused to concede, however, that the Jesuits were educated men, for

> [t]hey are trained, moulded, shaped, disciplined, pruned, bent, braced, pinioned, stereotyped, and, if you please, learned in their way, but they are not educated—because they have never been taught to think.[42]

To Beman the threat of the Catholics lay in their extensive activity in establishing schools and churches, their "endless" financial backing, and "a blind faith, and not investigation," that characterized their exertions. "This," he concluded, "is papacy on the banks of the Mississippi."[43]

If the battle for political control was to be fought in the West, Beman thought that every effort should be made "to plant another New England" beyond the mountains. To accomplish this objective, he argued for an im-

---

[40]Lois Kimball Mathews, *The Expansion of New England* (Boston and New York: Houghton, Mifflin Co., 1909) 197, 209; Beman, *Second Report*, 21.

[41]*Detroit Advertiser*, 21, 23 June 1845; *The Liberator* (Boston), 25 July 1845; *New York Observer*, 5 July 1845.

[42]Beman, "Collegiate and Theological Education," 63-64.

[43]Ibid.

proved educational system, better preachers, and more Protestant institutions in the West.[44]

Beman learned a great deal about the colleges receiving aid from the Society for the Promotion of Collegiate and Theological Education at the West, namely Illinois College, Wabash College, Marietta College, Western Reserve College, and Lane Theological Seminary. Illinois College in Jacksonville was typical. A Protestant institution formed in 1829 by members of the "Yale band," the school consisted of a few buildings on a plot of ground about a mile from the village. The town itself had about three thousand inhabitants and consisted of a huddle of log cabins clustered around a public square where a drab courthouse sat forlornly in a rectangle of mud and dirt. In 1845 the school had eighty-three students. Modeled after the New England colleges, the curriculum was predominately classical. Like other institutions being aided by the society, Illinois College was deeply in debt, and the trustees held serious doubts whether it could survive without assistance.[45]

Beman concluded that the facilities of the colleges he visited were adequate, the number of students satisfactory, and their influence on the communities desirable. Enough such schools, however, did not exist. "It is a simple matter of fact," he reported, "that the people are not educated—they are comparatively ignorant. . . . They are in a great measure destitute of institutions of learning; colleges, academies, and common schools do not exist there and bless the land and accommodate every district of country as they do among us."[46] More schools and a supply of good books, Beman felt, would accomplish much. He envisioned the young scholars bringing into the log cabin homes their books and lessons which the parents might also read and study.[47]

---

[44]Ibid., 70.

[45]*Third and Fourth Reports of the Society for the Promotion of Collegiate and Theological Education at the West* (New York: Trow and Co., 1846, 1847) 1846, p. 36, 1847, p. 13; T. A. Post, *Truman Marcellus Post* (Boston and Chicago: Congregational Sunday-School and Publishing Society, 1891) 49, 55; *New York Observer*, 1 March 1845. In a report issued the year after Beman's visit, the school's indebtedness was estimated at $28,000.

[46]Beman, *Second Report*, 21-22.

[47]Beman, *Influence of Sunday-Schools*, 4; *New York Observer*, 25 April 1846.

The spiritual condition of the westerners also distressed Beman. Many villages contained persons of almost every religious persuasion, but not enough belonging to any single denomination to support a church and a preacher. In some communities he found almost no interest in religion. In others, he observed, "there is no lack of men called preachers, who are destitute of every qualification for the sacred office—without talents, without learning, without evangelical sentiment, and, it is to be feared, without piety."[48]

Although he realized that something more was needed to supply the religious demands of these communities, Beman believed that Sunday schools might fill an important niche. If the children could be collected on the Sabbath and instructed in reading, writing, and simple religious principles, he thought that the learning acquired might lead the youngsters to seek more information. An account of western children walking to Sunday school one morning offers insight into Beman's feelings about the new land. Addressing the American Sunday School Union, he wrote,

> One of the sweetest pictures of Sabbath-school children I ever gazed upon was in the great forests of the Mississippi. It was in one of the northern counties of Illinois. I was riding to church the distance of several miles. It was a very warm day in the month of August. The timbered land and prairie were, in some measure, intermingled, and as I passed along the highway with others in a wagon, I discovered here and there, ever and anon, peering out from among the tall grass and hazle of the prairie and the thick undergrowth of the forest, a large number of little children threading their mazy way along the unnumbered foot-paths, which pursued their winding course in almost every direction. These little pedestrians alternately appeared and disappeared; but when I could catch the faintest view of them, I discovered that they were neatly dressed and each one carried in the hand a pocket handkerchief, white as the snow, and a little volume of your publications. As I thought of the influence of this school and of your books in this wild spot, far distant from my home and the scene of my labours, a warm tear filled my eye. My heart breathed a prayer for the success of such a holy work.[49]

At the conclusion of his tour, Beman told the Society for the Promotion of Collegiate and Theological Education at the West,

---

[48]Beman, *Influence of Sunday-Schools*, 6.

[49]Ibid., 3, 6, 8.

I have been over this field—I have explored it with some degree of accuracy and have seen its condition and importance; and I declare to you before high Heaven that, if it were necessary, we better give up any of our charities rather than this. Everything depends on this—the weal of the country and of the whole world.[50]

Because of this conviction, Beman became one of the most active members of the society, serving on the board of directors and later as a vice president. The West continued to exert an influence on Beman, leading him to approve not only his son's decision to settle in Minnesota, but motivating him to spend his last years in Illinois.

Upon his return to Troy, Beman assumed the presidency of Rensselaer Polytechnic Institute. President Nott had resigned in April and Beman had been elected to succeed him. Although Beman had served as a vice president and lecturer since 1842, he found that the new position afforded him new responsibilities and a greater challenge. Long a supporter of educational enterprises, Beman believed that knowledge was power and "by this power the world and all its elements are to be subdued and rendered subservient to the convenience and happiness of man." Only two years before, he had proclaimed, "The men who are to meet and answer the large demands of the current and the coming age of our country should be educated men," and went on to explain, "By education I mean the training of the entire man—physical, intellectual, and moral."[51]

Beman was peculiarly well qualified to head the engineering college. In addition to extensive teaching experience, he was particularly sympathetic to programs for educating the working class. Believing that the ploughboy might aspire to be president, the clergyman enthusiastically supported manual labor and Lancastrian schools, mutual improvement societies, and popular education. At Lincoln Academy shipbuilding and navigation had been included in the curriculum, and at Mt. Zion he had introduced a course of study stressing practical subjects for boys not planning to attend college. He thought that even the poorest young man should procure, little by little, a collection of books and, through reading and conversation with informed men, educate himself. He urged farmers to

---

[50]Beman, *Second Report*, 22-23.

[51]Beman, *The Claims . . . on Young Men*, 28, 32.

study the science of agriculture and recommended that every common school have an agricultural class.[52]

Above all, Beman believed that knowledge was not an end, but a means. He contended that the more practical its character, the more important it was to the purposes of human life. While he agreed that useful knowledge was important to every country, he believed it to be indispensable to the United States. "The resources of our wide domain can be explored and developed by no other means," he explained; "cities are to be built—railways constructed—agriculture improved and perfected—forests converted into cornfields . . . soils and climates . . . remain to be tested . . . marble quarries, iron, copper, lead and coal mines" to be worked.[53]

Rensselaer Polytechnic Institute had been founded to effectuate these very principles. The stated purpose of the school, as set forth by its founder Stephen Van Rensselaer in 1824, was to instruct "persons in the application of Science to the common pursuits of life." The school originally offered training in the sciences, surveying, mineralogy, "the laws regulating town-officers and jurors," and "social duties peculiar to farmers and mechanics." Ten years after its founding, the institute had expanded its curriculum to include a general course and departments of natural science and engineering. Students devoted the winter term to the general course, which included mathematics, composition, logic, rhetoric, geology, geography, and history. During the second session, they enrolled in either the science department or the engineering corps. So that even the poorest student might attend, fees were only one dollar a week.[54]

When Beman assumed the presidency, Rensselaer was one of only four engineering schools in the country. As president he continued to deliver his lectures on moral and mental philosophy, but he also early instituted an investigation that was to mark the beginning of an epoch in the school's

---

[52]Beman, *The Influence of Freedom*, 17, 24; Nathan S. S. Beman, *The Annual Fair* (Troy: R. V. Wilson, 1837) 13-14.

[53]Nathan S. S. Beman, *The Intellectual Position of Our Country* (Troy: N. Tuttle, 1839).

[54]*Religious Monitor*, December 1824, 317; Daniel D. Bernard, *The Life, Services and Character of Stephen Van Rensselaer* (Albany: Hoffman and White, 1839) 79; Palmer C. Ricketts, *History of Rensselaer Polytechnic Institute, 1824-1934*, 92.

history. In collaboration with the senior professor of the college, B. Franklin Greene, he began a careful study of the school and its curriculum. This study resulted in the complete reorganization of the institution in 1849-1850.

Prior to this restructuring, the course of study at Rensselaer was completed in one year and, while attendance throughout the two terms did not necessarily guarantee a degree, the average student who came to the school reasonably well prepared usually could pass the examination. Greene, who was a graduate of the class of 1842 and had taught at Washington College, felt that the standards were low and the requirements lax. After a study of European scientific and technical training, he submitted a new curriculum to Beman. After his approval and that of the board of trustees, the reorganization began in 1849, making the courses more in-depth with more rigid scholarship required. Although the curriculum was restricted to courses immediately related to architecture and engineering, the period of study of these subjects was increased from one to three years and stricter examinations were inaugurated. The division of the curriculum into the general course, followed by concentration in either science or engineering, was retained, but the amount of time devoted to each program was increased.[55]

Although the major share of the credit for the revision undoubtedly goes to Greene—and in 1850 his contributions were acknowledged when he was named the director—recognition must also be given Beman, for as president he assumed the ultimate responsibility for changes and innovations. Without Beman's assistance and support, Greene could never have effected the widespread modifications that were to alter vastly the program at Rensselaer and to influence other engineering colleges in years to come.[56]

For twenty-three years Beman was associated with Rensselaer Polytechnic Institute, serving as president from 1845 until his resignation in 1865 and assuming the duties of both president and director during 1859. Although in 1846 he was again offered the presidency of Middlebury College, he declined the invitation in order to remain in Troy. The institute grew rapidly throughout this period, doubling its enrollment during Be-

---

[55]Ibid., 92-94.

[56]Ibid., 91-92, 100.

man's first ten years as president. Hundreds of aspiring young engineers—dressed in the school uniform of dark green caps and frock coats—entered Beman's lecture room for instruction in mental and moral philosophy. Meeting the collegians on campus, he never neglected the opportunity to impress upon them their duty to themselves, their families, and society to increase their knowledge. He reminded them of the privilege of attending the institute and urged them to maintain a studious and honorable deportment.[57]

Throughout his association with Rensselaer, Beman continued as pastor of the First Presbyterian Church. The college was small and the duties of the president neither too time-consuming nor too demanding to prevent retention of his ministerial charge. He continued to attend meetings of religious and philanthropic societies, but with advancing age the clergyman was less active than he once had been.

---

[57]Ibid., 103, 108; Henry B. Nason, *Biographical Record of the Officers and Graduates of Rensselaer Polytechnic Institute, 1824-1886* (Troy: William H. Young, 1887) 30-34.

Chapter IX

Renewed
Religious Jousting

*If arrogance should receive an occasional
rebuke in what I write, I trust the reader
will see that necessity was laid upon me.*
—Nathan S. S. Beman to Bishop
John Hughes, D.D.

In 1849 Beman moved to the family farm at Hampton. Ever since the death
of his father four years earlier, he had longed to return. Because the property had belonged to the family since his early childhood, he was loath to
sell or to lease it. The opportunity to settle there was provided by the return to New York of his son Sam, who had gone to Alabama in 1843 to
live with William Yancey and to study law. Beman's older daughter Eliza
had long before married and departed from the family hearth and only
Louisa remained with the clergyman in Troy. Upon Sam's return, Beman
suggested that the three of them move to the farm and share the responsibilities of operating it. He proposed that Sam should have charge of the
actual farming, Louisa should manage the household chores, and he would
continue his pastoral and academic work, driving to Troy to perform his
duties. Sam reluctantly agreed, and the trio moved to the country that
summer.

This arrangement, which lasted for five years, was never entirely satisfactory to any of the participants. By October Sam was eager to return to Alabama, but Beman persuaded him to remain at Hampton.[1] Sam did visit in the South that winter, but sickness forced him to return to New York prematurely. Shortly thereafter Beman himself became so ill that for nearly a year and a half he was confined to the farm; the church hired an assistant pastor to handle his duties. Whenever possible Beman drove to Troy to preach, but he was compelled to spend many Sundays at home.[2] Under these circumstances Sam felt that he could not possibly contemplate leaving.

Differences in personality occasioned much of the mutual dissatisfaction of the three. Beman was accustomed to strict obedience; Louisa complied readily, but Sam often rebelled. Perhaps because of his deformity and dwarfed stature, Sam was oversensitive and inclined to aggressiveness. Coupled with these traits, he had his father's intelligence, strong convictions, and sharp tongue. Louisa was frequently sullen and withdrawn and in any dispute always sided with her father. Of his relations with his sister, Sam wrote to Ben, "Lou, you know, is as unlike me as though we had the blood of opposite climes in us. We do not think alike, our temperaments are utterly dissimilar. I love her more than she can ever know, but our sympathies run in different and often opposite channels."[3]

In addition, the three held sharply conflicting views on several subjects. One point of contention was Caroline. While Beman, as well as he was able, had prevented his wife from exercising any influence on Louisa, Sam was close to his mother and had spent much time with her in the South. He was also devoted to his stepbrothers. Thus, Sam tended to disagree with his father and sister on any matter affecting the Yanceys.

---

[1]Letter, Samuel Beman to Benjamin C. Yancey, 22 October 1849, Benjamin C. Yancey Papers, Southern Historical Collection, University of North Carolina Library, Chapel Hill.

[2]Letter from Robert Aikman, *Proceedings of the Centennial Anniversary of the First Presbyterian Church, Troy, N.Y., December 30, 31, 1891* (Troy: Troy Times, 1892) 71-72.

[3]Letter, Samuel Beman to Benjamin C. Yancey, 7 September 1851, Benjamin C. Yancey Papers.

The most frequent source of friction, however, was Sam's intemperance. Beman's feelings about the use of liquor were as strong as ever. In vain he tried to convert Sam to the cause of total abstinence. Finally, in 1852, the clergyman felt compelled to take drastic action. "I was," Beman later told Ben Yancey, "after many kind experiments, forced to take a decided course and say to him that he must give up rum forever or give me up; and he has chosen the former." He reported that Sam had not taken a drink since and concluded, "I think he has entirely reformed."[4]

Although Sam's new abstinence removed one cause of unrest in the household, harmony was preserved only by the most careful effort. However, in the autumn of 1852 Sam's dissatisfaction was temporarily dispelled by an invitation from the Whig party to campaign for a seat in the State Assembly as a representative of Washington County. Politically ambitious, Sam had already sought election to the United States House of Representatives during his residence in Alabama. While there he had been a candidate in a canvass to fill the vacancy occasioned by William Yancey's resignation in 1846. Although Yancey was a Democrat, Sam had run as a Whig. In this unusual circumstance, Yancey refused to take part in the campaign, although he did intervene once to denounce rumors damaging to Sam's personal character. When the votes were counted, Sam trailed his opponent by less than twenty-five ballots.[5] This taste of politics appealed to Sam and intermittently throughout the rest of his life he sought public office.

When the offer to campaign for the Whigs was made, Sam accepted willingly. Beman endorsed the decision and peace temporarily reigned at Hampton. Sam was a brilliant campaigner. As a public speaker, he was impassioned and vehement. He had an almost inexhaustable command of language and a style that was both concise and eloquent. Some contemporaries who heard both men claimed that Sam was superior to his more famous stepbrother. In later years, Sam attributed his ability as a speaker

---

[4]Letter, Nathan S. S. Beman to Benjamin C. Yancey, 6 April 1852, Benjamin C. Yancey Papers.

[5]John Witherspoon DuBose, *Life and Times of William Lowndes Yancey*, 2 vols. (New York: Peter Smith, 1942) 1:155-56; "The Late Samuel S. Beman," undated clipping from the *St. Charles* (Minnesota) *Press* in the possession of Catharine Marston Anderson, Seattle, Washington.

to the early training that he had received from his father. Certainly his skill in invective and sarcasm reflected the clergyman's example.[6]

Sam was victorious. The following January he took his seat in the State Assembly at Albany. Although he represented a small rural county and was virtually unknown at the time, Sam became one of the leading members of the assembly before the end of the session. His position on many questions—including violation of the Sabbath, corruption, and political responsibility—reflected Beman's influence and probably pleased the clergyman.[7]

Beman undoubtedly took greatest pride in his son's stand on the issue of temperance. Two weeks after the assembly convened, the State Temperance Alliance held its annual meeting in Albany. Sam attended several sessions and, although not an active participant, he was named a "counsellor" for the coming year. When the alliance submitted an antiliquor bill to the legislature, Sam was its most ardent champion. Although the legislators sought to avoid committing themselves on the controversial measure by tabling and postponing indefinitely its consideration, Sam attacked the actions as cowardly. Sounding much like Beman, he condemned the bill's opponents as representatives of "rum-rowdyism" and the unchristian element of the state. "Pass the Maine Law," he appealed, "and it will save more than one sinner from death and send joy to the most distant fireside."[8]

During the first months of his membership in the assembly, Sam was happy and proud of his efforts. Favorably known to the Whigs throughout the state, he was already setting his sights on another term or, perhaps, even the national legislature. Beman had also given him complete control of the farm and in March Sam wrote to Ben, "I have got to be a thorough farmer. I like the employment much and have a very pleasant situation on

---

[6]"The Late Samuel S. Beman"; DuBose, *William Lowndes Yancey,* 155-56.

[7]New York *Times,* 16 March, 15 April 1853; New York *Tribune,* 27 January, 15 April 1853; *Journal of the Assembly of the State of New York, 76th session, 1853* (Albany: Charles Van Benthuysen, 1853) 1:287.

[8]New York *Times,* 21 January, 6 April, 25 June, 11 July 1853; New York *Tribune,* 21 January, 25 June 1853.

the old homestead."[9] However, only two months later, Sam indicated that the earlier peace of the household had been disturbed.

> I am tired of farming at Hampton. I like the business well, but as we are situated it does not suit me. Lou, of course, cares for nothing beyond her own sphere. Father is a capital theologian. I think I am a very good farmer. But, it requires a harmony of interests to be successful in this pursuit.[10]

Sam had long expressed a desire to settle in the West, and a year later he set forth to explore Illinois and the surrounding area.[11]

Although Sam returned to New York, he had decided to remain in the West. The following summer he settled in Minnesota, where he spent the rest of his life. Beman and Louisa stayed on the farm for two years more, but in 1857 they moved to an eleven-acre farm near Troy. Although he was experiencing difficulty in getting Caroline to sign the deed so that he might sell the family homestead, even Beman was happy to see the project abandoned, for he confessed to Sam, "I feel quite relieved in throwing off the Hampton business, if indeed it is off!"[12]

Advancing age and illness, the responsibilities of his church and of Rensselaer, and his effort to maintain the farm combined to restrict Beman's activities during the years at Hampton. These duties, however, were not enough to deter Beman in his perpetual war against doctrines that he felt were undermining the country and the Protestant church. If he could not always confront the enemy in person, he could use the weapons of pen, press, and pulpit. Thus, in three controversies—among the most famous in his career—the clergyman conducted his campaign through the medium of the printed word. Significantly, the issues involved movements that had long occupied him: nativism, missions, and slavery. A fourth

---

[9]Letter, Samuel S. Beman to Benjamin C. Yancey, 15 March 1853, Benjamin C. Yancey Papers.

[10]Letter, Samuel S. Beman to Benjamin C. Yancey, 25 March 1852, Benjamin C. Yancey Papers.

[11]Letter, William L. Yancey to Benjamin C. Yancey, 17 October 1854, Benjamin C. Yancey Papers.

[12]Letter, Nathan S. S. Beman to Samuel S. Beman, 22 December 1857, in the possession of Catharine Marston Anderson, Seattle, Washington.

battle, designed to prevent modification of the New Measures, was waged in the General Assembly of the Presbyterian Church.

Throughout this period, Beman continued to be disturbed by the growing influence of the Catholic Church. He remained active in the American Protestant Society until that organization merged with the Foreign Evangelical Society and the Christian Alliance in May 1849. The new society, the American and Foreign Christian Union, had as its stated purpose, "to promote the salvation of Romanists at home and abroad." Beman was named one of the vice presidents. Others who were active included Edward Beecher, Albert Barnes, Chauncy A. Goodrich, president of Yale, and Governor Briggs of Massachusetts. Among the methods used by the union to win converts among immigrants was the employment of foreign-speaking missionaries—many of whom had left the Catholic Church—to distribute tracts and lecture the newly arrived settlers. In 1850 the union had seventy-eight men engaged in this work.[13]

The energetic promotion of Catholicism by Bishop John Hughes over the years evoked an increasingly bitter antipathy among the Protestant clergy. For some time Beman had viewed the bishop's activities with alarm. His antagonism was heightened by the recognition that prominent government officials accorded to the Catholic leader. In December 1847, John Quincy Adams, Calhoun, Douglas, Benton, and others asked the prelate to preach before Congress. Shortly after the outbreak of the Mexican War, Secretary of State James Buchanan invited Hughes to Washington to advise the president and even suggested that the Catholic clergyman be named envoy to Mexico. This "dabbling in politics," as Beman saw it, only increased his suspicion that the Catholic Church was determined to subvert the government and institutions of the country to its own ends.[14]

A widely publicized sermon by Hughes in November 1850 on the decline of Protestantism led to further deterioration in relations between the bishop and his critics. In 1851, during a visit to Rome, Hughes was named head of the newly created archdiocese of New York. Upon his return on

---

[13]*The American and Foreign Christian Union* 1 (1850): 251, 253, 259; 2 (1851): 172, 179.

[14]Henry A. Brann, *John Hughes* (New York: Dodd, Mead, and Co., 1892) 101; *Dictionary of American Biography* (New York: Charles Scribner's Sons, 1932) 9:352-55.

29 June, a large crowd assembled in St. Patrick's Cathedral in New York to welcome home and congratulate the priest. At this service, Hughes preached a sermon, which was reprinted in the Troy *Whig*, on the theme, "Christ tells Peter . . . 'Thou art, Peter, a rock, and on this rock I will build my Church, and the gates of hell shall not prevail against it.' Christ has built on a rock, and that rock is Peter."

In his sermon, Hughes contended that although "lying historians" had questioned the omnipotence of the Roman Catholic Church, the Church remained supreme, and "implicit obedience to the authority of the church" was demanded of all men. He attacked the forces of the Italian revolution that had compelled the pope to flee to Naples as a "dark conspiracy" and claimed that the pope had been "the first to extend liberty and privileges to a corrupt people who showed their ingratitude by attempting to subvert his throne and to overturn all social order."[15]

Upon reading the sermon, Beman reached the limits of his patience and unleashed an attack on his old adversary in a series of eleven letters published in the Troy *Whig*. In his opening letter, he announced that he intended to reply to Hughes's sermon and "other productions of a recent date, which seem to me to demand a notice." He claimed that he would discuss "in a plain and undisguised way, as becomes a Protestant and Republican, certain sentiments oft-repeated in these productions, both political and religious, which are palpably at open war with the rights of man and liberty of conscience. . . . If arrogance should receive an occasional rebuke in what I write, I trust the reader will see that necessity was laid upon me."[16]

Beman's first letter was published on 21 July, and subsequent letters appeared at the rate of two a week until 2 September. Essentially, they consisted of a refutation of three arguments advanced by Hughes, criticism of the Catholic Church, and vindictive personal attacks on the archbishop and Pope Pius IX. Throughout, the letters were bitter and vitriolic. In his second and third letters, Beman sought to refute Hughes's interpretation of the passage, "Thou art, Peter, a rock, and on this rock I will build my Church." Citing biblical sources and church history, Beman claimed

---

[15]Nathan S. S. Beman, *Letters to Rev. John Hughes, D. D.* (Troy: L. Willard, 1851) 5-11.

[16]Ibid., 12-13.

that Peter had not been a pope and that Christ, not Peter, had founded the Christian church. Attacking Hughes's call for implicit obedience to the Catholic Church, Beman replied that "Implicit obedience, except to the authority of God, is fit only for a slave. That mind is in slavery which renders it." Replying to the charge that the Italian revolutionists had attempted to destroy the social order, he sought to illustrate that the behavior of the triumvirate toward the people of Italy had been better than that of the Church.[17]

In addition to these rebuttal efforts, Beman introduced four attacks on the Catholic Church which he demanded that the archbishop answer. He argued that the rites of the Church were idolatrous, that the Papal State preferred monarchy to democracy, that the Church sought to suppress freedom, and that it exerted an undesirable influence within the United States. Beman quoted various Protestant missionaries and clergy to substantiate his charge of idolatry. In an attempt to convince his readers that the Catholic Church favored monarchy over democratic governments, he argued that the papal system itself was an absolute monarchy, that the pope was a temporal prince, and that the Church sought to overthrow any government that stood in its way. He asked, "What Catholic prince of Europe would you wish to see deposed from his throne and a free government established in his realm?"[18]

Beman apparently felt strongest about the alleged suppression of freedom in Italy. He cited evidence from letters and diaries to show that the inquisition had flourished in Rome both before and after the flight of Pope Pius IX. Since 1850, Beman said, "imprisonment, base and appalling indignities, and slow, lingering deaths [have been] inflicted on hundreds, I may say thousands and tens of thousands, who have never been regularly arrested or legally tried and who often know not the crimes which are alleged against them!" Throughout the letters, he contrasted conditions in Rome with those in America by reminders such as, "We are in the United States . . . where no despot, political or spiritual, has a veto upon the press and where no inquisition can put grappling irons on free minds. . . . This is not Italy, nor have you here minds to deal with that think by proxy and dare not speak but at the bidding of a priest. . . . You are in New York,

---

[17]Ibid., 16-22, 24, 33.

[18]Ibid., 29-31, 62-68.

where the people have the inconvenient habit of thinking for themselves, never having given it over into the hands of the priesthood."[19]

Finally, Beman claimed that the Catholic Church had exercised a deleterious influence upon the poor of America. "You literally fleece your poor by church exactions," Beman charged; "it is money, money for everything and on all occasions—and then your pillaged paupers are turned loose to sponge their living out of Protestants by begging." He accused the Church of trying to keep its communicants in ignorance, claiming that the most uneducated people in the country were Catholic immigrants from Hughes's native Ireland.[20]

Argumentum ad hominem characterized all of the letters. Beman unsparingly attacked Hughes and the Catholic hierarchy. In one letter he remonstrated the archbishop, saying, "Your papal-boasting, your abuse of Protestants, your self-congratulations, your dabbling in politics, and your courting of great men for the purpose of making an impression abroad in favor of the papacy and yourself are all clearly seen and have begun to attract public attention." In another letter, he called Hughes one of the pope's "tools and sycophants, without one drop of American blood in his veins, nor a fibre of real republicanism in his heart." He also criticized Hughes's style, triteness, arrogance, "priestly brass," and claims of "ghostly powers."[21]

He was even more denunciatory of Catholic officials, calling them "priests, monks, friars, whining beggars, and wiley Jesuits, numerous as the locust of Egypt and far more destructive to the hopes and happiness of man." He charged that popes "have been among the bloodiest tyrants that ever filled a throne or scourged our race." Pope Pius IX he regarded as "a traitor to freedom" and associated his name with that of Benedict Arnold.[22]

In his final letter, Beman summarized his arguments so that the archbishop might answer them. "Some of your friends think you will reply to my strictures," he wrote; "I hope you will." Inured to attacks by Protes-

---

[19]Ibid., 13, 26, 35-37, 47-49, 76.

[20]Ibid., 51, 71-72.

[21]Ibid., 13-15, 21, 23, 27, 45, 59, 68.

[22]Ibid., 25, 31, 53.

tants, Hughes failed to take public notice of the letters. When it became obvious that he did not intend to reply, Beman's letters were published in pamphlet form and distributed widely.

These letters were Beman's most famous anti-Catholic effort, although he remained active in the work of the American and Foreign Christian Union for several years. In 1859 he preached the principal sermon at the society's annual meeting. Entitled "The World a Missionary Field," the sermon reiterated many of the charges included in his attack on Hughes. In addition, Beman appealed for action throughout the world to convert Roman Catholics.[23] To the very end of his life, Beman remained suspicious of the Catholic Church, and in his will he left a small legacy to the American and Foreign Christian Union.[24]

A year after his attack on Hughes, Beman took part in an important debate at the General Assembly of the Presbyterian Church in Washington, D.C., in May 1852. The dispute concerned proposals to reorganize several agencies of the church. Following the division of the Presbyterian Church, the New School branch had experienced little expansion; many factors accounted for the lack of growth. Among them was the unsectarian—almost undenominational—spirit that pervaded the body. A large portion of the ministry, like Beman, were men born and educated in the Congregational Church or other denominations. Although zealous in their defense of their right to preach as they wished in 1838, these men shrank sensitively from enforcing their views on others or any appearance of proselytizing.

A second hindrance was the New School's financial condition; at the time of the division, most of the wealthy congregations had gone with the Old School. After a long and complicated law suit, so did most of the well-endowed institutions. Consequently, throughout much of its existence, the New School had been unable to support financially many projects that would have extended its influence.

A third handicap was the result of a mistake in judgment. Weary with past struggles, many Presbyterians came to regard the annual General As-

---

[23]Nathan S. S. Beman, "The World a Missionary Field," *The National Preacher* 2 (May 1859): 134-48.

[24]Last Will and Testament of Nathan S. S. Beman, Jackson County Clerk's Office, Murphysboro, Illinois.

sembly with disfavor. In 1840 this attitude led to meetings every three years. As a consequence, important matters often were postponed for two or three years, and ties between the member churches began to weaken.[25]

The inadvisability of triennial assemblies became apparent in 1846 when considerable business "of vast importance" was left unfinished and members were forced to call a special meeting for the following year. At the 1847 session, Thornton A. Mills presented a memorial in which he urged that means be found to reinvigorate the church through increasing the number of churches and ministers, providing itinerant preachers, and bringing the gospel to immigrants.[26]

Before the 1852 Assembly convened in Washington, members knew that the most important topic for consideration would be a report by Mills embodying specific proposals to meet the needs he had outlined five years earlier. In its report, the Mills committee recommended improvement in the education of ministers, in the work of home missions, and in the distribution of doctrinal tracts. The committee's proposal for each of the three areas involved essentially the same principle: stronger central control.[27]

No sooner had the report been presented than the Assembly divided into two camps. Beman's opposition to the plan could have been predicted. For years he had strongly supported the American Board of Commissioners for Foreign Missions, the Home Missionary Society, the American Sunday-School Union, the American Tract Society, and other interdenominational and voluntary religious organizations. Raised in an Episcopal home, educated and ordained as a Congregationalist, and occupant of a Presbyterian pulpit, he was inclined to be tolerant of theological differences among Protestant churches. Furthermore, as he was to indicate later, he could see no reason why Presbyterians, Episcopalians, Baptists, and Methodists could not unite to give away a Bible, establish a mission, or publish a religious pamphlet.[28]

[25]Johnathon F. Stearns, "Historical Review of the Church (New School Branch) since 1839," *Presbyterian Re-Union Memorial Volume, 1837-1871* (New York: DeWitt C. Lent and Co., 1870) 57-60.

[26]Ibid., 62-63.

[27]Ibid., 67.

[28]Nathan S. S. Beman, *Episcopacy Exclusive: or Two Series of Letters, Being a Review of Dr. Coit's Sermon and Pamphlet* (Troy: L. Willard, 1856) 5-14.

In the debate on the proposal, Beman was the leading spokesman for the opposition. Late in the afternoon on 25 May Beman began his speech, but he was soon interrupted by the hour for adjournment. The Assembly awaited with excitement his resumption the following morning; many members remembered the telling blows he had struck at the time of the division, while others already regarded him as a legend. According to the New York *Tribune*, Beman's address "is to be the great speech of the occasion."[29]

Resuming his remarks the following morning, Beman denounced the report as calculated to destroy the unity and cooperative spirit of the Protestant churches. "Ours was the spirit of evangelism," he contended, "a union spirit, keen-eyed to discern the image of Christ everywhere—a spirit which created the Bible, Tract, Sunday School, and Home Missionary Societies." He would not join in the work of breaking down so tried a system. If the voluntary associations had not achieved all that the New School desired, he claimed, any failures were largely the result of previous church dissension. Furthermore, he charged that the movement was simply a copy of Old School methods. The New York *Times* correspondent described the address as a "long and eloquent speech," "emphatic," and characterized by "earnest dissuasion."[30]

In the end, Beman emerged victorious—at least in part—for instead of adopting the report, the entire matter was referred to a special committee, with Beman as one of its members. The final report of that committee, which was later adopted by the General Assembly, reflects Beman's influence. None of the existing voluntary agencies was disturbed and the church agreed to continue cooperating with them. However, in acquiescence to compromise, the section of Mills's report proposing the creation of itinerant missionaries was incorporated into the committee's recommendations and adopted by the Assembly.[31]

Beman's visit to Washington was remarkable for another reason. Throughout his life he felt a deep love for his country. Born shortly after the American Revolution and nourished on the tales of heroism told by

[29]New York *Tribune*, 27 May 1852.

[30]New York *Times*, 28 May 1852.

[31]Stearns, "Historical Review of the Church," 68-71.

his father and uncle, Beman never forgot the sacrifices necessary to achieve democratic government. He felt a profound affection for the rugged hills of New England and awe and admiration for the rolling plains and vast forests of the West. Even his nativism and anti-Catholicism were inspired by a perverted kind of patriotism, a fear that alien forces might damage the institutions and ideals of America. Critics might accuse Beman of belligerence, intolerance, and a desire for personal recognition, but they could not doubt his patriotism.

Beman best expressed his veneration for the founders of the republic in a discourse delivered on the Fourth of July in 1841.

> Our Patriot Fathers . . . were no common race of men. God made them for the times in which they lived and acted, and the spirit of the times raised them to that eminence which they finally attained. When we consider their number, their talents, their virtues, and their achievements, it would be difficult, in the annals of the world, to find their equals, in any country during a single age. It may be truly said, that "there were giants in the earth in those days. . . . "
>
> I cannot tell you with what mingled emotions I have trodden the consecrated soil of Bunker Hill, once sprinkled with their blood, or stood at other times by some of their sepulchres. On the banks of the mighty Potomac, and near its calm and deep waters, I have thought of the struggles of the revolution—of the conflicts of mind which framed our constitution, and matured our systems of government—of the dark storm that had passed by, and of the scenes of future brightness, which may mark our country's progress through the long tract of coming ages, while I have mused in silence at the humble tomb of Washington.[32]

On Saturday morning, the General Assembly adjourned to visit Washington's grave; for most of the members it was their first visit. A reporter observed, "As I looked at these representatives of a large church which had borne such an important part in securing our freedom, reverently approaching the sacred spot . . . I thought it must be one of the choicest pilgrimages ever made by patriotism to the place."[33] On their return from Mount Vernon, the members visited Fort Washington and that

---

[32]Nathan S. S. Beman, *The Western Continent* (Troy: N. Tuttle, 1841) 25-26.

[33]New York *Tribune*, 25 May 1852.

afternoon they were received by President Fillmore in the East Room of the White House.[34]

These events made such a deep impression on Beman that he introduced a resolution in the General Assembly inviting each member to contribute a dollar to purchase a block of marble for the Washington Monument. Upon passage of the resolution, $161.75 was collected and given to the Washington National Monument Society. Beman must have been particularly proud of the resolutions adopted by the managers of the society in June. The first resolution thanked the General Assembly for its contribution. The second prescribed, "That the above resolution be handed to the Rev. N. S. S. Beman, D. D., and thanks of the Board are hereby conveyed to him for his offering and advocating the resolution of the Assembly referred to."[35]

For three-and-a-half years following his participation in the debate at Washington, the clergyman lived quietly. However, Beman seems to have been incapable of avoiding controversy for any prolonged period of time, and during the early months of 1856 he and the Episcopal rector treated all of Troy to a theological tempest. At seventy years of age, Beman showed no signs of mellowing. While the residents of the Hudson River city undoubtedly had long before accustomed themselves to the minister's penchant for argument, the dispute reminded them that the aging divine had not changed. Although no public demonstrations occurred, probably no other single action by Beman had aroused so much interest in Troy since the Weld riots of 1835.

From all appearances the controversy began innocently. The Reverend Dr. Thomas W. Coit, rector of St. Paul's Episcopal Church, addressed the Troy Bible Society on Christmas Eve, December 1855. Having served at St. Paul's for only two years, Coit took from his files a sermon that he had delivered several times elsewhere and presented it to the assemblage. Present were members of all of the Protestant denominations of the city. Since the occasion, as Coit noted in his introduction, traditionally was devoted to discourses vindicating some of the peculiarities that distinguished one denomination from another, he deemed it appropriate

---

[34]New York Times, 26 May 1852; National Intelligencer (Washington), 24 May 1852.

[35]National Intelligencer (Washington), 27 May, 2 June 1852.

to present a defense of the commonly charged exclusiveness of the Episcopal Church.[36]

The address was short and mild in tone. In the course of his defense, Coit compared the beliefs and practices of the Episcopalians to those of other Protestants. A lengthy account of the sermon appeared in the Troy *Daily Traveler* of 26 December.[37] Five weeks passed, during which no comment was heard, then the first of twelve letters from Beman appeared in the Troy *Times*. Although critical, these too were temperate. Since he had been out of the city and had not heard the actual speech, Beman based his attack on the newspaper account. Claiming he had been inaccurately reported, Coit printed a copy of the address, accompanied by explanatory notes. The notes were characterized by a vituperation that even Beman could not match. Beman responded with seventeen additional letters to the *Times*. The second series was far more caustic than the original group, but still fell short of Coit's level of personal abuse. Following the publication of Beman's second set of letters, Coit put out a revised edition of his address, accompanied by additional comments on the new letters. Beman followed with a publication of the entire series of twenty-nine letters in pamphlet form, and Coit replied with still a third edition of his speech.[38]

Although they probably could not always follow the two ministers through the labyrinth of theological argument set forth in the charges and countercharges, readers had no difficulty whatever in understanding the bitter personal attacks of the two antagonists. The reactions of other clergymen can be surmised. Those who had felt the sting of Beman's rebukes must have enjoyed seeing a newcomer baiting the old warrior. Others who shared Beman's convictions about Episcopalians probably sided with the Presbyterian. Regardless of their sentiments, the city's clergymen must have chuckled with devilish glee at the sight of the representatives of two of Troy's most distinguished congregations flailing away at each other.

Whether personal motives were involved in the dispute is difficult to determine. Beman had maintained amicable relations with rectors of the

---

[36]T. W. Coit, *Exclusiveness: A Lecture for Christmas Eve, Delivered on Monday, December 24, 1855*, 3d ed., rev. (Troy: William H. Young, 1856) 5-9.

[37]Ibid., 17-20; *Troy Traveler*, 26 December 1855.

[38]Coit, *Exclusiveness*, 5-8; Beman, *Episcopacy Exclusive*, 3.

other Episcopalian churches in Troy, so it does not seem likely that this factor led him to publish the letters. In addition, the first letters were not unduly harsh. Since newspaper controversies over religious doctrines were not uncommon, Beman's criticism should not have offended Coit. Furthermore, Coit had been involved in a similar debate with no less a theologian than Andrews Norton as early as 1834. Finally, that the dispute should have become so acrimonious is surprising in light of the background of the two men. Beman had been raised in an Episcopalian home, while Coit had been a member of the Congregational Church until he entered college. An explanation for the acidity generated in the course of the dispute may lie in Coit's frequent taunting of his non-Anglican colleagues. An address on Puritanism in 1846 had evoked a hostile reaction among Presbyterians, and perhaps Beman seized upon the Christmas Eve sermon as an excuse to answer Coit.[39]

Whatever the explanation, Beman found a worthy antagonist in Coit. Fifty-two years old, Coit was a native of Connecticut who had graduated from Yale and had attended both Andover and Princeton theological seminaries. He had served as rector of churches in Salem and Cambridge, Massachusetts, before filling the presidency of Transylvania University in Lexington, Kentucky, from 1835 to 1837. For ten years he had occupied the pulpit of Trinity Church in New Rochelle, and from 1849 to 1854 he taught church history at Trinity College in Hartford. In the latter year he accepted the charge in Troy, where he was to serve for twenty-five years. Among his publications was a version of the Bible that was highly prized among the Episcopalians.[40]

In answering the charge of exclusiveness of the Episcopal Church, Coit argued that his church was no different from others in believing itself superior and closest to the doctrines of the New Testament. Posing a dilemma, he claimed that each sect either believed in its own superiority or else it condemned itself by creating a mere schism in the church of God without good reason. "If this is exclusiveness," he contended, ". . . then

---

[39]*Dictionary of American Biography* (New York: Charles Scribner's Sons, 1930) 4:278; Beman, *Episcopacy Exclusive,* 47; *New York Observer,* 5 October 1845, 7 February, 28 March 1846.

[40]*Dictionary of American Biography* (1930) 4:278; *National Cyclopedia of American Biography* (New York: James T. White) 4:514-15.

we look fearlessly round upon every sect which upbraids us and say, the one that is without sin among you, let that one cast the first stone."[41]

Episcopalians had often been criticized for the failure of their church to participate in charitable and evangelical enterprises jointly sponsored by Protestant groups. Coit evaded this criticism by comparing his church to each of the leading denominations and concluded "that while Episcopalians think freely and speak freely of the *opinions* of other Christians, they are less free than any Christians I know in their judgments of the unseen condition of a fellow-creature's soul." "This is charity in the best sense of that holy word," he concluded; "nevertheless, the calumny flies round and round that if any Christian communion is preeminently exclusive, we are that one."[42]

In his letters, Beman pointed out that Coit had not refuted the charge that the Episcopal Church refused to work with other denominations. That the Episcopalians thought themselves closer to the true Christianity than others, he argued, was no reason for refusing to cooperate in religious endeavors. "The Episcopal Church and all 'the sects,' " he said, "have an inherent right to choose their own religious system, and adopt it, and carry out its principles. But it does not follow that they act correctly and exemplify the spirit of Christ and his gospel when they refuse to have 'dealings' in religious matters with one another. . . . There is such a thing as evangelical Christianity, and men who have the spirit of Christ and the gospel can act together in very many things in order to make the world better." Indulging in sarcasm, Beman suggested, "I can see no good reason why an Episcopalian, *pure* as his church is in his own estimation—and I would not disturb his self-complacency—may not give away a Bible in company with the Presbyterian, the Baptist, the Methodist—or even with 'the Socinian or Universalist,' without injury to any one or the sacrifice of any great Christian principle."[43] Long a supporter of several societies that derived their support from various denominations, Beman felt keenly about the half-heartedness of the Episcopal Church in this realm.

---

[41]Coit, *Exclusiveness*, 10-11.

[42]Ibid., 13-21.

[43]Beman, *Episcopacy Exclusive*, 5-14.

In attacking the sermon, Beman claimed that Coit was guilty of inconsistencies, of shifting his position, of factual errors, and of lapses in grammar and style.[44] Although the letters were mild and restrained for Beman, scattered throughout were enough jibes to arouse Coit's ire. Beman called the rector's style "rhetorical invective," "assuming, denunciatory, pugilistic," and possessing a "strong tendency toward hyperbole"; he labeled one argument "illiberal in spirit, inaccurate in point of historical fact, and quite unseemly and out of place as coming from an Episcopalian"; he referred to another as "one of the strangest paragraphs which has issued from the modern press." He undoubtedly irritated Coit when he said, "The Doctor ought to know this—and I think he does"; "Here the Doctor, very adroitly or very accidentally, has failed to finish his antithesis"; and, in reference to Coit's frequent use of the phrase "the Church": "In addition to its arrogance, it is certainly in bad taste to be forever blowing a loud trumpet about it. . . . It is verily sickening, coming from this quarter."[45]

Almost any man might become provoked by such insinuations, but even Beman was shocked by the flood of invective that they unleashed from the Episcopalian. Coit used such abusive epithets as: "like a leech," "sorry morality," "ludicrous errors," "queasy and churlish," "perverted," "sheer ignorance," "heretic," "raw and vipery testiness," "controversial defamer," "a mere popeling," "disgraceful," "unworthy," "his own dishonor," and "virulent." He accused Beman of being "an imitator of the archbishop's [Hughes's] faults, though by no means of his talent," of possessing an "old stereotyped Jesuitical sneer," called him an "object of mirthful pity," and claimed that Beman had become a Presbyterian simply for the sake of expediency—"and of course expediency with a silver clink in it."[46]

As the debate continued the two contenders ranged farther and farther from the original points of difference, devoting many paragraphs to quibbling over minor arguments and interpretations of obscure theological passages. In his final letter, although largely irrelevant, Beman probably made the Episcopalian's blood boil, for he devoted it to a minute

---

[44]Ibid., 11-12.

[45]Ibid., 12, 16, 22-23, 26, 29, 33, 35-36.

[46]Ibid., 39-41; Coit, *Exclusiveness*.

dissection of the grammatical errors and stylistic flaws in Coit's publications. Beman's parting shot reveals the low level to which the controversy descended before its termination. He ended his last letter:

> I have spoken of this pamphlet with as little severity as is compatible with its literary defects and blemishes. . . . And yet the author tells us that the production is "some ten or eleven years old," and "it has been delivered on different occasions and in places widely distant from each other." How any man of ordinary talents—though he has never seen the inside of a college—could keep such a literary production on hand for so many years and could read and preach it repeatedly, without detecting its glaring errors, is an inexplicable mystery. And then it must have been, with its author, rather a favourite, as "it has been delivered on different occasions, in places widely distant from each other." If this is an extraordinary sermon, it would be "singularly amusing," to borrow the Doctor's language, to any man's "recollections," to read or hear an ordinary one![47]

The controversy dragged on until the middle of the year, with Beman's pamphlet being published on 20 June and Coit's final revision not long after. Surely the dispute can have accomplished little. It did remind the citizenry that Beman remained unchanged in his outspoken denunciation of all that he regarded as hypocritical or theologically unsound.

---

[47]Beman, *Episcopacy Exclusive*, 102.

Chapter X

Slavery, Secession, and the Final Years

> In my old age, one of my strongest de-
> sires to live a little longer is to see this ex-
> isting and wicked rebellion put under the
> feet of genuine loyalty.
> —Nathan S. S. Beman

As the nation marched relentlessly down the road to civil war, attention turned increasingly to the subject of slavery and the related issue of disunion. Interdenominational disputes within the churches subsided; temperance and evangelical endeavors languished; and nativist sentiment gradually receded into the background of men's minds. As the conflict approached, Beman too became increasingly concerned with the great issue.

Although never a supporter of slavery, Beman had altered his attitude toward the institution over the years. While living in Georgia, he had opposed emancipation as "wild and destructive." After his marriage to Caroline Yancey, he was not averse to selling three slaves. Not until his return to the North did he publicly attack slaveholding. Disillusioned with colonization schemes, like many others in the 1830s Beman turned to abolition as a solution to the vexing problem. From this time, he repeatedly denounced slavery as "an immense evil" and a "heinous sin," and urged others in the ministry to oppose it. After 1835 he persistently agitated the slave question in the General Assemblies of the Presbyterian Church. Between 1835 and 1838, Beman contemplated accepting an appointment as a European agent of the American Anti-Slavery Society; and, while he did not actually represent the society, he was outspoken in his condemnation of slaveholding during his tour of England in 1839. By this time Beman was widely recognized as an opponent of slavery.[1]

Beman hoped to see abolition accomplished under the Constitution and through existing political agencies. By 1839 antislavery sentiment had become so strong that some were calling for a third political party. At a convention held in Warsaw, New York, in November, a small group of abolitionists nominated James G. Birney as a candidate for the presidency on the Liberty party ticket. When Birney declined the nomination because the convention had not been national in character, another convention was scheduled for Albany on 1 April 1840.

Beman went to Albany and on the first day, while members waited for the business meeting, he attempted to dissuade the delegates from their purpose in a lengthy address. He argued that the formation of a separate political party would endanger the antislavery movement. He ridiculed the party's chances of electing its nominees and urged, instead, support of General Garrison. The clergyman was unsuccessful. Failing in their purpose, Beman and his associates withdrew, and the convention went ahead with its plans and again nominated Birney. Following the split between the Garrison wing and the third-party sympathizers later that month, Beman aligned himself with the Garrisonians.[2]

On the Fourth of July 1841 Beman denounced slavery in a sermon that was published and distributed widely. The following September, he joined with several other leaders in calling an Anti-Slavery Union meeting to be

---

[1]*Anti-Slavery Record* 1:7 (July 1835): 81.

[2]Mary Theophane Geary, *A History of Third Parties in Pennsylvania* (Washington: Catholic University Press, 1938) 36-40; Theodore Clark Smith, *The Liberty and Free Soil Parties in the Northwest* (New York: Longmans, Green and Co., 1897) 38-39; Joshua Leavitt, *Memorial Sermon on Rev. N. S. S. Beman, Delivered December 17, 1871, in the First Presbyterian Church, Troy, N.Y.* (Troy: n.p., 1872) 60.

held in Albany.[3] After his tour of the West in 1845, he expressed concern over the influence of slavery in the Mississippi Valley.

Although he attended numerous meetings of antislavery organizations and repeatedly agitated the controversial question in the councils of the Presbyterian Church, Beman made his most famous pronouncements on the issue from his pulpit in Troy. The churches traditionally observed national holidays with special services and, on these occasions, ministers customarily delivered addresses of a political nature. During the 1850s Beman's forceful attacks on slavery attracted attention throughout much of the country. One of the reasons for the general interest was his relationship to William Lowndes Yancey, who was fast becoming known as a leading defender of slavery.

The inherent drama in the conflict between stepfather and stepson was heightened by the prominence of the two men, their known propensity for controversy, and the forcible and unyielding character of their public utterances. During the years when Beman was most vigorous in his denunciation of slaveholding, Yancey was gaining fame as a supporter of the institution. The younger man's political rise was meteoric. At twenty-seven he was in the lower house of the state legislature; at twenty-nine he was a state senator; and at thirty he won a seat in Congress. His reputation as an orator had preceded him, and his first speech at Washington and the resultant duel with Congressman Clingman made him for a time a national celebrity.[4] Thus, when Beman attacked slavery, his remarks acquired added interest because of his publicized relationship to Yancey.

Although Yancey's feelings on slavery at the time of his departure from the North are not known, shortly thereafter he took a firm stand against nullification in South Carolina. When he assumed editorship of the Greenville *Mountaineer* in 1834, his predecessor introduced him to the newspaper's readers as a man of "acknowledged talents and firm attachment to our glorious Union." In succeeding issues, the youthful Yancey poured forth a series of editorials for liberty and the Union with as much

---

[3]Nathan S. S. Beman, *The Western Continent* (Troy: N. Tuttle, 1841) 22; *The Liberator* (Boston), 1 October 1841.

[4]William Garrett Brown, "William Lowndes Yancey, An Interesting Sketch of the Great Southern Leader," *Montgomery Advertiser*, 28 May 1899.

ardor as he later devoted to secession.[5] However, over the ensuing years
he gradually changed. Probably one of the most influential factors in Yancey's conversion was his marriage in 1835 and subsequent acquisition of a
large number of slaves. Upon her marriage, his bride inherited a plantation and about thirty-five slaves. In managing the plantation Yancey came
to appreciate the high degree to which his livelihood—and that of the entire planter caste—depended on slavery. Although he usually defended
slaveholding on a legal and constitutional basis, Yancey came to believe
that the institution was positively beneficial to the blacks.[6]

Beman's influence upon his stepson, which in many matters seems to
have been considerable, ironically failed to prevent Yancey from embrac-
ing that cause which the cleric came to regard with the greatest abhorrence. So far as is known, Yancey never specifically discussed his
stepfather's abolitionist activities in public. However, a remark in his
maiden speech in Congress in 1845 may be construed to have been directed at the clergyman. In 1835 Beman had denounced slaveholders as
"men who sell the image of Jesus Christ in their slaves." Although other
abolitionists had used the same or similar language, Beman's remarks on
this occasion attracted considerable publicity. So in his first speech to the
House of Representatives, which was an attack on abolitionists, Yancey
employed almost identical language. He argued that those New Englanders who condemned slaveholders as men "who sold the image of Christ"
were the true disunionists and plunderers of the country. In view of the
publicity given to this particular remark by Beman, it seems unlikely that
Yancey would have been unaware of his stepfather's use of the phrase.
However, although Yancey's public speeches contain frequent comments
on his Northern boyhood, nowhere can a direct reference to Beman be
found.[7]

---

[5]*Greenville* (South Carolina) *Mountaineer,* 15 November 1834; Lillian Adele
Kibler, *Benjamin F. Perry, South Carolina Unionist* (Durham: Duke University Press,
1946) 198-99.

[6]John Witherspoon DuBose, *The Life and Times of William Lowndes Yancey,* 2
vols. (New York: Peter Smith, 1942) 1:33, 64, 70; 2:508.

[7]*The South Vindicated from the Treason and Fanaticism of the Northern Abolitionists* (Philadelphia: H. Manly, 1836) 168-70; Speech, William L. Yancey,
United States House of Representatives, *Congressional Globe,* 7 January 1845, 100-
102.

Yancey's support of slavery and states' rights was characterized by an unyielding adherence to principle. This trait, probably acquired at the feet of his stern stepfather or among the strict Calvinists at Williams College, earned him the appellation of "fire-eater." Although he probably was more denounced than any other man in the Union at one time, Yancey maintained that he was no disunionist or reckless troublemaker. "I tell you, gentlemen," he insisted, "my disunionism consists of this: I stand by the Constitution."[8] In 1846 Yancey resigned his seat in the House because he felt that the Democratic party had failed to support the principles set forth in the party platform. Following his resignation, Yancey spent the next fourteen years contending for slavery and states' rights. During this period, he consistently refused to stand for public office, but instead sought to arouse the people of Alabama and the South to stand firm in the face of Northern opposition and abolitionism. Even Beman would have found it difficult to match such determination and sacrifice of public favor for principle.

Yancey believed that the Constitution gave slaveholders the right to take their slaves into territories and that Congress was obligated to protect that right. Because the Northern states with their control of the House might try to interfere, he thought it essential to the protection of the South that legislation be enacted recognizing this Constitutional guarantee. To this end, Yancey fought determinedly in the Democratic National Convention of 1848. However, when a minority report embodying his position received but thirty-six votes, he walked out of the convention. Only one other Southerner accompanied him; however, twelve years later that tale was to end differently. The defeat served merely to spur Yancey to greater efforts in his crusade to rally Southern support for his point of view. For the next twelve years he stumped the state and attended political and commercial conventions throughout the South to urge secession if Southern states were denied their full rights in the new territories.

During the same period, Beman became increasingly involved in his antislavery activities. After 1850, his Thanksgiving and Fourth of July sermons and other addresses on special days dealt with the issue of slavery almost exclusively. On such occasions the church was crowded to the

---

[8]DuBose, *William Lowndes Yancey*, 1:151, 220, 319, 362; 2:439-40, 492, 497.

doors, with many from other societies swelling the ranks of the congregation that usually worshiped there.[9]

In his address, Characteristics of the Age, delivered on the Fourth of July in 1851, Beman expressed at length his opinion of the fugitive-slave law. Introducing his topic, he indicated that he was opposed to interfering with the institution of slavery in the South. "If they want slavery, let them have it," he said; "it is their own business and not mine. . . . But I have a right," he continued, "to think and say that I believe it is the deepest curse entailed upon the colonies by Great Britain, that it was most improvident and unfortunate that the fathers of the Republic did not devise an early plan for its abolition."[10]

Beman expressed his doubt of the constitutionality of the fugitive-slave law, but cautioned his listeners that "we have a tribunal to settle such questions, and the popular will is not the tribunal; it is the Supreme Court of the United States." At this time, Beman still hoped that the controversy might be settled under the laws of the country.

> It is certain that the Constitution makes provision for the return from the Free States to the Slave States of fugitives from service. This Constitution is the only admitted bond of union between the States. Repudiate or nullify this and the Union is broken up. While we continue one people, we must stand by this compact. We must observe good faith in carrying out its provisions, as a whole and in all its parts. If one man or one portion of the republic may disregard or trample down one provision, another man or another portion of the republic may disregard or trample down another, and we shall have no Constitution left.[11]

But whatever he thought of the constitutionality of the law, Beman felt the provision to be ugly and unfortunate. He believed that the law permitted a man to swear property into his own hands, that it erected a tribunal, and then offered a bribe to the judge by giving him twice the amount in fees for sending a man into slavery than it gave him for pronouncing

---

[9]"Pulpit Giants," Proceedings of the Centennial Anniversary of the First Presbyterian Church, Troy, N.Y., December 30, 31, 1891 (Troy: Troy Times, 1892) 98; Leavitt, Memorial Sermon, 60.

[10]Nathan S. S. Beman, Characteristics of the Age (Troy: Young and Hartt, 1851) 18-19.

[11]Ibid., 19-20.

him free. In spite of these flaws, Beman urged his listeners to enforce the law, for, he said, "If we expect the protection of the law, we must protect law and see that its provisions are carried out."[12]

Beman's confidence in adherence to the law was badly shaken by the Dred Scott case. The five-to-four decision, announced by Chief Justice Taney, supported the Southern contention that the right of property in slaves was distinctly affirmed in the Constitution. Under this interpretation, neither Congress nor the territorial legislatures could prohibit the importation of slavery into any territory, for Congress itself not only had no power to deprive any owner of his property, but also could not delegate to the territorial legislatures authority that Congress itself did not possess.

In his Thanksgiving Day address of 1858, Beman attacked the Dred Scott ruling. In introducing his discussion of the slavery controversy, he defended his right to speak on the topic. "Men talk very foolishly who resolve to stop all agitation on this subject," he said; "you might as well have a convention to stop the wind blowing."[13] Beman then condemned the influence of slaveholders on the founders of the country, complained of the disproportionate power wielded by the South in national affairs, and attacked the reasoning of Judge Taney in the Dred Scott decision.

Beman believed that the framers of the Constitution had intended as rapidly as was practicable to carry out the principle that all men are created equal. That this was the hope of the Founding Fathers, he argued, was indicated by their vote to exclude the terms "slave" and "slavery" from the Constitution so that these words might not appear in future ages. However, Beman continued, "It may be easily seen that Satan, in the impersonation of the slave-power, stood at the right hand of our Joshuas when they formed our Constitution. . . . Several positions were taken which never would have been assumed and maintained if the evil genius of slavery had not stood at the right hand of the framers of the Constitution to resist their better and noble purposes."[14]

According to Beman, the forces of slavery had persuaded the founders to protect the slave trade until 1808 in spite of Jefferson's opposition. He

---

[12]Ibid., 20-21.

[13]Nathan S. S. Beman, *Antagonisms in the Moral and Political World* (Troy: A. W. Scribner and Co., 1858) 25.

[14]Ibid., 26-27.

contended that the return of fugitive slaves should never have received the sanction of those states where slavery existed in name only. Beman also argued that in fixing the ratio of representation in Congress, the framers of the Constitution had offered a bounty for the encouragement of slavery. Counting five slaves as equal to three free men, Beman estimated that the South had twenty members on the floors of Congress "not by the census of men, but of property." His fourth condemnation was that no provision had been incorporated into the Constitution providing for the gradual manumission of slaves.[15]

Beman also contended that the South wielded a disproportionate influence in national affairs. Although the 1850 census showed that the free white population of the North was more than double that of the Southern states, Beman argued that the South had supplied a majority of the country's presidents, Supreme Court justices, cabinet ministers, and foreign ministers. By threats of disunion, liberal use of government funds, and judicious distribution of offices, Beman asserted, the South was generally able to control even Congress. They tell us what must be done, the minister said, or they will secede, and we have some men who tremble at the consequences.[16]

Beman regarded Judge Taney's argument in support of the Dred Scott decision as illogical. Refuting the judge's claim that the phrase "all men are created equal" excluded blacks, the clergyman cited statements of Jefferson and Benjamin Rush and the petitions of the New England colonies, New Jersey, Pennsylvania, and Virginia opposing slavery. "What a marvelous document this would be," Beman exclaimed, "if it were written out according to Judge Taney's interpretation: 'We hold these truths to be self-evident that all *white* men are created equal; that all *white* men are endowed by their Creator with certain unalienable rights, among which is life, liberty, and the pursuit of happiness.' "[17]

One of Beman's most impassioned attacks on slavery concluded his 1858 Thanksgiving address:

---

[15]Ibid., 26-30.

[16]Ibid., 30-31.

[17]Ibid., 32-34.

Democracy and slavery—what a brotherhood! It seems to me like an alliance between Jerusalem and Sodom, a friendly league between an archangel and Lucifer, the consummation of nuptials between benevolence personified and one of the seven Furies, a treaty of amity and commerce and mutual defense between heaven and hell! This must be a spurious democracy. What is the nut worth when the kernel is gone, and nothing but the shell is left. Away then with this last and most loathesome phase of political hypocrisy. It would put Benedict Arnold to the blush—it would lead Judas Iscariot to cast down thirty pieces of silver and go and hang himself.[18]

Beman was particularly irritated by President Buchanan's tolerant attitude toward slavery. The clergyman described Buchanan as watching slavery "till his heart, which was never known to have any other fibre in it than that of ambition, actually began to soften, and he almost fell in love with it." The longer the president gazed, according to Beman, the more beautiful slavery became. "It was so near faultless that it would be unconstitutional and unkind to resort to the use of coercion in dealing with it." So, Beman asserted, Buchanan adopted a policy of coaxing, not coercing the secessionists. "This tame policy," he concluded, "has wellnigh made ship-wreck of this republic."[19]

Almost as disconcerting as the Dred Scott ruling and the president's vacillating attitude on slavery must have been the publication in 1858 of Yancey's famous Slaughter letter. In that remarkable document, Yancey proclaimed his disillusion with the Democratic party as a source of protection for Southern rights and urged the organization throughout the South of committees of safety in imitation of the associations of 1776. The purposes of the committees were to "fire the Southern heart, instruct the Southern mind, give courage to each other," and "at the proper moment by one organized, concerted action . . . to precipitate the Cotton States into a revolution." The motto of the League of United Southerners, as the committees were known, was "A Southern Republic is our only safety." In cooperation with Edmund Ruffin and Robert Barnwell Rhett, Yancey

---

[18]Ibid., 35.

[19]Nathan S. S. Beman, *Our Civil War: The Principles Involved, Its Causes and Cure* (Troy: A. W. Scribner, 1862) 11-12.

set about the task of launching the association and quickly succeeded in organizing committees in three Alabama communities.[20]

Exactly what Beman thought of his stepson's plan cannot be determined. That he was acutely aware of the likelihood of revolution, however, is revealed in his Thanksgiving Day sermon of 1858 when at one point he abandoned his manuscript, stepped to one side of the pulpit, and prophetically warned the congregation, "Don't allow yourselves to be deceived with the idea that these men are going to allow this question to be settled by the result of a ballot. . . . I have lived among these men, and I know them and I tell you they mean blood."[21]

The harsh criticism that the League of United Southerners encountered forced Yancey and his associates on the defensive. They tried to explain that it was not a disunion movement. In the summer of 1859 Yancey modified his approach. He feared that if his group stayed out of the Democratic party, a popular sovereignty platform would be adopted and Stephen A. Douglas named to run on it. He, therefore, seized upon the Dred Scott ruling as justification for his demand for a slave-code plank in the party platform. While Beman and the Northern abolitionists regarded the decision as treacherous and unjust, Yancey accepted it as confirmation of what he had long claimed. However, he was not content to let the matter rest there. Insisting that ways of circumventing the decision existed, he demanded that Congress enact legislation guaranteeing the right of Southerners to carry slaves into the territories.[22]

In 1860 Yancey went to the Democratic National Convention in Charleston supported by an Alabama delegation committed to this position. The attention of the entire nation was focused on Charleston during those ten days, for the public knew that on the outcome of that conflict

---

[20]Laura A. White, *Robert Barnwell Rhett: Father of Secession* (New York: Century Co., 1931) 146; Henry H. Simms, *A Decade of Sectional Controversy, 1851-1861* (Chapel Hill: University of North Carolina Press, 1942) 205-206; Avery Craven, *Edmund Ruffin, Southerner* (New York: D. Appleton and Co., 1932) 162.

[21]Beman, *Antagonisms*, 30-31; Martin I. Townsend, "Historical Address," *Proceedings of the Centennial Anniversary*, 26.

[22]White, *Robert Barnwell Rhett*, 146; Craven, *Edmund Ruffin*; George Fort Milton, *The Eve of Conflict* (Boston and New York: Houghton, Mifflin Co., 1934) 396.

might rest the future of the Union. Yancey, too, recognized the seriousness of the step he was about to take; he took no part in the preliminary skirmishes and was to be seen walking the streets alone and seemingly in deep thought, late at night.[23]

On the sixth day, during the debate on the platform, Yancey rose to speak. For him it was the culmination of a long struggle. In an eloquent address termed "the speech of the convention," he defended his position. It grew dark before he finished, and the combination of the flickering gas-jets, crowded hall, and Southern cries contributed to the drama of the occasion. At the conclusion of his address, historic Institute Hall reverberated with cheers and applause. The ladies in the gallery waved their handkerchiefs and covered the feet of the eloquent Alabamian with bouquets of spring flowers.

The speech was an "unspeakably glorious triumph" for Yancey. It roused Southern spirit as had no other address on the subject. From that point, Yancey exercised undisputed control over the actions of the Southern delegates. When the Douglas-controlled convention rejected his demands, Yancey withdrew. He was followed by virtually all of the delegates from the lower South. Remembering his humiliating defeat in 1848, Yancey must have found the victory doubly sweet. That night the seceders paraded through the city to serenade their hero. In response to this courtesy, Yancey told them, "Perhaps even now the pen of the historian is nibbed to write the story of a new revolution," and the crowd gave three cheers for the new Southern republic.[24]

In separate conventions at Baltimore—called after the Charleston convention had failed to nominate a candidate—the seceders nominated John Breckinridge for the presidency and the remaining delegates named Douglas as their standard bearer. That autumn Yancey undertook an extensive speaking tour of the North in support of Breckinridge's candidacy. Although he probably converted few listeners on the trip, Yancey attracted large crowds wherever he spoke. The Yankees were curious to see and hear a man reported to be an outright secessionist. In fact, Yancey's

[23]Helen Reed Powell, "Yancey the Conservative," Alabama State Department of Archives and History, Montgomery.

[24]*Charleston Mercury,* 28 April 1860; Murat Halstead, *Caucuses of 1860* (Columbus: Follet, Foster and Co., 1860) 49; Milton, *Eve of Conflict,* 440-41.

identification with the Southern cause had become so complete that he threatened to eclipse Breckinridge.[25]

In the public imagination, Yancey stood as the symbol of Southern chivalry and bravado, and his reputation for eloquence was near-legendary. In his speeches, Yancey urged the people to support Breckinridge and the Southern platform or else, he warned, there would be disunion. Included in Yancey's itinerary was an address in Albany on 15 October 1860. The conflict between Yancey and Beman might reach a dramatically satisfying climax if one could report that a confrontation took place in the New York capital. However, no evidence exists to show that Beman heard the address or that Yancey visited his stepfather. It seems likely, however, that on that day both men paused to recall the tempestuous decade they had shared in Troy and to ponder the circumstances that had directed their footsteps along such disparate paths.

When the Southern states, as forecast by Yancey, seceded from the Union following Lincoln's election, Beman vehemently condemned the action. He argued that the "right" of secession, whether by individuals, groups, or states, was "a bald absurdity." If any state or individual could withdraw at will, he contended that all law and order would cease to exist. According to him, no nation could survive if parts of it were permitted to withdraw their allegiance whenever an unpopular action occurred. Under such a doctrine, he alleged that all powers of government, all agreements and alliances, and the very nationality of a country were destroyed. Thus, he concluded, the man who holds this doctrine is a traitor who ought to be punished.[26]

In spite of Yancey's role in dividing the country, Beman regarded John Calhoun as the man chiefly responsible for the secession of the Southern states.[27] However, he did not entirely absolve Yancey from blame. Whether the secession of the Southern states, the outbreak of actual hostilities, or Yancey's effort to win recognition of the Confederacy in Europe convinced the pastor of the dangerousness of his stepson is not known. Regardless of the cause, Beman seems to have reached this decision in

---

[25]*Montgomery Weekly Post*, 6 August 1860.

[26]Beman, *Our Civil War*, 12-14.

[27]Ibid., 14-17.

1861, for in his Thanksgiving Day sermon that year he attacked Yancey in public and by name.

"But a few weeks ago," Beman announced, "William L. Yancey declared in London that the abolition of the slave trade was in repugnance to the Constitution. . . . To justify this revolution and to authorize disobedience to the established government of any country, revolutionists are required to make out a clear and indisputable case of wrong and oppression." But, Beman contended, the secessionists have not done this. Although they claimed that the same love of liberty that led to the American Revolution prompted them to take up arms, Beman argued that the two wars were not parallel. The American colonists, he claimed, had no voice in the government or in the selection of the judiciary, while the South had furnished a majority of the country's presidents and for more than sixty years had controlled the Supreme Court. Why then do they complain? "Why, simply because the Northern mind holds slavery to be a moral and social evil—a curse to the master and a wrong to the slave, and because we like to speak freely on this subject as on all others."[28]

As far as can be determined from extant copies of Beman's lectures and sermons, his attack on Yancey in 1861 constituted his only public opposition to his stepson. Even then, Beman deleted the reference from the address when preparing it for publication and referred to Yancey only as "one of the great men of the South, now paying court to the pioneer anti-slavery Kingdom of Europe."[29]

For both personal and political reasons, the war greatly distressed Beman; he still had "family" in the South. Although Caroline had died at William's home near Montgomery in December 1859,[30] William and Ben were aligned with the Southern cause. In spite of their political differences, Beman remained on good terms with his stepsons and maintained correspondence with both up to the outbreak of hostilities. Also of concern to Beman was Carlisle and his family who resided in the South throughout the war.

---

[28]New York *Herald*, 21 November 1861.

[29]Nathan S. S. Beman, *Thanksgiving in Times of Civil War* (Troy: A. W. Scribner and Co., 1861) 31.

[30]*Montgomery Mail*, 3 January 1860.

Politically, Beman regarded the conflict as a trial of self-government. "The cry has already been lifted up all over Europe that the democratic principle has been tried and found wanting," he contended, and if the Union were destroyed he feared that the defeat would strengthen despotism everywhere. Furthermore, Beman believed that if the Southern states were successful in their effort to secede, other states might take the same course later, and the disintegration, once begun, would eventually ruin the nation.[31]

To Beman, one of the disappointments of the war was the failure of the English to support the North. He was not surprised at the attitude of "the wily Frenchman . . . or his half-starved and unstable millions," but England! "Who would have expected such a voice from England?" He attacked William Ewart Gladstone and Lords Palmerston, Russell, and Brougham for their sympathetic leanings toward the South, but praised John Bright, John Stuart Mill, and Reverend William Arthur for their support of the Union. Of the Trent affair, Beman announced,

> It was a dark, dark day in English intellect. A general lunacy broke loose among the people at that period. . . . Here is a nation turning to . . . [what] they call a "strict neutrality" in favor of a slaveholding rebellion, prompted only by ambition and love of power. England has done this in the very face of all her former declarations and acts against human bondage—thus blotting with ineffaceable stains the fairest page of her history.[32]

Beman felt so keenly about the English position because of his high regard for the country and its early abolition of slavery.

In his Thanksgiving Day sermon of 1862 Beman expressed disappointment over the errors and failures of the Union in prosecuting the war. He cited the mistaken assumption that most of the Southern people were loyal to the Union and claimed that the administration seemed to think that the rebellion could be conquered without warfare. "Nothing is ready when it is wanted," he asserted. The blockade of the South had proved a failure; six months ago the army was about to press the foe "to the wall," but the wall had not been reached yet; last spring the Mississippi was to be opened, but the river still remained closed. Of delays and reverses, "surely we have

---

[31]Beman, Our Civil War, 17-21.

[32]Ibid., 22-27.

had enough to fill the cup of our national humiliation to the brim," Beman proclaimed. The venerable clergyman saw God's hand in the reverses. He regarded the failures as chastisement of the nation for its complicity with slavery, the great sin of the republic.[33]

Reports of alleged Southern atrocities horrified Beman. Taking his information from *The Report of the Joint Committee on the Conduct of the Present War* given to the Senate on 30 April 1862, Beman cited instances of attacks on wounded Union soldiers, the dismemberment of men killed in battle, the stripping of clothing from the dead, crowding of prisoners into filthy prisons, shooting captives, denying water to the dying, and boiling of flesh from corpses in order to secure human bones for ornaments. The report, undoubtedly flagrantly exaggerated, said, "The outrages upon the dead will revive the recollections of the cruelties to which savage tribes subject their prisoners."[34]

When President Lincoln issued his Emancipation Proclamation in September 1862, Beman hailed the pronouncement. In spite of critics' charges that it was ineffectual, Beman regarded it as "a dagger in the heart of the rebellion." "It was a bold step," he said; "I honor the man who could take it."[35]

In his last public statement on the war, Beman movingly concluded his antislavery activity. To his congregation he said,

> When the year of Jubilee shall come, as come it will, and come it must—whether it be with the dawn of 1863 or at some later period—then this broad, goodly land, one and indivisible forever, shall celebrate the second birthday of freedom and the nations of the earth and emancipated Africa among them shall unite in one grand anthem, and the earth and the heavens shall join in the universal chorus, as with "the voice of many waters, and the voice of mighty thunderings, saying Allaluia: for the Lord God omnipotent reigneth." Though seventy-seven years old today, I hope yet to live long enough to see these bright visions of the future fully accomplished. Amen.[36]

The fear that he might die before secession and slavery had been crushed

---

[33]Ibid., 28-34.

[34]Ibid., 48-49.

[35]Ibid., 52.

[36]Ibid., 52.

apparently was of great concern to Beman. In a letter the same year he repeated this sentiment, saying, "In my old age, one of my strongest desires to live a little longer is to see this existing and wicked rebellion put under the feet of genuine loyalty."[37]

Beman lived to witness the grand victory; but one of his stepsons was not to observe the end of the war, for on 27 July 1863, William Lowndes Yancey died. For Yancey, the apex of his career had been the night of his triumph in Charleston. Thereafter his star began to dim. In 1861 he had been sent as a representative of the rebel government to England and France, and in 1862 he had been elected to the Confederate Senate, but never was he accorded the honors and offices that his leadership at Charleston probably led him to expect. Only after his death was his role in the rebellion recognized. The Richmond Whig said, "He was more, perhaps, than any other person instrumental in producing the separation of the Southern from the Northern States." The Gulf City, Alabama, Home Journal claimed that "his great mind more than any other" set in motion the forces that led to secession, and the Columbus, Georgia, Times called him "the master spirit of the revolution." Similar tributes poured in from across the entire South.[38]

When the day of victory arrived, Beman was far from the familiar scenes of Troy, for on 17 June 1863, he had resigned his pastorate, having served the congregation of the First Presbyterian Church for forty of his seventy-seven years. During that time, hundreds of Trojans had grown to maturity knowing no other theology than that preached by Beman. In this period, he had received into the church 1,840 members, 26 of whom had become clergymen, and had built the First Church into one of the largest in the state. At a farewell ceremony, his congregation paid their respects to the minister and announced that they had voted him a life annuity of $1,000.[39]

---

[37]Letter, Nathan S. S. Beman to L. S. Cist, 18 January 1862, Pennsylvania Historical Society, Philadelphia.

[38]Undated newspaper clippings copied from a scrapbook found at "Longwood," the home of F. Raoul, Mt. Meigs, Alabama (photostatic copies at Alabama State Department of Archives and History, Montgomery).

[39]Henry B. Nason, Biographical Record of the Officers and Graduates of the Rensselaer Polytechnic Institute, 1824-1886 (Troy: William H. Young, 1887) 30-34.

Although Beman remained in Troy for a little more than a year after his retirement, his successor was unable to induce him to preach again.[40]

In 1864 Beman and Louisa moved to Carbondale, Illinois. Ever since his tour in 1845 Beman had been interested in the West, but why he selected Carbondale cannot be determined. Fragmentary evidence suggests that his older daughter Eliza may have lived in the Illinois town at the time. If so, this undoubtedly was the reason for his choice. Beman purchased a small homestead consisting of a house, barn, and garden on the outskirts of town. Shortly after his arrival, he bought a horse and a cow and calf. Although Beman and his daughter lived simply, they need not have. After a lifetime of hardship, Beman was in a comfortable financial position. His annuity more than covered his expenses, and at the time of his death, in addition to his property, he owned more than $20,000 worth of stocks and bonds.[41]

Not long after moving to Carbondale, Beman paid a visit to his son Samuel in Minnesota. Two years after settling in St. Charles as a prosperous farmer, Sam's entire life had been changed with his marriage to Caroline Whiton, a quiet Quaker girl; together they had three children. Sam also pursued his political ambitions and was elected to the Minnesota legislature. The desire to meet Sam's wife and to become acquainted with his grandchildren prompted Beman's journey.[42]

Apparently the visit was a memorable one, for nearly a century later family members were still recounting stories concerning it. Recalling past disputes, Sam took every precaution to prevent any possible irritation of his father. An overdose of "hell-fire and damnation" in his father's household had considerably dimmed Sam's religious fervor. As a result, his children were permitted to choose any Sunday school they wished to attend—

---

[40]Letter from Marvin R. Vincent, *Proceedings of the Centennial Anniversary*, 64.

[41]Last Will and Testament of Nathan S. S. Beman, Jackson County Clerk's Office, Murphysboro, Illinois.

[42]"The Late Samuel S. Beman," undated clipping from *St. Charles* (Minnesota) *Press* in possession of Catharine Marston Anderson, Seattle, Washington; Letters, Samuel Beman to Benjamin C. Yancey, 17 June 1857, and Samuel Beman to Caroline Beman, 10 May 1859, Benjamin C. Yancey Papers, Southern Historical Collection, University of North Carolina Library, Chapel Hill.

and each went to a different one. But before Beman's arrival Sam coached his family in what to expect and prepared them for the lengthy evening and morning prayer sessions upon which he knew his father would insist.[43]

To Sam's gratification, the children endured the long and solemn religious rites with patience. However, trouble came from another quarter. Although Sam's wife did not have the advantages of education enjoyed by her husband and father-in-law, she was courageous and independent. When Beman requested some shaving paper on one of the first mornings of his visit, the young wife dutifully provided the article. But when he started to wipe his razor on the paper instead of taking it from her hands, she dropped the pack and walked from the room. Thereafter relations deteriorated rapidly. Father and son engaged in countless arguments, and by the end of Beman's visit the situation had become sorely strained. Upon departing, the minister tossed a twenty-dollar gold piece on the table and walked out to the waiting carriage. In anger, Sam picked up the money and threw it at the receding figure of his father. According to family legend, after Beman was well out of sight, practical-minded Caroline and the children lighted a lantern and searched the yard until the gold piece was found. One great-granddaughter of Beman relates, "Our family are still laughing about this incident—I am glad it happened."[44]

In 1870 Beman returned to Troy where he remained during the greater part of a year, receiving the affectionate attentions of old friends and parishioners. One of his most enjoyable experiences was the service that he attended in celebration of the reunion of the Presbyterian Church.[45] Two contemporaries later recalled Beman's visit. A Rutland, Vermont, editor wrote,

> We shall ever cherish the hour spent with him scarcely a year ago, one beautiful summer afternoon. We heard the footsteps of feebleness and age slowly ascending the stairs to our editorial rooms. We hastened to render assistance, and met our venerable friend who at once recognized us, saying "I have come to see you once more." Although feeble in body, his mind

[43]Letter, Catharine Marston Anderson to author, 8 June 1957.

[44]Ibid.

[45]Vincent, *Proceedings of the Centennial Anniversary*, 63; *The New Era* (Carbondale, Illinois), 26 August 1871.

impaired, yet with evidences left of his great intellect and noble soul, he reverted to tender memories of earlier years with the affection of a child.[46]

William Lee recalled,

> I remember Dr. Beman's visit, as an old man, to the scenes of his former victories. There was something even then of the old leonine look in his aged pathetic face—like the heads of the grim lions which, from the four corners of your Greek temple, have through all these years looked calmly down on the passers-by. They always made me think of Dr. Beman as I saw him in this extreme old age: that feeble old man, leaning on the top of his staff, revisiting the place where he had once reigned supreme.[47]

After his return to Carbondale, Beman's strength gradually ebbed. During those last weeks he said little about his views on death, but the few remarks he did make were enough to satisfy those near him that when death came on the morning of Tuesday, 8 August 1871, his faith in Jesus Christ was the light and hope of his soul.

Looking back on Beman's life from the vantage point of more than a century, what is the appropriate means for measuring his contribution and conduct? Edmund Burke, in his speech to the electors of Bristol who were considering whether he should continue to be their Member of Parliament, urged them to examine his representation of them carefully, "but with discretion, with an attention to all the circumstances, and to all the motives." Look to the *whole tenor* of your member's conduct, he admonished.

> He may have fallen into errors; he must have faults; but our error is greater and our fault is radically ruinous to ourselves if we do not bear, if we do not even applaud the whole compound and mixed mass of such a character. Not to act thus is folly; I had almost said it is impiety. He censures God who quarrels with the imperfections of man.

Any appreciation of Beman must be based on the *whole tenor* of his life. Beman's accomplishments and contributions—as well as his failures—are fairly easy to document. Understanding the private man is more difficult.

---

[46]"Nathan Sidney Smith Beman, D.D.," undated clipping from the *Rutland* (Vermont) *Herald* in possession of Catharine Marston Anderson.

[47]Letter from William Lee, *Proceedings of the Centennial Anniversary*, 81.

During the eighty-five years that his life spanned, Beman exercised a decisive influence on the country and his fellowman. He participated in many of the important events in the formative years of the new nation. Born not long after the American Revolution, Beman was raised among and by patriots, many of whom had actually fought in the war. Their commitment to the new country and republican principles influenced him throughout his life. These beliefs and values, inculcated in childhood, shaped his perceptions and positions on major issues affecting the country's political processes, religious institutions, moral stance, and foreign relations. They were particularly important in determining his response to the War of 1812, foreign immigration, slavery, secession, and the Civil War.

Strongly influenced by the religious teaching of his childhood, the example of hard-working, frugal parents and neighbors, and a deep belief in the worth of education, Beman toiled throughout his life—as a clergyman, educator, editor, writer, lecturer, and agitator—to extend Christianity, to perpetuate the values of his New England upbringing, and to encourage learning.

His greatest influence was as a religious leader. He rose to national prominence within the Presbyterian Church and helped shape its course. He was an active supporter of a wide assortment of religious causes and reforms. As a revivalist, preacher, hymnodist, and spiritual mentor to thousands of Troy Presbyterians for forty years, he was a major figure in the religious events of the time.

Throughout most of his life, Beman was also deeply involved in education. After overcoming family opposition and inadequate finances in order to attend college, Beman became a dedicated supporter of education. Beginning with his teaching in the humble, one-room Fair Haven school, Beman went on to become preceptor of Mt. Zion Academy in Georgia, promoter of manual labor schools for the poor, and lecturer, vice president, and president of Rensselaer Polytechnic Institute. Closely related to Beman's religious and educational activities was his involvement in reform movements ranging from the eradication of prostitution, duelling, intemperance, gambling, and violations of the Sabbath to the abolition of slavery.

In all these causes, Beman strove to influence not only through his preaching and lectures, but also as a writer and editor. Publication of his exchanges with Bishop Hughes and Dr. Coit, his letters from his British and American western tours, many of his sermons and speeches, and his editorship of the Mt. Zion *Missionary*—albeit brief—served to extend his ideas to an unknown number of readers.

In looking to the *whole tenor* of Beman's life, one must also seek to understand the private man. This perception is complicated by the controversy surrounding him and his complex and seemingly contradictory personal qualities. In any attempt to perceive the private man, it would be unfair to impose contemporary standards upon his conduct. His belief in Draconian discipline as an educator, in the almost total subservience of a wife to her husband's wishes, and in an Anglo-Saxon United States, for example, are currently unacceptable attitudes, but they were widely accepted at the time, and Beman was a man of his time. Nor does it reflect unfavorably upon the man that he was sometimes mistaken. His early support of schemes for sending free blacks back to Africa, his manual labor schools for the poor, and his efforts to curb prostitution all show a certain naiveté, but are evidence of a sincere concern for the plight of the disadvantaged.

Beman's personal qualities, "the whole compound and mixed mass" of his character may be the key to understanding the man. Beman possessed many admirable qualities that earned him the respect of his associates and the affection of followers and contributed to the progress of the causes and reforms he espoused. These traits included a devout religious conviction, moral strength, determination, perseverance, and courage. For a man of such zeal, he often displayed an unexpected compassion for others, as illustrated by his concern for prostitutes, seamen, slaves, and the poor and the way they lived. He knew sorrow, illness, and adversity, but he labored on.

Yet, one cannot help notice certain imperfections. At times his zeal was excessive. One wonders whether his relations with family members, especially Caroline, and his parishioners might not have been happier had he been less resolute and obdurate. At times he seemed to display an almost total intolerance of any difference of opinion. On occasion, he had a tendency to overreact, as seen by the venomousness of his denunciation of critics of his early Troy revivals, his personal attacks on Bishop Hughes and Dr. Coit in their theological exchanges, and his near vindictive treatment of his second wife.

Had Beman been confronted with these allegations of misconduct and excess, he probably would have replied as did Burke to the Bristol electors:

The charges against me are all of one kind, that I have pushed the principles of general justice and benevolence too far, farther than a cautious policy would warrant and farther than the opinions of many people would go along with me. In every accident which may happen through life—in pain, in sorrow, in depression, and distress—I will call to mind this accusation and be comforted.

Beman believed that one had a duty and moral obligation to work for reforms and causes that would benefit the people, without regard for public opinion. Like Burke, he asked only, "Applaud us when we run, console us when we fail, cheer us when we recover; but let us pass on. For God's sake, let us pass on."

Bibliography

Unpublished Materials

Letters and scrapbook of Nathan S. S. Beman in possession of Catharine Marston Anderson, Seattle, Washington.

Letters of Nathan S. S. Beman, Pennsylvania Historical Society, Philadelphia, Pennsylvania.

Last Will and Testament of Nathan S. S. Beman, Jackson County Clerk's Office, Murphysboro, Illinois.

Charles Grandison Finney Papers, Oberlin College Library, Oberlin, Ohio.

Minutes of the Board of Trustees of the University of Georgia, University of Georgia Library, Athens, Georgia.

Minutes of Hopewell Presbytery, Presbyterian Historical Foundation, Montreat, North Carolina.

Minutes of the Presbytery of Georgia, Presbyterian Historical Foundation, Montreat, North Carolina.

Minutes of the Board of Trustees of Rensselaer Polytechnic Institute, Library, Rensselaer Polytechnic Institute, Troy, New York.

Letters of Isaac M. Wales and Nathan S. S. Beman, University of Georgia Library, Athens, Georgia.

Benjamin C. Yancey, Jr., Papers, Southern Historical Collection, University of North Carolina Library, Chapel Hill, North Carolina.

William L. Yancey Papers, Alabama State Department of Archives and History, Montgomery, Alabama.

Published Works of Nathan S. S. Beman

A Sermon Preached at Fairhaven, Vermont, June 18, 1812, at the Dedication of the New Meeting House. Middlebury, Vermont, 1812.

A Sermon Delivered at the Meeting House of the Second Parish in Portland, August 20, 1812, on the Occasion of the National Fast. Portland: Hyde, Lord and Co., 1812.

A Sermon Delivered February 27, 1820, Before the Mt. Zion Auxiliary Education Society at the First Annual Meeting. Mt. Zion, Georgia, 1820.

Oration Pronounced at Middlebury before the Associated Alumni of the College on the Evening of Commencement, August 17, 1825. Troy: Tuttle and Richards, 1825.

Four Sermons on the Doctrine of the Atonement. Troy: Tuttle and Richards, 1825.

An Appeal to the Presbyterian Church: Review and Vindication. New York: Daniel Appleton, 1831. These articles also appeared in The Philadelphian, July, August, September 1831, and in the Christian Advocate, August 1831.

A Discourse Delivered in Stephentown, December 25, 1828, and in Troy, January 11, 1829, before the Temperance Societies of Those Towns. New York: John P. Haven, 1820.

A Discourse Delivered at the Opening of the General Assembly of the Presbyterian Church, on the 17th of May, 1832. Philadelphia, Pennsylvania, 1833. This address also appeared in the Cincinnati Journal, 22 June 1832.

The Influence of Ardent Spirits in the Production of Cholera. Troy: n.p., 1832.

Sacred Lyrics; or, Selected Hymns Particularly Adapted to Revivals of Religion and Intended as a Supplement to Watts. Troy: N. Tuttle, 1832.

"Punctuality in the Payment of Debts," American National Preacher 11:11 (April 1837).

The Intellectual Position of Our Country. Troy: N. Tuttle, 1839.

The Old Ministry: Being a Lecture Delivered in London, May 19, 1839. London: John Snow, 1839.

The Gospel Adapted to the Wants of the World. Boston: Crocker and Brewster, 1840.

The Claims of Jesus Christ on Young Women. Troy: N. Tuttle, 1841.

The Western Continent. Troy: N. Tuttle, 1841.

The Claims of Our Country on Young Men. Troy: N. Tuttle, 1843.

Christ, the Only Sacrifice: or the Atonement in its Relation to God and Man. 2d rev. ed. New York, 1844.

The Influence of Freedom on Popular and National Education. Troy: Young and Hartt, 1846.

"Collegiate and Theological Education at the West," American National Preacher 21:3 (March 1847).

Characteristics of the Age. Troy: Young and Hartt, 1851.

Letters to Rev. John Hughes, D. D. Troy: L. Willard, 1851.

Episcopacy Exclusive: or Two Series of Letters, Being a Review of Dr. Coit's Sermon and Pamphlet. Troy: L. Willard, 1856.

The Annual Fair. Troy: R. V. Wilson, 1857.

Antagonisms in the Moral and Political World. Troy: A. W. Scribner and Co., 1858.

"The World a Missionary Field," The National Preacher 2 (May 1859): 134-48.

Thanksgiving in Times of Civil War. Troy: A. W. Scribner and Co., 1861.

Our Civil War: the Principles Involved, its Causes and Cure. Troy: A. W. Scribner and Co., 1862.

Newspapers

Bath (England) Chronicle
Bath (England) Herald
Bath (England) Journal and General Advertiser
Bath and Chiltenham (England) Gazette
Bristol (England) Mercury
Bristol (England) Times
Charleston (South Carolina) Mercury
Detroit Advertiser
Detroit Journal and Courier
Felix Farley's Bristol Journal (England)
The Friend of Man
Georgia Journal (Milledgeville)
Hancock Advertiser (Mt. Zion, Georgia)
Journal of the New British and Foreign Temperance Society (London)
The Liberator (Boston)
The Missionary (Mt. Zion, Georgia)
Mobile Tribune
Montgomery (Alabama) Advertiser
Montgomery (Alabama) Mail
National Intelligencer (Washington, D.C.)
New Era (Carbondale, Illinois)
New York Evangelist
New York Herald
New York Observer
New York Times
New York Tribune
Philadelphia Presbyterian
St. Louis Bulletin
Troy (New York) Budget
Troy (New York) Post
Troy (New York) Sentinel
Troy (New York) Traveler
Troy (New York) Whig

Articles and Periodicals

The Adviser, or Vermont Evangelical Magazine 2:8 (August 1810): 255.
The Anti-Slavery Record 1:7 (July 1835): 81.
The Christian Advocate, August 1831.
The Congregational Magazine (London), June 1839, 373; September 1839, 600-604.
"Letter from Nathan S. S. Beman to Rev. L. L. Beman, January 18, 1801," New York History 28:2 (April 1847): 197-98.

Literary and Philosophical Repository 2:3 (March 1815): 375-78.
The Missionary Magazine and Chronicle (London) 3:37 (June 1839): 82-93.
Religious Monitor 7 (December 1835): 382.

Contemporary Secondary Sources

The American and Foreign Christian Youth, vol. 1 (1850), vol. 2 (1851).
Beecher, Charles, ed. *Autobiography of Lyman Beecher, D.D.* New York: Harper and Brothers, 1865.
Beecher, Lyman. *A Plea for the West.* Cincinnati: Truman and Smith, 1835.
Brief Account of the Origins and Progress of the Divisions in the First Presbyterian Church; Containing also Strictures upon the New Doctrines Preached by the Rev. C. G. Finney and N. S. S. Beman, with a Summary Relation of the Trial of the Latter before the Troy Presbytery, By a Member of the late Church and Congregation. Troy: Tuttle and Richards, 1827.
Brockway, Josephus. *Apology to the Rev. Nathan S. S. Beman, With the Facts in the Case.* Troy: Troy Sentinel, 1827.
_____. *Delineation of the Characteristic Features of a Revival of Religion in Troy, in 1826 and 1827.* Troy: Francis Adancourt, 1827.
Burns, Dawson. *Pen Pictures of Some Temperance Notables.* London: National Temperance Publication, 1895.
Catalog of Officers and Students of the Lenox Academy, March, 1830.
Coit, T. W. *Exclusiveness: A Lecture for Christmas Eve, Delivered on Monday, December 24, 1855.* 3d ed., rev. Troy: William H. Young, 1856.
Collection of the Maine Historical Society, vol. 8, p. 166.
Dwight, Timothy. *Travels in New England and New York.* London: W. Baynes and Son, 1823.
Engles, William M., ed. *Minutes of the General Assembly of the Presbyterian Church in the United States of America from 1821 to 1835.* Philadelphia: Presbyterian Board of Publications, 1835.
Finney, Charles Grandison. *Memoirs.* New York: A. S. Barnes, 1876.
French, J. H. *Gazetteer of New York.* Syracuse: R. Pearsall Smith, 1860.
Gillett, Ezra H. *History of the Presbyterian Church in the United States of America.* Philadelphia: Presbyterian Board of Publications, 1864.
Goodell, William. *Slavery and Anti-Slavery.* New York: William Goodell, 1853.
Greeley, Horace. *Recollections of a Busy Life.* New York: E. B. Treat, 1872.
Halstead, Murat. *Caucuses of 1860.* Columbus: Follett, Foster and Co., 1860.
Jay, William. *An Inquiry into the Character and Tendency of the American Colonization and American Anti-Slavery Societies.* New York: Leavitt, Lord and Co., 1835.
Journal of the Assembly of the State of New York, Seventy-sixth Session, 1853. Albany: Charles Van Benthuysen, 1853.
Miller, Samuel, Jr. *Report of the Presbyterian Church Case: The Commonwealth of Pennsylvania vs. Ashbel Green and Others.* Philadelphia: William S. Martien, 1839.

Morse, Jedediah. *The American Universal Geography.* Boston: Isiah Thomas and Ebenezer T. Andrews, 1796.

Noble, Jonathon H., Memorial Sermon in Marvin R. Vincent, *Memorial Sermon on Rev. N. S. S. Beman, D.D., LL.D., Delivered Sunday Evening, December 17, 1871, in the First Presbyterian Church, Troy, N. Y., by Rev. Marvin R. Vincent, D.D., Pastor.* Troy: A. W. Scribner Co., 1872.

Permanent Temperance Documents of the American Temperance Society. Vol. 1. Boston: Seth Bliss and Perkins and Marvin and Co., 1835.

Perry, Benjamin F. *Reminiscences of Public Men.* Greenville SC: Shannon and Co., 1889.

Report of the Wesleyan-Methodist Missionary Society for the Year Ending April, 1839. London: Wesleyan-Methodist Missionary Society, 1839.

Reports of the New British and Foreign Society for the Suppression of Intemperance. London: J. Pasco, 1837, 1838.

Reports of the Society for the Promotion of Collegiate and Theological Education at the West. New York: J. F. Trow, 1844, 1845, 1846, 1847.

Sherwood, Adiel. *A Gazetteer of the State of Georgia, 1827.* Athens: University of Georgia Press, 1939.

————. *A Gazetteer of the State of Georgia.* 3d ed. Washington: P. Force, 1837.

The South Vindicated from the Treason and Fanaticism of the Northern Abolitionists. Philadelphia: H. Manly, 1837.

Sprague, William D. *Annals of the American Pulpit.* New York: Robert Carter and Bros., 1859.

Stearns, Johnathon F. "Historical Review of the Church (Old School Branch) since 1837," *Presbyterian Re-Union Memorial Volume, 1837-1871.* New York: DeWitt C. Lent and Co., 1870.

Troy Directory (1830 to 1845). Troy: N. Tuttle.

Tyler, Bennet. *Memoir of the Life and Character of Rev. Asahel Nettleton, D.D.* Boston: Congregational Board of Publications, 1856.

Vincent, Marvin R. *Memorial Sermon on the Rev. N. S. S. Beman, D.D., LL.D., Delivered Sunday Evening December 17, 1871, in the First Presbyterian Church, Troy, N.Y., by Rev. Marvin R. Vincent, D.D., Pastor.* Troy: A. W. Scribner Co., 1872.

White, George. *Statistics of Georgia.* Savannah: W. Thorne Williams, 1849.

Willis, William. *Journals of the Rev. Thomas Smith and the Rev. Samuel Deane, Pastor of the First Church in Portland.* Portland: Joseph B. Bailey, 1849.

Index